THE WORLD ALMANAC GUIDE TO
NATURAL
FOODS

THE WORLD ALMANAC GUIDE TO

NATURAL FOODS

SHIRLEY ROSS

World Almanac Publications

New York, New York

Interior and Cover design: Janet Froelich
Cover photograph: Michael Breskin

First published in 1985.

Distributed in the United States by Ballantine Books, a division of Random House, Inc., and in Canada by Random House of Canada, Ltd.

Library of Congress Catalog Card Number: 85-050746
Newspaper Enterprise Association ISBN: 0-911818-55-3
Ballantine Books ISBN: 0-345-32628-8

Printed in the United States of America

World Almanac Publications
Newspaper Enterprise Association
A division of United Media Enterprises
A Scripps Howard company
200 Park Avenue
New York, NY 10166

10 9 8 7 6 5 4 3 2 1

We owe it to ourselves not only to understand what constitutes health, but also what is required of us to retain it in a normal condition. Since happiness and health go together, we should pay as much attention to the building up and preservation of health as we do to attaining happiness.

— Mahatma Gandhi

CONTENTS

INTRODUCTION

Today, more than ever before, people are concerned about becoming better informed about nutrition. To this end, people are questioning the kinds of foods they eat, what those foods consist of, and where those foods come from. In addition, most people are becoming aware of the importance of exercising discretion about the additives and artificial substances they allow into their bodies.

You know that the way you feel and look is specifically related to the food you eat; if you eat a deficient diet, your system won't keep you healthy and feeling good. You can literally commit nutritional suicide by being uninformed (or misinformed) about the food you eat and how it affects you.

However, good nutrition is more than bare vitamins, minerals, and protein. You won't benefit from eating tasteless, colorless foods, even though they have all the nutritional requirements. A good diet must take into account your feelings towards what you eat. Whatever foods you choose, they should be fun to make and to eat. The goal of this book is to teach you the basics of eating that is both delicious and healthy without forcing you to read through a confusing mass of scientific research and technical material.

Finally, a healthful diet is only one part of a long and happy life. To be truly healthy, you must know who you are and what you believe in. Establishing and maintaining your own health—mentally, physically, and spiritually—will put you well on the road to a joyful, fulfilling life.

THE BASICS OF EATING NATURALLY

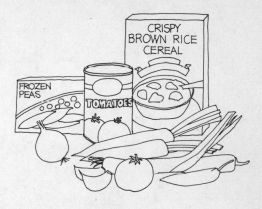

NATURAL FOODS, HEALTH FOODS, AND SUPERMARKETS

Many people believe that health foods, natural foods, and organic foods all mean the same thing. This is not true. "Health food" is a term used to describe many kinds of foods that supposedly are more healthful than foods purchased in supermarkets. Writing about health foods, advertisers and food faddists try to make you believe they are of superior quality, free of additives and preservatives. This is not entirely true. Health food stores and supermarkets are both dominated by brand names, and many of their products can be purchased in either store. These brand names often extract a higher price but are not necessarily better-quality products, especially in regard to vitamins and minerals.

Many people are tired of the overchemicalized and overprocessed foods that predominate in supermarkets. Yet many of the products available in a supermarket are cheaper but no less or more nutritious than those sold in health food stores. For example, fruits and vegetables, if they are not organic, are not usually any better in a health food store than in a supermarket. And they are more expensive in the health food store. Much of the produce in health food stores also sits for longer periods of time than in supermarkets and is consequently less fresh when purchased.

Diet products, many brands of crackers, and grains and cereals sold in health food stores are also sold in supermarkets—at a cheaper price and under the same brand names. Notice, too, that many products, especially diet products, contain additives and preservatives. Some products, cornflakes for example, are equal in food value whether purchased in the supermarket or the health food store, unless the flakes are made from whole corn.

Many foods purchased in a health food store are more nutritious than those sold in a supermarket; nevertheless, there is an abundance of nourishing food in your supermarket. It is your responsibility to find out the nutritional content of food and what your nutritional needs are for a balanced diet. Being knowledgeable about food allows you to make accurate decisions about what to purchase in the health food store and what you can buy in the supermarket. You must read all product labels carefully. Do not sacrifice nutritional quality for convenience.

5

Natural food stores try to help you learn the difference between good and bad varieties of similar foods, for example, the nutritional value of honey versus sugar. Or to realize that frozen or canned produce is not natural.

Organically produced food conforms to exact specifications (see the next section). You must be very cautious when buying organic produce. Ask the salesperson or owner where the food came from and in what kind of soil it was grown. If they cannot give you a satisfactory answer, chances are the food is not organic, although it is being sold for a much higher price than other produce. Remember, too, that no matter how hard we try to "buy organic," water and air pollution and acid rain surround us. It is getting harder each day to call organic organic.

ORGANIC FARMING, INORGANIC FARMING, AND HOME-GROWN FOODS

ORGANIC FARMING
One alternative to eating artificially colored, flavored, and preserved food is to purchase organic food. Organic food is food that is grown organically and that is processed without preservatives, hormones, antibiotics, or synthetics being added. For example, white bread is not an organic food because the whole wheat has been refined in the processing. The problem here is that millions of people want organic food, but there are very few organic farmers.

Organic farming is a very expensive and very difficult method of producing food. To begin with, the organic farmer uses better plant varieties than those used by commercial farmers. The organic farmer gives back to the soil the nutrients depleted by other plants, allowing all possible minerals to be restored to the soil and, ultimately, to those who eat the plant. Restoring the soil naturally is done by treating the soil with an organic material (humus). Organic materials include plant compost, animal manure, peat moss, blood, sawdust shavings, and leaves. The billions of bacteria, fungi, and other organisms in this humus allow the soil to feed large amounts of nutrients and minerals to the roots of the growing plants. Humus also absorbs and holds water very well, allowing the plant to use it easily. Organic farmers use no pesticides, herbicides, or potentially hazardous synthetic fertilizers.

Organically grown produce varies in quality depending on the area and climate in which it is grown, but it always has a better taste than supermarket produce. Organic food has blemishes, but, especially with fruit, they can be a mark of quality.

What are the nutritional advantages? If you continually use organic produce, your body's intake of minerals and other nutrients will be higher and more balanced than if you consume inorganic produce.

INORGANIC FARMING

Chemical fertilizers are made soluble by adding acids and other processing chemicals. The chemicals not used by the plants build up in the soil and, after many years, can alter the structure and tilth of the soil. Many commercial soils have less than 1 percent humus; such soils produce less food because they interfere with water absorption and the active biological life necessary for healthy soils. The diminished microbial action causes trace-mineral problems, and maintaining a healthy growing environment is almost impossible.

In a natural environment, plants get their nutrients from insoluble sources. The soluble chemical fertilizers drench the roots of plants with an overabundance of one nutrient and force the plant to use what is given to it rather than what it needs, causing the nutrients in the soil to become unbalanced.

When pesticides and herbicides are used on produce, they are not evenly dispersed and may not be washed off thoroughly during processing. Vegetables grown above ground may have large amounts of these pesticides, root vegetables little, if any. Food scientists are concerned about how much damage pesticides can do to the body. Long-term unfavorable effects on health may have terrible consequences.

Organic farming is by far superior to inorganic. Nevertheless, the following points can be made in the favor of inorganic farming: (1) Organic farming is not practical if we are to feed millions of people; (2) pesticide use can increase the amount of food grown; (3) after processing, the pesticides that remain are not harmful; and (4) government inspection prevents an inordinate amount of pesticide from reaching the consumer.

HOME-GROWN FOODS

Growing vegetables at home is advisable during warm months. You can then learn to freeze or preserve foods for the winter. And you can learn how to condition the soil, using ladybugs and praying mantises for biological regulation. Growing a variety of vegetables promotes the presence of many insects; this, in turn, keeps the number of any one species in check.

FRESH, FROZEN, AND CANNED FOODS

Stored food, deteriorates from drying, by going stale, from dirt and chemical contaminants, and by insect contamination.

The major cause of spoilage is microorganisms, which are everywhere — on hands and in the air, soil, dust, and sewage. Special care must be taken to prevent microorganism growth. This can be accomplished by killing the organisms or by preventing their further growth. This is why we freeze, can, and dry foods.

There is reason for the belief that frozen and canned fruits and vegetables are inferior to fresh. In some instances, however, the frozen variety can be a better-quality product.

Vegetables grown for canning and freezing are not bred for toughness because they are frozen within hours after harvesting and are usually harvested when ripe. Fresh produce is bred for toughness at the cost of a softer, juicier, and more flavorful and nutritious product. Fresh produce is picked unripened and is ripened during storage; and the product the consumer buys has a poor quality and is low in nutritional value. Also, pesticide residues have a better chance of being absorbed into fresh produce, making washing and peeling less than adequate precautions. The quick processing of frozen food includes cleaning, sorting, and then steam blanching for 1 to 3 minutes, depending on whether the food needs a short or long cooking time. This processing almost completely eliminates spoilage due to enzymatic action and any invasion from pesticide residues.

FROZEN VEGETABLES

A few different methods are used in quick-freezing vegetables; one is cooling them between cooled plates and another is the fluidized method, which blows cold air through food that is kept in motion to keep each piece separated. The latter method is especially useful with peas and vegetable pieces. Once frozen, these vegetables can be purchased in large pour-and-store packages. The consumer need use only the amount wanted, and the rest of the package can be returned to the freezer. There is also cryogenic freezing, which uses low-boiling liquids (nitrogen or Freon). With this method, the food is submerged or sprayed, and the freezing is done so quickly that the food maintains its original shape and true color. Most quick-freezing is accomplished in 5 to 15 minutes.

Frozen foods are stored at 0° F and then shipped. Most vitamin A is retained in fruits and vegetables during processing. The loss of vitamins and minerals is very little compared to the loss that occurs when fresh produce takes two weeks to be shipped from California to New York in unrefrigerated trucks. And there is no damage to the frozen produce from loading and unloading it, or from handling it in the supermarket.

Frozen produce is a high-grade product when it leaves the processing plant; but because improperly stored frozen produce is hard to discover, abuses in shipping occur frequently. Truckers may ship the frozen food in unrefrigerated warehouses or in "coolers" rather than freezers. And once the frozen foods reach the supermarkets, they are often piled too high in freezer cases, thus allowing the packages on top to thaw. Produce can be refrozen without any noticeable damage, however.

Frozen foods must be stored in your freezer at temperatures of 0 degrees F or below. Kept at these temperatures, the quality of the frozen product can be superior to that of the fresh. Avoid buying frozen vegetables processed with sauces. The sauces usually have artificial coloring and flavoring, which is not desirable.

It is difficult to detect bad frozen foods. To be on the safe side, avoid buying any product that has the following:

- Misshapen box.
- Stains on the boxes. This indicates the leakage (and loss) of thawed juices.
- Juice is rich in nutrients and also can give bacteria an excellent place for breeding.
- Pour-and-store bags with vegetables clumped together. This indicates that the product has been thawed and refrozen.

9

Except for spinach and corn-on-the-cob, always cook frozen vegetables by adding them to boiling water without prior thawing.

FROZEN, CANNED, AND DRIED FRUITS

Frozen fruits are available and are processed without any cooking. The texture will be soft from the freezing procedure. Frozen fruits can be purchased sugared, free of sugar, or with a syrup.

Avoid buying packages with juice stains or frost on the outside of the package. This indicates previous thawing.

Canned fruits lose approximately one-third of their water-soluble nutrients in their liquid. Fruits canned in their own juices (without sugar) are higher in nutrients.

Dried fruits have little nutrient value after processing. With vacuum-dehydrated fruits, the texture is extremely crisp with only 1 to 3 percent water; there is less nutritional loss and a better rehydrating capacity than with regular dried fruits.

Fruit sauces, such as apple or cranberry sauce, have a very high loss of nutrition.

FREEZING FOODS AT HOME

The easiest and fastest method to retain nutrients and preserve vegetables and fruits is to freeze them. Some vitamin C is lost during the process of freezing fruits; when freezing vegetables, there is a loss of vitamin C, vitamin B (riboflavin), and minute amounts of other water-soluble vitamins and minerals.

Freezing is not meant to destroy microorganisms but to slow down their growth and slow down enzyme action. Slow freezing causes large ice crystals to form within the food; when food is thawed, a considerable loss of juices causes it to have a soggy and flabby texture and some nutritional loss. Quick freezing at temperatures below 0° F forms large numbers of small ice crystals within the food structure and rarely penetrates the cell walls to cause a heavy leaking of juices.

The following vegetables can be frozen successfully: peas, green beans, corn, broccoli, cauliflower, lima beans, eggplant, peppers, beets, spinach, squash, sweet potatoes, kale, and pumpkin. Foods with a high water content—lettuce, celery, tomatoes — cannot be frozen.

With fruits, freezing produces a soft, soggy texture and a cellular breakdown similar to cooked fruit. The cause is the separation of water from the fruit during freezing; only a small amount is reabsorbed. Fruits best for freezing are fruits with good flavor and color. They will retain their firmness better than other fruits. Melon or any high water content fruit does not freeze successfully. Serving the fruit slightly frozen will make the fruit more palatable. If spoilage does occur with frozen fruits, it is harmless fermentation that occurs naturally.

Freezing Vegetables

Have everything necessary for blanching and freezing in front of you. Speed is extremely important in retaining taste, nutrition, and freshness during the preparation of vegetables for freezing.

What follows is a step-by-step procedure from the market to your freezer.

1. When buying vegetables for freezing, pick young, tender vegetables with few damaged spots. Choose vegatables that have not completely ripened.

2. Clean vegetables thoroughly, removing any damaged areas. Cut into sizes desired.

3. If the vegetables are to be blanched: in a pot with a cover, heat to boiling 1 gallon of water to every 1 pound of vegetables. Or prepare a steamer for steaming. Boil or steam for the following number of minutes:

Vegetable	Boil(minutes)	Steam(minutes)
Asparagus	3	4
Green beans	3	3
Lima beans	3	3
Beets	30-60 (until tender)	
Broccoli, cut in pieces	3	5
Brussels sprouts	4	5
Carrots, whole small or halved	4	5
Carrots, sliced	2	4
Cauliflower flowerets, separated	3	4

11

Corn on the cob	10	no
Corn removed from the cob	4	no
Kale	2	no
Green peas	2	2
Spinach	2	no
Summer squash	3	4
Winter squash	20	no

4. Cool the vegetables quickly by immersing them in cold water or by running them under cold running water. Drain well. Dry on absorbent towels.

5. Packaging in suitable containers is an extremely important step. Proper containers will prevent further contamination from microorganisms, will prevent moisture from escaping, and will eliminate as much air as possible. Use glass jars or freezer containers, allowing ½-inch space at the top for expansion. No "headroom" is necessary for asparagus, broccoli, or similar vegetables because they should be packaged loosely. When using moisture-proof wrapping materials, make sure they wrap tightly. If foods are not packaged properly, moisture will escape, causing dehydration, which destroys flavor texture and color and results in a loss of nutrients. Moisture escaping from packaged foods will also cause frost buildup on the freezer walls and the outsides of packages.

6. Label your containers. Indicate the package contents and the date of freezing. Vegetables should not be frozen longer than 12 months. Except for spinach and corn on the cob, cook vegetables without thawing. Cook them only until tender. Don't forget that blanching has partially cooked the vegetables.

Freezing Fruits

1. Select fruits that have no decayed or bruised areas and are not overly ripe.

2. Wash gently but thoroughly and quickly. Note that apricots need to be blanched for 2 minutes before freezing.

3. Slice the fruit if necessary. Place in a bowl.

4. Add sugar and gently mix the fruit and sugar until all sugar is dissolved.

5. Place the fruit, along with the juice that forms, into containers suitable for freezing. Shake containers gently to pack the fruit as tightly as possible without crushing. Leave ½-inch space at the top for expansion. Cover tightly.

6. Label with name of fruit and date of freezing.

CANNED FOODS

Canning produce requires two more steps than freezing. First, a diluted brine is added to vegetables, or a syrup is added to fruits. (Sometimes only water is added.) This liquid is added during the time that the cans are being filled or immediately after filling. Second, salt is added to most canned products (only peas and limas beans add salt in the commercial frozen product.) Some canned products contain added sugar and artificial coloring; by law, such additives must be put on the label.

The can is heated in a vacuum to expel air and gas. The internal pressure after the can has cooled will be less than the pressure of the atmosphere. This is called "exhausting" and is a process that prevents color deterioration and any oxidation. The cans are then hermetically sealed.

Sterilization is the next step; the cans are heated at a temperature of 250° F for 60 minutes. At this temperature most organisms are destroyed. After sterilizing, the cans are cooled down with water, although the contents can remain warm for 3 days causing nutritional loss. A further loss of nutrition occurs if cans are stored in warm locations in the home. Canned products should be kept in the coolest storage place you have. The most desirable temperature for canned foods is just above freezing.

Before opening a canned product, clean off the top of the can to rid it of any dirt or insecticide used in the supermarket. To prevent metal slivers from falling into the food, always open a can starting past the side seam and not cutting through it.

When buying canned food, avoid cans with large dents. These dents can cause content leakage. Small dents will not harm the contents. The net weight on the label of the can refers to the combined weight of the liquid and solid food.

Store leftover food from cans in separate containers. An opened can can be covered and refrigerated, but if the food has an acid content, a metallic taste will result from storage in the can.

Canned food has already been completely cooked. Thus cooking time should be extremely brief, only enough to heat the product.

DRIED FOODS

There are other methods of preserving food. The oldest method is drying, which can be exemplified by peas, coffee, tea, raisins, currants, sultanas, and dried soups and fruits. Drying prevents microorganisms from growing and reproducing. The quality of dried produce has improved significantly as a result of new, rapid-drying methods.

Freeze-drying is an expensive procedure but a widely used method of preservation. The ice of food that has been frozen is converted directly into water vapor by reducing pressure and heating quickly, without structural changes. Rehydrating and heating is all that is necessary to prepare freeze-dried foods for eating.

ADDITIVES AND CONTAMINANTS

New technology has increased food supplies for the burgeoning world population and has also produced new kinds of foods. But the present-day farmer is not able to produce food by his own methods alone. He needs extensive help from fertilizer factories and oil refineries. What is worse is that the farmer cannot package his own foods. Packaging is done in canneries, packing plants, and dairies.

All the steps necessary to get food in large quantities from the farmer to the consumer have brought about an increase in chemical compounds, preservatives, emulsifiers, and artificial flavors and colors. Many additives from chemicals used to destroy pests are unintentionally added to the foods we eat. Contamination from handling in the processing and preparation of foods (e.g., mineral oil which is used as a lubricant but causes "off" flavors) are also unintentional additives.

In the process of planting and growing foods, the major chemicals used on or around them are pesticides, herbicides, and fertilizers.

Pesticides are sprayed directly onto both growing plants and stored crops to destroy insect infestations that ruin food supplies meant for humans and animals. Some insects can carry diseases through infected plants. Research has shown that most pesticides remain on the surface of the plant, can be washed off, and are not absorbed into the plant. Few pesticides alter the composition of a plant.

Herbicides remove any objectionable vegetation surrounding plants, either generally or selectively.

Insecticides can contaminate the soil by chance or directly when used to control soil-borne pests. Insecticides are used mainly on stored grain. Rodenticides are also used on stored grain.

Chlorinated hydrocarbons used in dust and spray forms contaminate livestock, either directly or by contaminating animal feed. Many animal diseases are treated with chemicals that enter the fatty tissues of the treated cattle, pigs, sheep, and poultry and such by-products as eggs, milk, and other dairy products. Dairy products made from the milk of contaminated cows contain insecticides. Egg yolks show high levels of chlorinated hydrocarbons from poultry feed or direct ingestion by the poultry.

Fumigation and preharvest sprays are used on plants to reduce postharvest decay. Postharvest fungicides are used during harvesting and processing to prevent fungi and insects from infesting the plants. In the United States and Canada, these sprays are washed off before marketing. Removal by any other means is not effective.

Rodenticides are also used to control rodents; molluscicides to control slugs and snails (zinc compounds, nontoxic to humans and animals); and nematocides to control a worm that damages crops. There are also chemicals that control the time of flowering and stimulate root cuttings.

Food contains carbohydrates, fats, proteins, vitamins, minerals, and water, all of which are necessary for life. Besides these wonderful natural ingredients, many additional components are added during flowering and storage, as we have just discussed. Let us now discuss those that are added during processing.

To increase shelf life, to allow cooking and baking to be done more easily, to intensify food color and prevent any texture or taste alteration, to increase nutritive value, and to prevent the chemical and rancid spoilage of foods (enzyme action caused by a reaction with oxygen in the air, the growth of microorganisms), we have added chemicals to our food.

The food industry does not agree on what "additives" are. Food technologists interpret them as any matter (natural or not) added during any stage of processing that remains in the product when it is put on the market for the consumer. Food manufacturers interpret them as anything other than the basic food. These added substances are the result of prearranged controls over processing and packaging of foods.

Additives do not include the pesticides or other products used in growing the plants. An additive may or may not have a nutritional quality. It can be there by accident, serving no useful purpose in the final product.

The use of most chemicals in food is controlled by government laws; nevertheless, there is no such thing as a completely safe chemical. Problems with chemicals may not surface for years. The government weighs any risk involved against the benefits when deciding whether or not to allow a certain chemical to be used.

Those defending the use of additives claim that most people will never suffer from any form of toxicity caused by added food substances and that they make useful new foods available. For example, protein usefulness has been improved by adding synthetic lysine (an amino acid) to fortify whole wheat. On the other hand, adding vitamin C to imitation fruit juices only deprives the body of vitamins and minerals available in the natural juices.

Defendants of additives also say that food additives are less expensive than natural ingredients. This is not true; in fact, they cost more. For example imitation fruit juices cost about half as much as fresh juice but contain one-tenth the juice, thus costing five times as much as fresh juice per ounce.

GOVERNMENT FOOD CONTROL

The Food and Drug Administration (FDA) is part of the U.S. Department of Health and Human Services. The main function of the FDA is to enforce the Food, Drug and Cosmetic Act of 1938 and thereby assure that the foods we eat are safe, pure, and wholesome.

Chiefly, the law provides health safeguards and sanitary controls. The law prohibits deception; requires label statement; assures the safety of food containers, colors, and other additives; establishes the allowable residue of pesticides; limits the amount of deleterious matter that can be used in the manufacture of foodstuffs; prohibits in interstate commerce any food that is unsafe or injurious to health; and bans the sale of contaminated or decomposed food. False or misleading food labels and misleading food containers are also prohibited.

Other laws include the following:

Color-additive amendment of 1960: No food or color additive may be used in food unless the Food and Drug Administration has determined by scientific evaluation that it is safe at its intended level of use.

Delaney clause: No food substance can be considered safe if it is found to produce cancer when fed to man or animals, or can be shown to induce cancer by any appropriate tests. (However, additives such as sugar and salt have been shown to induce cancer under special conditions.)

GRAS (generally recognized as safe): Included here are additives proven safe by qualified experts for their intended use.

Many health problems have been linked to an insufficient amount of traditional foods and the eating of fast foods and junk food.

COMMONLY USED ADDITIVES
The following is a list of additives frequently used in the foods we eat.

Flavor additives
There are more than 1,400 different kinds, making flavor additives the largest and most diversified of the additives used. The consumer has brought about the increased use of flavor additives by demanding that food have a uniform flavor at all times. Also, natural additives do not always endure processing as well as artificial flavor additives. And acquiring natural food additives is very expensive; the supply is not available all year round and is usually available in very small amounts. Some of the flavors added are aromatic flavors (cherry, walnut, strawberry, etc.), natural spices (cloves, ginger, citrus, oils, etc.), ketones, proteins, alcohol, esters, ethers, and aldehydes.

MSG
MSG (monosodium glutamate) is a flavor enhancer with no taste. As table salt is a sodium salt of hydrochloric acid, MSG is a sodium salt of

17

glutamic acid. Glutamic acid is an integral part of gluten, which is a protein of wheat, the tacky part of flour that makes flour stand up when it is used in baking. Glutamic acid is an organic amino acid; however, it is not an essential amino acid. This substance is processed from sugar beets and molasses. Because of the large demand, MSG is also produced very cheaply by fermenting with a bacteria solution of glucose containing simple nitrogen compounds.

Emulsifiers
Emulsifiers (Mono- and di-glycerides) allow tiny particles (molecules) that normally do not mix well together, like water and oil, to blend. Emulsifiers are also used in salad dressings and mayonnaise. In baked goods, emulsifiers preserve and disperse the ingredients evenly, causing good texture and volume. On fresh chocolate, a gray color will appear unless an emulsifier is used to prevent this development.

Stabilizers and thickeners
Stabilizers and thickeners, many from natural sources, are used in liquids to swell, gel, and thicken, and to cause a smooth uniformity of body and texture. They keep particles from sinking to the bottom, for example in containers of chocolate milk. They hinder the formation of ice particles in frozen desserts. Used are magnesium phosphate, magnesium salicylate, magnesium and calcium stearate, sodium silicate, sodium phosphate, and calcium heptenoate.

Lecithin
Lecithin prevents the formation of fat particles and stabilizes salad dressings and oils. It is widely used to improve the texture of baked goods. Lecithin also helps prevent spoilage in baked products. The smoothness of ice cream is increased by using lecithin. In the United States, lecithin is processed from soybeans, but it can also be obtained from peanuts and cottonseed.

Sequesterants
Sequesterants, or chelating agents, prevent staleness, rancidity, and bad flavor. These chemicals bind metal ions such as calcium, iron, and copper. The most widely used are EDTA, a sodium salt of ethylene diamine tetraacetic acid used in milk, salad dressings, and juices, and SAAP, sodium acid pyrophosphate, which prevents an ion sequestering property

from turning potatoes black after cooking. Here are a few more: phytic acid, lecithin, pyrogallol, citric acid, ascorbyl palmitate, some amino acids, polyphosphate, oxalohydramic acid, cheledemic acid, aminopropionic acid, aminopropionic acid, oxydipropionic acid, and throdipropionic acid.

Humectants
Humectants prevent the caking and drying out of foods and keep them free flowing. Products can cake from moisture or from processing. Calcium silicate is used in baking powders. Aluminum calcium silicate, calcium, and magnesium or tricalcium silicate are used in common table salt. They also maintain moisture in some foods.

Dessicants
Dessicants prevent lumping and solidification in packaged products. Silica gel, made into tiny packets, is placed in the package separately.

Surfactants
Surfactants are surface-active agents used mainly in bread. They keep the bread fresh for a longer time and give the product a soft texture. Sucrose esters are the surfactants most commonly used.

Antibiotics
Antibiotics enter our food as preservatives, to fight plant and animal diseases, and to improve animal growth when used in feed. Antibiotics can also enter our food as contaminants. There is a tremendous concern about antibiotics in milk.

Stilbestrol
Stilbestrol is a synthetic female hormone used in animal feed and plants to increase muscle growth. The U.S. Department of Health has prohibited the use of stilbestrol with chickens because of a cancer risk, but it is still used on cattle grown for human consumption.

Thickening agents
Thickening agents are food or chemical substances that have the ability to expand liquid. They are used both in the food industry and in home cooking. The most common thickening agents are meat and fish gelatins, casein, flour, isinglass, starch syrups, cellulose, agar agar, tragacanth, alginates, peelins, gums made from carob flour, dextrines, carrageen, and

algin (ammonium calcium alginate, propylene, glycol alginate, sodium alginate amylopertin). Thickeners add no flavor to food.

Sorbic Acid

Sorbic acid (potassium sorbate) is used as a preservative with dried fruits. These fruits have been rehydrated only partially to give them a softer texture and a more appetizing appearance. For example, apricots will have a bright orange appearance and very moist texture. Dark-colored fruits have no preservatives. They are pasteurized after they have been partially rehydrated, eliminating the need for additional chemicals. Fruits without sorbic acid are called "moist pack." Labeling on dried fruits must list additives

Acidulants

Acidulants are used in minute amounts as antoxidants and leavening agents. Citric acid, phosphoric, fumaric, tartaric, lactic, adipic, and malic are a few of the acidulants used in food. As an example of their use, fumaric acid makes egg whites stand up better and decreases whipping time. It also allows the egg white to be overbeaten without any deterioration.

Amylose

Amylose is used to produce edible membranes for foods such as sausage products, some meats, and many specialty items.

Waxing

Waxing is used on many fruits and vegetables. It extends the life of the produce by covering the pores, which prevents water loss.

The flavor and texture of waxed fruits and vegetables last longer. The most frequently waxed fruits and vegetables are apples, lemons, oranges, tangerines, grapefruit, cantaloupes, turnips, tomatoes, green peppers, cucumbers, and russet potatoes. Never eat the skin of a fruit or vegetable that has been waxed; health hazards have been suggested.

Scald inhibitors

Scald inhibitors are oiled paper, shredded, that is used as a blotter or is wrapped around individual pieces of fruit to prevent scald, a disease of fruit.

Antistick sprays

Antistick pan sprays are excellent antistick agents, safe and effective. Lecithin is removed from crude oil during its refining and is used as an antistick spray. There may be danger in breathing the propellents from spray cans, but these sprays can be purchased in other forms. Some brands also have artificial flavor additives.

Coffee taint

Coffee taint can be caused by several contaminants. The soil in northern Brazil contains iodoform, which can be assimilated by the plant, causing an off flavor. Noxious matter from asphaltic subsoils and soils containing petroleum also cause off flavors. DDT, BHC, aldrin, and other insecticides used as tar-oil emulsions, as well as faulty storage, can also cause off flavors.

Leavening agents

Leavening agents serve to make food light in texture. Although air and steam sometimes act as leaveners, yeast, baking powder, and baking soda are by far the most important agents. Without the acids and alkalies that make up baking powder and baking soda, a number of cakes, biscuits, waffles, and muffins could not be made. Most of them depend on the chemical release of carbon dioxide to produce their light texture and volume.

Baking powders consist of three basic ingredients: sodium bicarbonate (baking soda), an acid salt or acid reacting component, and edible starch (to absorb moisture during storage). Sodium bicarbonate, when heated, makes carbon dioxide, but a soapy-tasting residue, sodium carbonate, remains unless the food includes an acid ingredient to neutralize this. When water is added, the acid reacts with the sodium bicarbonate to produce carbon dioxide. The residue is a tasteless salt.

Baking powders are tailored to meet specific needs. Some fast-acting baking powders are mainly for home use; slow-acting baking powders are used in commercial bakeries so that large batters can be held for several hours or even refrigerated until the next day.

Water

Our water supply is polluted by industrial wastes, among them chlorine, phenol petroleum oil, and chlorophenols. Cleaning residues in equipment used for processing foods can cause off-flavors; in addition, depending on the type of equipment used, they can add a metal flavor to foods.

Detergents

Detergents can cause off-flavors in beer and soft drinks. They can also cause biological growth and the growth of organic matter such as algae (some can be toxic), fungi, filamentous bacteria, and aquatic actinomycetes.

Trace elements

Some trace elements, such as copper, zinc, and cadmium, are added to foods to increase nutritional quality or come from the packing or equipment used in food processing. Excessive amounts can cause vomiting. Also, copper gives dairy products a bad flavor and can destroy vitamin C in frozen or processed fruits and vegetables.

Mineral oil is used in the baking industry to facilitate the removal of baked goods from baking pans.

Radioactive fallout

The most crucial food contaminant today is the radioactive fallout (radionuclides) contaminating the biosphere. We drink it in our water and eat it in the fruits, vegetables, and meat we consume. Fallout comes to earth through snow, rain, or wind. It settles on land and water, spreading to tributaries and polluting fish and other seafood.

A nuclear blast test causes large particles to fall to earth quickly. Smaller particles survive in the stratosphere for years, although they lose some of their intensity.

NUTRITION
HANDBOOK

A BALANCED DIET

What is a balanced diet? There is no single answer. Every human being must reason out the best diet for himself or herself. Each individual varies in nutritional needs. No one food contains all the nutritional requirements necessary to substain life. Proper nutrition involves receiving, in sufficient quantities and proper balance, vitamins, minerals, proteins, fats, and carbohydrates. A varied assortment of foods, consumed in the right quantities and on a regular basis, will provide proper nourishment. Normally, if you eat foods that contain the B vitamins, especially thiamin (B1), riboflavin(B2), and niacin (B6), other vitamins will be included.

No matter what kind of diet you live on, you will gain or lose weight in direct proportion to the amount of food you eat, whether you exercise, and how your metabolism works. More calories equal more weight. To keep trim and healthy, a good diet and perhaps a change of life-style and attitude are necessary.

DIET INCLUDING FLESH FOOD

To be properly nourished, you must eat, daily, foods from the following six food groups:

1. Meat, fish, eggs, poultry, and legumes
2. Breads and cereals (whole grains)
3. Milk and milk products (cheese, yoghurt, etc.)
4. Dark green leafy and yellow vegetables
5. Other vegetables and fruits
6. Fats and oils (preferably unsaturated)

VEGETARIAN DIET

There are moral, ethical, aesthetic, health, ecological, and economic reasons for becoming a vegetarian. There are no semivegetarians. A vegetarian does not eat flesh foods at any time.

A beginner must decrease flesh intake gradually. The basic guideline is to eat a large and wide variety of foods, not only one or two, to receive the proper nutrition.

By eating meat, you get all your proteins from less food. Plants lack

25

some of the essential amino acids, but a combination of varied vegetable proteins, if chosen carefully, can supply all the essential amino acids. Consult the section on Protein to learn how to combine plant proteins that complement each other.

There are different vegetarian diets. The kind of diet you choose will determine how easily nutritional requirements can be met. On a vegan diet, you refrain from eating any foods of animal origin, fish, poultry, meat, eggs, all dairy products, gelatin, and honey. On a lacto-vegetarian diet, you eat dairy products but no eggs. On an ovo-lacto vegetarian diet, you eat eggs and dairy products.

If you plan to eliminate flesh foods, you must take the following points seriously:

1. Your diet should revolve around whole grains, seeds, whole grain yeast, raised bread, legumes, vegetables (especially green vegetables) and fruits.

2. You should eat more small meals rather than three large meals. Between meals, eat fresh or dried fruit, unsalted nuts, or yoghurt with fresh sliced fruit.

3. If dairy products are not part of your diet, a B12 supplement from desiccated liver, yeast, fortified brewer's yeast, fortified soymilk, and other soy products must be consumed. Soymilk is a good source of calcium, although it contains only 25 percent of the calcium found in whole milk. Also, riboflavin, generous in animal products, is difficult to supply. A vegetarian must eat large amounts of dark green and leafy vegetables and whole grains: broccoli, spinach, kale, collards, turnips, dandelion greens, soybeans, okra, almonds, rutabaga, unhulled sesame seeds, tahini, sunflower seeds, wheat germ.

4. The vegetarian diet usually contains more polyunsaturated fats than a conventional diet. If you eat dairy products, you can enjoy more milk products and eggs than a meat eater because of your low daily cholesterol and saturated fat intake.

5. You have to be careful about getting a sufficient amount of calories. A vegetarian diet is high in bulk but low in calories.

If the body lacks calories, it will use protein for energy and, as a result, your diet to be low in protein.

PROTEINS

There is protein in all animal and vegetable life, and it is essential to human life. Aside from water, protein is more abundant than any other substance in the human body. There is an endless number of different forms of proteins. Proteins are formed from diversified combinations of the twenty-two amino acids. These combinations are linked into chemical chains; each is unique and each has a role prearranged by DNA (deoxyribonucleic acid), the molecule of heredity. Examples of different types of proteins include the following:

- Albumen (egg white)
- Casein and lactalbumin (milk and dairy products)
- Collagen (bone cartilage, ligaments, tendons)
- Glutenin (wheat)
- Glycinin (soybeans)
- Zein (corn)

Protein consists mostly of carbon, hydrogen, and oxygen; unlike carbohydrates and fats, which are less complex substances, protein contains as much as 16 percent nitrogen. All proteins are similar in one aspect: they all consist of amino acids, the basic constituents of protein. Some proteins contain small amounts of phosphorus, sulfur, iron, iodine, and copper.

Humans and animals cannot build protein in the body by using the nitrogen in the air or the nitrates of the soil. They must depend on plants and other animals for protein intake. Plants manufacture their own protein from the carbon dioxide in air and water and from minerals in the soil that contain nitrates. Some plants, such as legumes, peas, beans, clover, make protein by using the nitrogen in the air. With the assistance of bacteria, they manufacture it in the nodules in their roots.

A molecule of an amino acid is identical whether found in plants or animals. There are differences between plant and animal proteins, but an amino acid is always the same.

During digestion, proteins are broken down into separate amino acids. These acids are carried to the many cells in the body through the blood-stream. In the cells, a synthesis of new body protein tissue takes place and is used for repair and growth. This synthesis occurs only when all of what are called the eight essential amino acids are present at the same time and in the right amount and patterns.

The body is unable to synthesize the eight essential amino acids; they have to be provided by the food we eat. Foods containing all eight essential amino acids are called complete proteins. Such food are meat, fish, fowl, dairy products, and soybean products. About half the twenty-two amino acids are synthesized by other amino acids or from organic acids. These are nonessential amino acids, but are also necessary to meet the dietary needs in the body. A food containing an inadequate amount of one or more of the essential amino acids is called an incomplete protein.

If you eat meat, you can get all your proteins from less food. Plants lack some of the essential amino acids, but a combination of varied vegetable proteins, if chosen carefully, can supply all the essential amino acids. Vegetable protein is cheaper to eat then animal protein. If you eliminate flesh foods from your diet, your diet should revolve around whole grains, whole grain yeast, raised bread, legumes, vegetables, and fruits. Between meals, eat fresh or dried fruit, unsalted nuts, and yogurt with fresh sliced fruit. And don't forget that soybean products—tofu and miso—are complete proteins.

One-tenth of our protein is in muscle tissue, one-fifth in bone and cartilage, and one-tenth in the skin. The remaining protein exists in the tissue and fluids.

Protein quality is the amount of protein in food that can be used by the body, its digestibility, and the configuration of the essential amino acids. It is measured in terms of Net Protein Utilization (NPU).

There are many proteins in the blood. Hemoglobin moves oxygen from the lungs to tissues and returns carbon dioxide to the lungs; 95 percent of this molecule is protein, 5 percent is iron. Antibodies offer resistance to infection and occasionally exemption from disease. Bile and urine are the only body fluids that contain no protein.

ESSENTIAL AMINO ACIDS

A description of the eight essential amino acids follows. These acids aid in the absorption of the nonessential amino acids.

Lysine retains nitrogen during the process of tissue formation. Eat eggs, dairy products, nuts, liver, beef; liver concentrate is an excellent substitute for beef.

Methionine contains sulfur, a catalyst to protein manufacture. Methionine creates cysteine, a nonessential amino acid that improves muscle definition by assisting in burning excess fat. Methionine prevents protein from being used as an energy source. Red meat is the richest source.

Tryptophan maintains the nitrogen level in existing cells to prepare for new cells. It uses vitamins for conversion of substances into energy. Tryptophan cannot be used by the body without the presence of B-complex vitamins and riboflavin. Eat eggs and beef to provide both. Tryptophan has been found to be effective against insomnia.

Isoleucine/leucine break down cholesterol and aid in sugar metabolism and glycogenic activity, and serve in the process of enzyme digestion. B vitamins are necessary for isoleucine to function efficiently.

Valine is the primary source of nitrogen and the most important amino acid for the growth process. Valine helps manufacture an enzyme that is extremely important to the production of energy. It is also found in the nervous system to keep it functioning properly. Eat fish, cottage cheese, eggs, beef.

Threonine is necessary for other amino acids to be broken down for replacement purposes. Along with the B vitamins, threonine helps lower stress levels. Threonine aids in building tissues in the body and aids in the use of nutrients. Eat fish, beef, dairy products.

Phenylalanine aids in the formation of the hormones, epinephrine (adrenaline), and thyroxine, which are the thyroid's most important regulators of growth. Phenylalanine is also associated with the utilization of vitamin C. It is found in all animal sources.

Cereals (grains) are low in lysine but high in tryptophan and methionine. Legumes (beans, peas, lentils) are low in methionine and tryptophan but high in lysine. Eaten together, the protein will be complete. This is referred to as complementation. Some other examples follow:

- Brown rice: low in isoleucine and lysine, but mixed with beans it is high in isoleucine and lysine and gives you a complete protein.

- Legumes: low in tryptophan, methionine, and cysteine; high in lysine and isoleucine.

- Grains (wheat, oats, rice, barley, millet, corn, etc.): low in lysine and isoleucine; high in tryptophan, methionine, and cysteine.

- Seeds/nuts: low in lysine and isoleucine (but cashews and pumpkin seeds are not low in these amino acids); high in tryptophan, methionine, and cysteine.

- Milk products: low in nothing, high in lysine.

- Eggs: low in nothing; high in tryptophan, lysine, methionine, and cysteine.

- Vegetables: low in isoleucine, methionine, and cysteine; high in tryptophan and lysine.

NITROGEN

All protein is made up of approximately 16 percent nitrogen. Nitrogen is burned off during the manufacturing of protein; the ammonia odor of our excretions is created by this process.

When there are not enough carbohydrates from an energy source, nitrogen takes it upon itself to use amino acids and protein as fuel. During exercise, as the muscles are being stressed, nitrogen aids the anabolic process that takes place.

A cell lives longer when it retains nitrogen, allowing other amino acids to produce new cell growth. When this is not the case, the amino acids have to be used to replace of dying cells.

PROTEIN AND ENERGY

When too much protein is consumed and the body cannot convert it to building tissue or supplying energy, the liver will convert it to fat. The average 154-pound male needs only 23 grams of protein per day; he normally consumes about 94 grams per day. Fear, anxiety, pain, anger, heat, cold, and stress increase the need for protein.

If there are not enough calories available for fuel, the body will metabolize protein for energy. Hence protein should always be consumed along with carbohydrates and fat; otherwise, protein will be used as an energy source, and without fat, the carbohydrates will be incompletely used and this can cause headache, sickness, and a loss of appetite.

CARBOHYDRATES

Along with proteins, fats, water, vitamins, and minerals, carbohydrates are one of the six principal categories of nutrients. Carbohydrates are commonly referred to as sugars and starches.

Carbohydrates, which are formed in the process of photosynthesis in plants, are an extremely important part of our food. Carbohydrates are basically energy foods; they satisfy our hunger.

On a dry basis, three-quarters of the weight of a plant consists of carbohydrates. And, under certain situations, carbohydrates can be altered into simpler compounds and oxidized to provide energy. The majority of organic compounds found in plants are obtained from carbohydrates.

Fifty to 60 percent of the food we consume consists of carbohydrates. Foods high in carbohydrates are cereals (whole grains), baked products, legumes, fruits, vegetables, nuts, and enriched cereal products.

Carbohydrates are broken down into simple sugars during the process of digestion. These sugars are assimilated into the bloodstream and then into tissues where their energy is released. As the glucose level rises, the pancreas secretes insulin (a hormone that transforms a portion of the extra glucose into glycogen). The excess glucose is changed into fat and stored in the body. There is no other way in which carbohydrates can be absorbed into the body.

It is impossible for the body to digest fat without the presence of carbohydrates. If fat cannot be completely digested, the residue causes physical discomforts.

MONOSACCHARIDES

The most familiar monosaccharides, or simple sugars are glucose and, fructose. Glucose (dextrose) is a white solid, a sugar present in grapes, cherries, apples, plums, and other ripe fruits, and in fruit juices and nuts. Honey consists of approximately 35 percent glucose. Onions and unripe potatoes contain rather large amounts. Glucose is widely used in liquid form, especially in soft drinks where it is added to stabilize flavor and color and increase body without adding too much sweetness. In its liquid form, glucose can create combinations of sweeteners that can be used to enhance flavor. Glucose is also used in canning and preserving fruit to preserve the flavor, color, and form.

31

Fructose (fruit sugar or laevulose) is also found in the juice of many fruits and in honey. It is also found in combination with glucose.

Monosaccharides are formed in the fat and protein in living cells.

DISACCHARIDES

Disaccharides (sucrose, maltose, lactose) incorporate two connected nonsaccharide units, which may be similar or totally different.

Sucrose (ordinary sugar) is a white crystalline solid. Like most sugar, it dissolves in water. Sucrose can be obtained from almonds, many fruits, tubers, and the saps of some trees.

Sugar is processed from sugar cane, which is obtained in tropical countries only, or from sugar beets, which are grown in temperate climates. The sugar processed from these two sources is identical in flavor, texture, and color.

POLYSACCHARIDES

The polysaccharides are starch, dextrine (wheat products, honey), cellulose, glycogen (an animal starch in liver), enulin (Jerusalem artichokes), pectic substances and gum. Polysaccharides are nondigestible carbohydrates.

Plants use starch to store their energy. Starch is found in all plant life, but larger quantities are found in seeds, tubers, and root vegetables. Starch must be cooked in order for the body to digest it properly. When heated in water, the water enters the starch granules and they become pliable and expand, sometimes forming a paste.

Cellulose and pectin, referred to as fiber or roughage, provide bulk within the intestinal tract, thus allowing food to travel freely without any hindrance. Cellulose and pectin are not a source of energy because they are nondigestible.

Some cellulose foods contain phytic acid, which combines with iron or calcium to create an indigestible, insoluble mixture. If the phytic acid is not cooked and, consequently, useless, it will combine with the calcium and iron of other foods eaten along with it, destroying their food value. Phytic acid also can affect calcium and iron stored in the body.

CARBOHYDRATES AND ENERGY

Carbohydrates are an important food, but refined carbohydrate products must be avoided. Eating products with refined sugar raises the blood sugar level, giving a feeling of tremendous energy. But, this feeling dissipates quickly, causing the blood sugar to be lowered rapidly; it can cause tiredness and a craving for more sugar.

Carbohydrates are the most practical and economical way to obtain energy. Being selective about them is very important. Choose foods that first supply vitamins, minerals, and protein and then choose from the whole foods high in unrefined and complex carbohydrates, such as whole grains, seeds, beans, nuts, vegetables and fruits.

FATS AND OILS

Fats and oils (lipids) are a large group of organic substances that are either water insoluble or ether soluble. They are easily digested and utilized by the body. Almost all foods, including fruits and vegetables, contain fats or oils.

Fat and oil are not two separate substances. Oil is a fat that is liquid at normal room temperatures and becomes solid when cooled; fat remains solid or partially solid at room temperature and will become a liquid when the temperature is raised. Some fats contain large amounts of oil, but as long as they remain solid at room temperatures, they are considered fats.

Fifteen percent of the germ in whole grain cereals is fat, but it is processed out during milling along with the fat-soluble vitamin E. Nuts are very good sources of fat: walnuts, 64 percent; peanuts, 45 percent; and pecans, 73 percent. Animal products are fine sources of fat. We also add fat to food, with shortening, in frying, or as salad dressing during food preparation.

Fats serve a variety of purposes in the human body:

1. Fats provide an essential fatty acid, linoleic acid. This acid cannot be produced by any other food composition. Linoleic acid prevents cholesterol from building up on the walls of arteries.

2. Fats emphasize the flavors of food because most flavors are fat soluble.

3. Fats slow down intestinal mobility, decreasing the feelings of hunger.

33

4. Fats transport the fat-soluble vitamins, A, D, E, and K, and essential fatty acids throughout the body.

5. Gram for gram, fat supplies more than double the amount of energy that proteins or carbohydrates supply. (9 calories per gram fat, 4 calories per gram from proteins or carbohydrates).

6. The fat under the outer layer of skin prevents heat loss. This surplus is readily available when needed as fuel.

7. Fat cushions the vital organs, protecting them against injury.

8. Fats cannot be totally digested unless carbohydrates and proteins are present. If they are not present, a residue remains, which can cause headaches.

KINDS OF FATS

There are different kinds of fats. Broadly, fats are grouped into saturated and unsaturated; all fats contain both types, with one in a greater proportion.

Saturated fats have a tendency to be solid at room temperature. They are processed mainly from animal sources (lard, butterfat). Coconut oil and palm oil have large amounts of saturated fats and are found mainly in imitation dairy products. Saturated fats contain cholesterol but do not spoil quickly.

Unsaturated fats are liquid at room temperature. They are processed from vegetables, nuts, or seeds. Unsaturated oils used in frying can change their composition during the frying process to become saturated. Unsaturated oils, such as soya oil, soybean oil, and corn oil, containing vitamin E, an antioxidant, remain stable and do not change their nature. Unsaturated oils spoil more easily than saturated ones.

An extremely good source of unsaturated fat is a product made from sesame seeds called tahini. It is used as a spread in sauces and in humus. Tahini is richer in calcium than milk.

Monosaturated fats (oleic acid) contain no cholesterol. Two such fats are olive oil and peanut oil.

A high intake of polyunsaturated fats (linoleic acid), such as cottonseed oil, soybean oil, sesame oil, corn oil, and safflower oil, regulates the newly formed cholesterol by keeping the level low and mobilizing deposits on the artery walls. One or two teaspoons of corn oil, or its equal, each day will supply a substantial amount of linoleic acid.

Animal fats deteriorate more quickly than vegetable fats. All fats and oils spoil quickly if submitted to high heat (due to loss of significant amounts of vitamin E), light, some metals, and oxygen. Synthetic additives have very little effect on retarding spoilage and are usually not required. In the pure state, fats have no color. The yellow color that most oils have is caused by the pigments carotene and xanthophyll.

Lecithin is added to some oils as an emulsifying agent. Some commercial oils are a mixture of triglycerides of a few different fatty acids. Purified oils contain minute amounts of other compounds that usually have no effect on flavor.

Commercial vegetable oils are submitted to boiling temperatures, which destroys vitamin E and other vitamins. In order to get more oil, the vegetables, seeds, or grains are treated with petroleum-based chemical solvents; then the oil is bleached and deodorized. High-quality oils for cooking and baking are sesame and corn oils. Sesame can be purchased in a light or dark oil. The dark oil comes from roasted seeds with a rich, nutlike flavor. The light oil is processed from raw seeds.

Health food stores sell sesame and corn oils manufactured by a process called cold processing. Cold processing presses the oil from the seed or vegetable at low-heat temperatures. Cold-pressed oils have a flavor similar to the original seed or grain. The nutritional content is not lost, and no bleaches or solvents are added. These oils also do not spoil as quickly as commercial oils because the vitamin E content is intact; it is lack of this vitamin that causes rancidity. To prevent rancidity and prevent vitamin E loss, keep fats and oils refrigerated (the cloudiness that may occur does not affect the quality) or in a cool, dark cupboard, preferably in brown or opaque glass bottles. And keep them tightly sealed.

VITAMINS AND MINERALS

Vitamins, which are organic components, and minerals, which are inorganic substances (chemicals), are needed in tiny amounts and are best obtained from foods that retain their organic molecular structure. Packaged, processed, and preserved foods can alter their vitamin and mineral content through processing.

Vitamins and minerals cannot be manufactured by the body. However, they are easily produced by synthetic chemical compounds in a laboratory, and the nutritive value is equal to that of the natural vitamin. A possible difference is that the natural form may contain other substances of nutritional value that are not present in the synthetic form. The body cannot distinguish between the molecules of natural or synthetic vitamins and minerals.

There are more than twenty minerals in the body. With the exception of vitamins A and D, vitamins and minerals are nontoxic and are either stored for later use or excreted as waste. Vitamins and minerals are not food but are catalysts in organizing the body's living processes. Minerals control water balance and regulate acid-base balance, structural components, and constituents of enzymes and hormones.

Vitamins are different from other nutrients in that they do not form groups. Each has a specific function in maintaining the process of life, tissue repair, and the production of growth and energy. Vitamins also help process fats and proteins. Some vitamins are liquids, some solids; some are water-soluble, others fat-soluble. No vitamin has the ability to do the work of another.

A lack of vitamins and minerals will lead to bad health. A serious deficiency may even lead to disease.

Be careful not to become complusive about vitamin intake. Do not take vitamins lightly; reading and experimentation are the best ways to improve your health. The diet best for you may take a long time to formulate, but it can be found in live food intake if a wide range of food is regularly eaten.

If you feel you are lacking in one vitamin or mineral, you are probably deficient in others as well. Supplements can be used, but unless a doctor recommends a specific vitamin or mineral, a daily multiple vitamin is more than enough until you know exactly what you are doing.

For vitamins and minerals to fulfill their functions, they must be taken along with live food. The purpose of vitamins and minerals is to guide food into its proper function in the body. Unless you eat a large breakfast, lunch time is the best time to take supplements.

The body cannot be allergic to a vitamin or mineral supplement, but it can be allergic to the filler binder or capsule. Find out the ingredients, and if necessary switch to another make of vitamin.

The body excretes any excess vitamins and minerals every four hours. If you are taking large amounts of vitamins C and B, space them out during the day to prevent loss of vitamins, minerals, and money.

The only incompatible vitamin and mineral are iron and vitamin E. Iron supplements prevent vitamin E absorption. This causes no problem except for a loss of vitamin E.

Once a vitamin bottle is opened, it should be refrigerated. The temperature of a refrigerator is more constant than that of a room, and refrigerating will prevent changes in the supplement. Also, some compounds are light sensitive, which can affect the product's quality.

ENZYMES

Enzymes are proteins and organic catalysts. In the living cells, they alter a chemical reaction without causing a chemical change. Enzymes are made or synthesized in the body's tissues and organs. Taking enzyme preparations or those found in food does not aid the digestive process in the human body.

ANTIVITAMINS AND PROVITAMINS

In a chemical reaction, an antivitamin is an antagonist and can be a substitute for a vitamin.

The structure of provitamins is similar to that of vitamins. The body can change a provitamin into the chemical structure of a vitamin and performs in the same way as the active vitamin. Foods that contain provitamins are good sources of the vitamin. For example, carotene becomes vitamin A.

VITAMINS

Vitamin A (Retinol)

Vitamin A protects the linings of mucus membranes throughout the body, especially those of the throat, bronchial tubes, sinuses, and retina. It protects the skin, manufactures the visual purple that helps prevent night

37

blindness, and helps prevent colds and other illnesses. Any overabundance of vitamin A is stored in the liver until needed. A few provitamins contribute largely to the body's vitamin A intake: alpha, beta, gamma carotenes, and crystoxanthin, the yellow-orange pigment in most fruits and vegetables. Beta yellow, is so intense that it is used commercially as a coloring agent in processed foods; this also increases the vitamin A content of the food.

Vitamin A is produced in the intestine from carotene, a coloring agent. No plant food contains true (preformed) vitamin A. Preformed vitamin A is found only in liver, milk fat, egg yolks, and foods of animal origin.

Vitamin A is fat soluble, insoluble in water, and occurs in the stable form in most food. Steaming, boiling, or soaking does not lessen the vitamin A content. Frying causes some loss of vitamin A; fats that undergo oxidative rancidity quickly lose their vitamin A.

Vitimin A is found in yellow and orange fruits (apricots, peaches, nectarines) and vegetables, tomatoes, green vegetables (spinach, watercress, cabbage), margarine, milk and dairy products, fish, liver, kidney, liver oil, and egg yolk.

Vitamin B Complex

All the B vitamins are water soluble and must be supplied daily. There is no living tissue or food without all the B vitamins near each other. They complement one other; if one is a little short, another may help by doing its work. A balance is necessary; you should have plenty of all the B vitamins rather than large amounts of only a few.

The B vitamins play an essential role in metabolizing energy from carbohydrates, fats, and proteins, and in the functioning of the nervous system. The B vitamins are easily destroyed by heat.

VITAMIN B1 (THIAMINE): Vitamin B1 is important to the health of the nervous system, eyes, and skin. It prevents beriberi; aids metabolism and growth; and helps process carbohydrates, fats, and proteins. It aids maintaining a good appetite by promoting the growth and production of hormones and digestive juices.

When the body is releasing energy, vitamin B1 helps the burning of glucose. A minute amount of B1 is produced by the body, but the majority must be obtained, daily, from the food we eat.

Vitamin B1 is found in brewer's yeast, wheat germ, legumes (peas, soybeans), beans, potatoes, nuts, milk, eggs, fish roe, yeast extract, fish, pork, bacon, liver, lean meat, oranges, and whole grains.

VITAMIN B2 (RIBOFLAVIN): This is the one B vitamin that is not best taken in raw form, as its catalytic action is much more effective after cooking. Frying, roasting, and canning, however, cause a large loss of this vitamin. Riboflavin in solution (milk) is damaged by exposure to light.

Vitamin B2 is involved in energy production and the utilization of nutrients. It also helps activate B6, folic acid, and B13.

Vitamin B2 is found in brewer's yeast, meat, milk and dairy products, beans, nuts, enriched cereals, whole grains, and leafy greens. Liver has the most vitamin B2.

VITAMIN B3 (NIACIN OR NICOTINIC ACID): Vitamin B3 maintains healthy skin. Eating enough protein influences the B3 intake. The amino acid tryptophan is converted to niacin in the body. Vitamin B3 is involved in energy production. Foods containing B3 are in the indigestible form and need to be cooked; very little is destroyed in the cooking.

Vitamin B3 is found in broad beans, potatoes, chocolate, cereals, brewer's yeast, liver, kidney, bread, peanuts and peanut butter, yeast extract, legumes, and whole grains.

VITAMIN B6 (PRIDOXINE, PYRIDOXAL PHOSPHATE): Vitamin B6 is necessary for a few chemical reactions in the enzyme system, for the conversion of protein, and for the arrangement of blood cells. It is necessary for healthy skin, for growth, and for the nervous system. Twenty to 50 percent of the vitamin is lost in cooking.

Vitamin B6 is found in bananas, peanuts, fish, liver, yeast, potatoes, prunes, raisins, egg yolk, brewer's yeast, whole grains, and vegetables.

VITAMIN B12 (COBALAMINE, CYANOCOBALAMIN): Degeneration of nerve cells in the spinal cord, pernicious anemia, and other forms of anemia that result from a lack of vitamin B12. The vitamin is essential to the nervous system, digestive tract, bone marrow, and all cells.

Vitamin B12 contains cobalt, which is necessary in the structure of red blood corpuscles. Some B12 is created naturally in the large intestine when microorganisms interact with cobalt. Whether this is enough for the body without any additions is still a controversy. Twenty to 50 percent of the vitamin is lost through cooking.

Research has recently discovered that B12 can be found in foods other than animal sources, such as milk, meat, fish and eggs. There is B12 in fermented soybeans (miso) and sea vegetables. In yogurt, the B12 in the milk is depleted by the bacterial action of fermentation.

Folic Acid (Folacin)
Folic Acid interacts with B12 to produce red blood cells and the synthesis of nucleoproteins. Up to 90 percent is lost in cooking meats and up to 100 percent is lost in cooking fruits and vegetables. Folic acid is found in meats, fruits, dark green leafy vegetables, liver, kidney, leaf lettuce, legumes, oranges, bananas, mushrooms, nuts, and grains.

Pantothenic Acid
Pantothenic acid is necessary for healthy skin and body growth; it fights infection through the production of antibodies and transforms fats and carbohydrates into energy.

Pantothenic acid is found in brewers yeast, wheat bran, green vegetables (especially peas, lima beans, broccoli), milk, raw mushrooms, egg yolk, and cereals. Liver and kidneys are the richest source.

Biotin
Biotin is necessary for the healing process of the skin. The body produces small amounts of biotin in the intestine, but additional amounts must be obtained from food. Biotin plays a role in the utilization of carbohydrates, fats, and proteins.

Raw egg white contains a substance called avidin, which makes biotin non-usable in the body. Cooked egg white does not have this effect.

Biotin is found in raw oatmeal, nuts, egg yolk, cheddar cheese, milk, bread, beans, cauliflower, leeks, liver, kidneys, oysters, canned salmon, brewers yeast, mung bean sprouts, cooked soybeans, some fruits and vegetables, and nuts.

Inositol and Para-Amino-benzoic Acid (PABA)
This is a vitamin-like substance related to the B complex vitamins.

Vitamin C (Ascorbic Acid)
Vitamin C is important to small blood vessels (capillaries), connective tissues, body structure, wound healing, normal metabolism, and the pre-

vention and treatment of scurvy. It is needed in combination with calcium and phosphorus for clean skin, healthy gums and teeth, and bones and cartilage. Vitamin C is water soluble and must be replenished every day. It is needed in increasing amounts during times of infection (colds); whether long-term megadoses are healthful or harmful is controversial. Vitamin C is oxidized by heat and light and exposure to air; fifty to 80 percent is lost in most cooking, and 100 percent is lost in steaming.

Large amounts of vitamin C are available in red and green peppers, Brussels sprouts, broccoli, parsley, cabbage, strawberries, citrus fruits, fish liver oils, kale, rose hips, melon, cauliflower, potatoes, bean sprouts.

Vitamin D (Calciferol, Cholecalciferol)

Known as the sunshine vitamin, vitamin D is fat soluble. Excess is stored in the body fat and is toxic in overdose. Vitamin D is nonexistent in plants. Its major source is the manufacture in our bodies (from the ultraviolet rays in sunlight or sunlamps) of a substance called ergosterol, which lies under the skin.

Calcium and phosphorus need the interaction of vitamin D; otherwise, they are excreted from the body instead of being absorbed through the intestinal walls into the blood (increasing phosphate levels) to develop sound teeth and bones. A small amount of vitamin D is used in maintenance and repair. It is not lost by cooking in water or destroyed by heat; however, because it is fat soluble, it is destroyed by deep frying.

Vitamin D is found in cod liver oil, butter, margarine, milk, cheese, egg yolk, herring, mackerel, sardines, shrimp, and tuna.

Vitamin E (Alpha Tocopherol)

Vitamin E is a fat-soluble vitamin destroyed by frying only. It is a controversial vitamin claimed to do the following:

- Prevent heart disease.
- Act as an antisterility compound and strengthener of the heart.
- Prevent formation of blood clots.
- Act as an agent in healing fibers.
- Prevent circulatory disease.
- Prevent polyunsaturated fats from oxidizing before the body can use them.

41

- Help form new skin over wounds and burns.
- Promote better circulation by enlarging arteries.
- Create new arteries or blood vessels around damaged portions.
- Maintain muscles.
- Promote healthy sex organs.

The main sources of vitamin E are wheat germ oil, wheat germ, green vegetables, whole wheat bread, wheat flour, whole grains, roasted peanuts, seeds, peanut oil, butter, cheese, milk, corn oil, soya oil, cottonseed oil, liver, and eggs.

Vitamin K (Menadione, Phylloquinone)

Vitamin K is fat soluble; it is synthesized by bacterial action in the intestines. It acts in the process of blood coagulating and promotes the healing of cuts and wounds. Without it, we would bleed to death from the slightest scratch. It is destroyed only by frying.

Vitamin K is found in green vegetables (kale, cabbage, spinach, green peas), alfalfa sprouts, cauliflower, soybeans, liver, kidney, whole grains, wheat germ, wheat bran, egg yolk, potatoes, and tomatoes.

MINERALS

Arsenic

Not too much is known about arsenic, but it may have a role in body structure and phosphates. Small traces are found in urine.

Boron

Very little is known about boron. Traces are found in urine.

Calcium

Calcuim is the most abundant mineral and is the major ingredient in bones and teeth; it is essential for their growth and durability. Calcium can be taken from the bones if needed for other reasons; thus, calcium must be replaced daily. It is also found in muscle and extracellular fluid in the body. Calcuim helps maintain the heartbeat.

The calcium/phosphorus ratio is important to the way calcium is absorbed; also, ascorbic acid and lysine (an amino acid) help fortify calcium absorption. Phytic acid (bran cereals) and oxalic acid (organic acids

— spinach, rhubarb, chard, beet greens) combine with calcium, hindering absorption; however, these foods are necessary in the diet as long as they are eaten in small quantities. Favoring calcium absorption is the lactose found in sugar in milk.

Excess fat will combine with calcium in the intestines to form calcium soaps that become insoluble, making calcium unavailable to the body.

Calcium is found in all dairy products, green vegetables, turnips, soybeans, nuts, sesame seeds, oatmeal, flour, bread, hard water, sardines, canned salmon, figs, apricots, and dates. Small amounts are found in grains and in blackstrap molasses.

Chlorine
Chlorine forms hydrochloric acid in the stomach. It serves as an antiseptic factor in the system. It is excreted through the urine and must be supplemented daily.

Chloride
Chloride maintains acid-base balance in body fluids. It is found mainly in table salt, milk, meat, and eggs.

Chromium
Chromium is necessary in the body for the formation and utilization of insulin. It helps improve the glucose intake by interacting with insulin. The body will not accept chromium in pill form.

Chromium is found in fruits, whole grains, vegetables, and brewers yeast.

Cobalt
A structural consitituent of vitamin B12, cobalt is used in the formation of read blood cells. It is found in flesh foods, milk, seaweed, limited amounts in land plants.

Copper
The exact function of copper in the body is not completely known; however, copper exists in all living things. It is a catalyst for the formation of hemoglobin; along with ascorbic acid, it helps in the formation of elastin, a connective tissue in the heart. It helps in the formation of another connective tissue, collagen.

Melanin, a dark pigment in hair and skin, is produced from an amino acid, tyrosine or tyrosinose, a copper-containing enzyme necessary to produce this pigment. Copper also takes a part in the formation of the insulation for nerve fibers, the myelin sheath formed from phospholipids.

Fluorine
Fluorine is found in the bones and teeth and is most widely known for preventing tooth cavities. It is found in fish bones, sardines, tea, water, toothpaste, sodium fluoride in drinking water, seafoods, and seaweed.

Iodine
The majority of iodine is utilized by the thyroid gland, located in the neck, to produce thyroid hormones (thyroxine), which are important to mental and physical health, the regulation of energy metabolism, protein synthesis, cholesterol production, the conversion of carotene to vitamin A, and carbohydrate assimilation. The remaining iodine is used by all the cells. Iodine must be kept in proper balance; too much or too little severely upsets the body's system.

Iodine is found in fish, shellfish, watercress, onions, table salt (iodized), powdered kelp, and other edible seaweed. The content in milk and eggs depends on what the animals have been fed.

Iron
Iron is important primarily in supplying and conditioning red blood cells. A portion of the hemoglobin in red blood corpuscles carries oxygen through the body to provide energy. Iron is stored in the liver and used over and over before being excreted; however, a constant supply is needed for the creation and replacement of red cells. The iron available in food can be increased by 100 to 400 percent when food is cooked in iron cookware.

Iron is lost through bleeding, digestive juices that are secreted, sweating, and in cutting the hair and nails. Iron combined with pytates (phytic acid or oxalic acid) impedes the absorption of iron and will cause it to pass through the body (iron in wheat). The cellulose in fruits and vegetables, starch, antacid preparations, and pancreatic secretions diminish iron absorption. Egg yolk not only inhibits iron absorption from the yolk but other foods as well; however, sugar, iron salts (dietary supplements), asscorbic acid, and hydrochloric acid in the stomach all hasten absorption.

Iron digested and used by the body can be found in liver, pumpkin seeds, molasses, almonds, raisins, nuts, potatoes, cabbage, apricots, water, meat, egges, leafy greens, dried fruit, whole grain bread and cereals, and soybean products with the exception of soy oil.

Magnesium

Magnesium is essential for muscular tissues and bones, retains calcium in the teeth, and is part of the fluid that surrounds nerve cells to conduct nerve impulses that relax muscles after contraction and in the brain. Most of the magnesium in the body is stored in the bone structure. An important ingredient in chlorophyll, the green substance found in vegetation, magnesium is necessary for proper metabolism. Magnesium releases thyroxine to assist the body to adjust to a cold environment.

Magnesium is present in most foods, mainly fresh green vegetables, seafood, seaweed, soy flour, nuts, tofu, whole grains, molasses, and sesame seeds.

Manganese

Manganese is an important aid in sexual functioning, normal bone formation, and tissue respiration. It is found in all green leafy vegetables, blueberries, wheat bran, nuts, whole grains, tea, legumes, peanut butter, and fruits.

Molybdenum

Molybdenum is found in an enzyme used in the construction of uric acid and is a component of the enzyme that influences iron reserves. It is found in organ meats, legumes, cereals, and brewers yeast.

Nickel

Nickel is related to pigmentation throughout the body.

Phosphorus

Phosphorus works in conjunction with calcium. A daily supply of phosphorus is necessary for proper bone structure (90 percent of phosphorus is stored in the bones) and tooth formation. It is part of every cell and tissue of the body. It also plays a part in releasing energy.

Calcium and phosphorus need to be taken on a one-to-one ratio. Excessive phosphorus intake decreases calcium absorption in the body. The shortage of calcium will be drawn from the calcium stored in the bones.

Phosphorus exists in all foods, especially flesh foods, milk, eggs, cereal grains, wheat germ, whole grains, oatmeal, cashews, peanuts, dried beans, peas, and brewers yeast. Vegetables and fruits are low in phosphorus.

Potassium

Potassium is an important regulator of body fluids; it is prominent in muscles and blood cells. United with phosphorus, potassium aids brain cells, helps heal injuries and assists in the absorption of energy by the cells and in the control of the acid-base balance. It acts as a catalyst in the metabolism of energy, making energy convenient for use by carbohydrates, fats, and proteins.

Potassium is found in avocados, mushrooms, potatoes, winter squash, bananas, cauliflower, nuts, yeast, prunes, beef, brewers yeast, bran, molasses, and oranges.

Selenium

Selenium works with vitamin E to help prevent injury to red blood cells. It is present in all tissues, hair, liver, and kidneys. It can be toxic at high levels.

Selenium is found in brewers yeast, onions, garlic, eggs, seafood, seaweed, milk, and wheat cereals.

Silicon

Silicon aids in the making of collagen (protein) in connective tissue.

Sodium

Besides being one of the two components of table salt (sodium chloride), sodium controls the acid-base balance and helps maintain the proper amount of water in the tissue. Sodium works with potassium to render the absorption of many nutrients, including glucose, and to convey nerve impulses.

Excess salt is harmlessly eliminated in perspiration and urine in a person without health problems. A lack of salt prevents protein digestion and causes loss of necessary body fluids.

Sodium is found in all foods, especially meat, milk, eggs, seafood, seaweed, and table salt.

Sulfur

Sulfur is a component in hair, nails and skin. Sulfur is found in every cell in the body. It is also a crucial part of the B vitamins, thiamin, pantothenic acid, and biotin.

Sulfur is obtained from protein foods containing the following amino acids: crystine, cysteine, and methionine. It is also found in wheat germ, cheese, peanuts, lentils, kidney beans, lean beef, and clams.

Vanadium

Vanadium reduces cholesterol formation and promotes teeth strengthening by replacing amounts of phosphorus.

Zinc

Zinc helps fortify the outer layer of the body's skin. It enables the blood to carry and release carbon dioxide by being a part of an enzyme (carbonic anhydrose) that is prominent in this release.

Zinc is found in cheese, liver, eggs, seaweed, oysters, herring, pumpkin seeds, whole grains, legumes, and some brands of brewers yeast.

THE NATURAL
FOODS PANTRY

EGGS

There are three main parts to an egg: the white, the yolk, and the shell. Shell colors include white, brown, and blue. The quality of the egg is not influenced by the color of the shell. The breed of hen determines shell color. Paying a higher price for white shells is foolish.

Eggshells are not digestible and are discarded. Shells are porous and can absorb moisture, gases, and other contaminants. Cracked eggs also can be contaminated with bacteria; wash eggs well before use. Never wash and then store eggs because the wet surface will increase the chance of contamination.

Inside the egg's shell are membranes, which are only noticeable if the egg is hard cooked. One membrane covers the shell, another surrounds the content of the egg (if a raw egg is broken, both membranes adhere to the shell). A third membrane surrounds the egg yolk. Attached to each end of the yolk is a white substance called chalaza (threadlike), which keeps the egg yolk centered within the egg. (These threads should be removed before cooking as they can cause a lumpy consistency in foods such as custards.) Chalaza is an edible egg white protein.

The color of the egg yolk is derived from the carotenoid group (vitamin A). The color comes from plants like yellow corn, green grass, and alfalfa. The color does not affect the nutritional content. Hens that are allowed to have access to the above plants and that are exposed to sunlight will lay eggs with dark pigmented yolks, thick whites, and thick shells (organic eggs). When such an egg is broken into a skillet, the egg will remain in place, without the white running all over the pan like eggs from a supermarket. Supermarket eggs are fragile; they have watery whites and light yellow yolks.

The vitamin A and B content of an egg is directly related to the hen's feed. Fertile and non-fertile eggs have the same nutritional content. The majority of eggs are nonfertile because hens produce more eggs when separated from the rooster. Outdoor hens yield ten times as many eggs as confined hens. There is a higher nutritional content in eggs from range-fed hens.

Egg yolks are an extremely important source of vitamin D. One yolk contains 10 to 15 international units. The yolk also contains phosphorus, calcium, magnesium, chlorine, potassium, sodium, sulfur, iron, and ash.

Egg yolk is high in lecithin, and one egg contains 200 to 300 mg of cholesterol. Cholesterol comes partly from the food fed to the hens and partly from the development of the yolk. The fat found in an egg is in the yolk alone, and the triglycerides are predominately saturated fatty acids.

The white of an egg contains sulfur, potassium, sodium, chlorine, phosphorus, calcium, magnesium, iron, and ash. Egg white is a valuable source of riboflavin, but no other vitamin is abundant. Iodine and copper vary from egg to egg.

High-quality complete protein is found in every part of the egg. In the raw state, avidin, a protein in egg white, blends with biotin (a vitamin), forming a complex that is indigestible. This process does not occur when the egg is cooked.

Whether chemical additives and hormones added to the feed, systemic pesticides, and antibiotic residues in eggs may cause health problems is not known. Care must be taken to determine whether the eggs in health food stores are truly organic.

Eggs should not be kept for too long, or an air sac will form at one end of the egg and become more alkaline due to loss of carbon dioxide. Alkalinity will cause the whites to become runny; the egg yolk will enlarge, causing the membranes to weaken; flavor will deteriorate; and a green coloring, caused by iron and sulfur-forming ferrous sulfide, will appear on the surface of a hard-cooked egg. (This coloring can also be caused by not cooling the egg quickly enough. In either case, the color is not harmful to eat.)

Buy eggs that have been refrigerated. Eggs are easily stored, in or out of the shell. Egg whites and yolks, covered with a thin layer of water to prevent a thick film from forming over the yolk, can be stored, tightly covered, in the refrigerator for a few days. Whole eggs should also be stored in the refrigerator. It is best to store them in covered containers because the porous quality of the shells enables them to absorb other odors. For best quality, use eggs within a week of purchase. Yolks, whites, and the two mixed well will freeze successfully.

EGG GRADES AND SIZES

The grading of eggs and egg size are not related. Any size egg can be any grade. The grade and size are on every carton. All grades of eggs have the same nutritive value.

GRADES	DESCRIPTION
AA	An all-purpose egg of high quality
A	Best used for frying and cooking
B	An all-purpose egg at the best price

EGG SIZE	OUNCES
Jumbo	30
X-Large	27
Large	24
Medium	21
Small	18
Pee Wee	15

Most recipes in cookbooks are based on medium-size eggs. Low to moderate cooking temperatures should be used in cooking egg protein.

HARD-COOKED EGGS IN THE SHELL

To prevent eggs from cracking when they are put in boiling water, make a small hole, with a needle, at the large end of the egg. Simmer medium eggs for no longer than 10 minutes. After it is cooked, a hard-cooked egg should be firm and white with an opaque yolk and no green discoloration (either from old eggs or overcooking or not cooling quickly enough).

For soft cooking, always simmer, rather than boil, and the cooked egg will have a very tender quality.

POACHED EGGS

Eggs, out of the shell, can be poached in water or milk at simmering temperatures. Use very fresh eggs, preferably organic eggs, because the whites are not as runny as those of other eggs. Bring the liquid to a boil; break and add the egg quickly, to thicken in one mass. Turn off heat, cover, and let sit for 3 to 4 minutes, until the consistency you want is reached.

FRIED EGGS

For sunny-side eggs: Heat butter or margarine, using enough to spoon over the cooking egg and to prevent the egg from sticking to the pan.

Break the egg carefully so as not to break the yellow. As the egg cooks to desired consistency, spoon fat over the egg to complete cooking. If cooking temperature is too high, the egg will be browned on the edges and bottom. The white should be opaque; the yellow should be partially hard or in a liquid state.

For easy-over eggs: Use less fat then with sunny-side eggs, but use enough to keep the egg from sticking to the pan. Cook until almost done, then very carefully turn the egg over and cook until desired doneness is achieved.

Frying Without Fat

A nonstick coating on a frypan or one of the nonstick sprays can be used. Heat the pan, add the egg and a few teaspoons of water. Cover and simmer until the egg is cooked to desired consistency.

One large egg, cooked without fat, is 80 calories; add 1 teaspoon (5 ml) of fat and it is 110 calories.

EGG SUBSTITUTES

One egg substitute is made from soy or milk products; another is made from the egg whites only. Egg substitutes have less sodium, half the fat, and half the calories of natural eggs. The fat in natural eggs has been replaced by corn oil, making the fat content higher in polyunsaturates; however, the flavor of egg substitutes is poor, and egg substitutes will not thicken in cooking.

CHEESE

Cheese is made from pasteurized whole milk, nonfat milk, or a mixture of whole milk and cream or certified raw milk (for natural cheese). It takes 10 (4.5 k) pounds of milk to make 1 pound (450 g) of cheese. The milk is coagulated and then the curd (casein) is separated from the whey. Cheese can be purchased in solid or semisolid form.

The precipitation of casein can be done in several ways: by acid added directly to milk; by acid produced by bacteria from lactose; or by rennin, an enzyme from the stomach of young calves. The most popular method is the combination of acid and rennin.

After the milk gels, the pieces are cut up and heated. The curds shrink and are separated from the whey, which is the liquid left after the curd is removed. (The whey contains soluble vitamins and minerals and whey protein. Whey is used for animal feed, cheeses, and gelatin desserts; its flavor is mild and sweet.) The curds are then treated with starters and fermented to create the many cheeses we buy in the markets with their varying degrees of texture and flavor.

During the process of making cheese, the B complex vitamins are lost except in the rind of aged cheeses (this rind is not usually eaten). Cheese made from whole milk is a good source of vitamin A and riboflavin. For example, 5 ounces (140 g) of American cheese has the approximate food value of 1 quart (1 l) of milk. Most cheeses are high in saturated fat, but cottage cheese has a low fat content.

Most cheeses preserve the original milk protein (a complete protein), calcium, and iron. While cheese is ripening, the lactose is transformed into lactic acid, making cheese a highly digestible food product. The lactose remains only in such fresh cheeses as cottage cheese.

CURING CHEESE
Soft unripened cheeses (cottage, cream, ricotta, and Neufchatel) have a high moisture content; therefore, due to rapid spoilage, there is no curing or ripening involved in making them. Salt and cream are added occasionally.

Soft ripened cheeses (Brie, camembert, and limburger) are inoculated with molds or strains of bacteria, which grow on the surface of the cheese. The cheese acquires its distinctive flavor and texture as the curing advances from the outside rind into the center.

Semisoft ripened cheeses (Bel Paese, Brick, Muenster, and Port du Salut) are ripened with the help of a bacterial or mold culture or both, and the curing progresses from both the interior and exterior.

Firm ripened cheeses (cheddar, Colby, Edam, Gouda, Provolone, and Swiss) age with the inoculation of a bacterial culture in the entire cheese.

In very hard ripened cheeses (Parmesan, Romano, and Sap Sago), curing advances very slowly with the aid of enzymes and bacterial cultures. Curing is extremely slow because of the high salt content and small amount of moisture in these cheeses.

In blue-vein ripened cheeses (blue, Gorgonzola, Stilton, and Roquefort), a mold culture and bacteria grows in the interior of the cheese to produce the distinctive flavor and appearance.

BUYING, STORING, AND COOKING WITH CHEESE

When buying cheese, buy natural-color (creamy white) cheese. If a cheese is orange, make sure carotene was used to obtain the color and not an artificial coloring.

The price of a cheese is determined by its flavor, not its nutritional value, and by the length of time it took for ripening. Normally the length of time for ripening determines the flavor, body, and texture of a cheese.

Cheese should be refrigerated. Storage life is limited and is determined by the kind of cheese: Soft unripened cheeses spoil quickly. Hard and semihard cheeses deteriorate slowly and should be stored in their original packaging. Cut cheeses must be wrapped in plastic or other sealant to hinder the drying process.

The mold that forms on older cheese is not harmful and needs only to be removed before the cheese is eaten. White deposits are crystals of the amino acid tyrosine and are not harmful.

Most cheeses do not stand up well to freezing. They become dry and crumbly or, with cottage cheese, powdery. Cheddar and Jack cheeses freeze if cut into chunks 1 inch (2.5 cm) thick; they can also be grated and frozen. Processed cheese and cream cheese can also be frozen.

If you are using cheese in cooking, you should chop or grate it before adding it to any cookery. Keep at a low cooking temperature and cook for a short length of time. It will curdle and have a grainy texture.

If you are melting cheese, a high cooking temperature will cause the cheese to shrink and the texture to become tough and rubbery due to moisture loss. The cheese will liquefy more quickly if the cheese has a high fat content. When making toasted cheese sandwiches, therefore, cook slowly to avoid a rubbery, stringy cheese.

CHEESE PRODUCTS

Processed cheese

Natural cheddar cheese is heated to isolate the fat from protein. Water and emulsifiers are added, and then the mixture is whipped. The result is a homogeneous product.

Cheese food
To make this product processed cheese is added to nonfat dry milk; it has a higher water content than processed cheese. Losses of protein, calcium, iron, and vitamins A and B are substantial.

Cheese spread
This cheese product is processed with more water than is used in cheese food.

Imitation dairy products
Some imitations are entirely synthetic, others have proteins or nonfat milk solids.

YOGURT

Yogurt is fermented milk, but the fermenting process gives the product a sour taste and a thick consistency. Natural-style yogurts (e.g., Dannon) are fermented with lactic and bacterial cultures in skim milk. Fruit preserves are used for flavoring and have to be mixed with the yogurt before eating. Natural-style yogurt has no additives or preservatives. Swiss-style yogurt is processed and the flavoring is premixed in the product. Swiss-style yogurt has additives and preservatives to obtain a smooth texture and tasteful flavor. Disease-causing bacteria can find their way into yogurt, but the antibacterial properties in yogurt kill most of these bacteria.

Yogurt is considered a low-calorie food, although flavored yogurt has as many as 260 calories in an 8-ounce (250 ml) serving. Only plain yogurt (the flavor is not pleasant to most people) is really low in calories; it has 130 calories in an 8-ounce (250 ml) serving.

The protein quality is slightly higher in yogurt than in milk because dry milk powder is added to commercial varieties of yogurt to increase the texture. Except for vitamin B2 the vitamin and mineral nutritional value of yogurt is equivalent to milk.

Most people believe that yogurt contains the acidophilus bacteria that prevents disease, and some attribute life-lengthening properties to it. Though scientific study shows yogurt to be a nutritious milk product, there is no proof it can lengthen the lifespan.

MILK

Milk is consumed in its natural state and contains all food nutrients necessary for good health. However, milk cannot be used as a complete diet. Nutrients such as iron, copper, manganese, and some vitamins are not available in the proper quantities to supply a balanced intake for good health.

There is a negative factor to having iron and copper in milk. They catalyze oxidation, which destroys some vitamins and can give milk a metallic taste. Normal babies are born with enough of these nutrients in reserve to keep them healthy until they can eat foods containing all nutrients; however, vitamins C and D should be added to their diets.

Milk fat, casein (a protein), and lactose (milk sugar, the principal carbohydrate in milk) are not available in other foods. Lactose increases the absorption of calcium, phosphorus, magnesium, and barium in the intestine and also enables nicotinic acid to synthesize in the intestines preventing rickets and pellagra.

The principal protein in milk is casein. Other proteins in milk are lactalbumin and traces of lactoglobulin and immunoglobulin. Milk contains all the essential amino acids except those that contain sulfur. It is low in the amino acid lysine, making milk complementary to cereals also low in lysine. The protein in one quart of milk equals that in five ounces of meat or fish, four ounces of American or cheddar cheese, five large eggs, or sixteen slices of bread.

Due to the large amount of water in milk (14 ounces per pint), it is a low energy food containing 320 calories in one pint. Fat supplies 50% of the total calories, lactose 25%, casein 21%.

Milk fats are both saturated and unsaturated. They are easily digested, and, consequently, cause fewer digestive disturbances than any other edible fat.

Milk is an extremely good source of calcium and has an excellent calcium/phosphorus ratio. Other minerals in milk are potassium, magnesium, sodium, chlorine, sulfur, iron, copper, bromine, manganese, copper, iodine, fluorine, zinc, cobalt, selenium, strontium, rubidium, mercury, and lead. It also contains vitamin A, all B vitamins, and vitamins C, D, and E.

STORAGE AND BUYING TIPS

The flavor of cow's milk, when first removed from the cow, is slight with a very mild taste and a hardly discernible sweetness. The flavor most people associate with milk develops after it is drawn from the cow. The flavor has nothing to do with the nutritive value of the milk.

Milk must be refrigerated to control any bacterial growth and enzyme activity. If you purchase milk in large containers, do not return the milk that has been removed for table use to the original container. Any glass or pitcher the milk is put into has a small amount of bacteria on it; if the milk is then mixed with fresh milk in the original container, bacteria will encourage spoilage.

Light contributes to the deterioration of some vitamins in milk. It is inadvisable to purchase milk in translucent containers or milk that has been stored near high intensity fluorescent lighting. These conditions allow oxidation, causing a flavor decrease two to four hours after the milk has been subjected to the light. The riboflavin and ascorbic acid content will decrease in direct proportion to the amount of light the milk is exposed to.

Homogenization stabilizes the emulsion of fat in milk and, consequently, the last serving of milk poured from a container has essentially the same concentration of fat as the first serving. A noticeable cream separation will not occur.

Pasteurization destroys bacteria that hastens spoilage as well as disease-causing bacteria. It also inactivates enzymes, such as natural milk lipose, that can cause the quality to deteriorate.

MILK PRODUCTS

Cream is the part of milk rich in milk fat that rises to the top when unhomogenized milk is allowed to stand. It can also be separated by centrifugal separation. The cream products generally available and their makeup are:

- Light cream, coffee cream, or table cream must be at least 18 percent fat, but not more than 30 percent fat.

- Light whipping cream is 30 percent to 36 percent fat.

- Heavy whipping cream should have a minimum of 36 percent fat.

Usually, the higher fat content increases the viscosity of cream. However, various lots of cream with the same fat content may vary in viscosity.

• Half and half is a combination of milk and cream. It has approximately 11.5% milk fat and is usually homogenized.

Eight ounces (250 ml) of skim milk contains 90 calories, 316 mg of calcium (more than in whole milk), 500 I.U. vitamin A, only 6 mg fat and a very low cholesterol content of 5 mg. All its other nutrients are similar to those in whole milk, except for fat and the fat-soluble vitamins (such as A and E) which must be supplemented from other food sources for a balanced diet. Skim milk is made by removing all the cream or milk fat from whole milk.

In low sodium milk, the salt content has been reduced from 550 mg to 50 mg per liter. Although small amounts of the B vitamins and possibly some calcium may be lost, low sodium milk has essentially the same nutritive value as whole milk.

Genuine buttermilk is the fluid left over after butter has been churned out of whole milk. Buttermilk is rarely available for sale except as a dried product sold to be used in baking. The buttermilk commonly found in supermarkets is cultured buttermilk. It is prepared from skim milk or low fat milk by fermentation with the bacteria Streptococcus cremoris and L-citrivorum. This buttermilk generally contains more salt than skim milk. It has less vitamin A and less fat than whole milk or fortified skim milk.

Sweetened condensed milk is a mixture of milk and an appropriate nutritive sweetener from which the water has been partially removed. The sweetener acts as a preservative. Sweetened condensed milk is pasteurized and can also be homogenized.

Canned (undiluted) evaporated milk is also called unsweetened condensed milk. One cup contains generally smaller quantities of vitamins (although it is an excellent source of vitamin A), but roughly double the amount of other nutrients as in whole milk. Evaporated milk is prepared by removing sixty percent of the water from whole milk by evaporation. The milk is then homogenized and the containers are heated either before or after sealing to prevent spoilage. This sterilization process causes a cooked flavor in the milk. Evaporated milk also contains an emulsifier and a stabilizer to ensure a smooth, creamy product.

Raw milk is unpasteurized. It contains phosphates, important to infants, that are destroyed in pasteurization. Raw milk also contains an enzyme necessary to fat utilization and one with a germicidal effect.

Cows that produce raw milk are inspected daily, shampooed daily, and milked by machines that are sterilized before each use. Raw milk must be delivered as soon as possible to the market. It is usually found in health food stores at a high price. After tasting the richness of raw milk, you will realize how sour pasteurized whole milk tastes.

Goat's milk has a soft curd and is naturally homogenized which makes it easier to digest than cow's milk. Soft curd means that it forms smaller, softer curds in the stomach, aiding digestion.

The milk of all species contains the same types of proteins. The chemical formation of goat's milk is similar to cow's milk with a vitamin content that is essentially the same. However, the folic acid and vitamin B content of goat's milk is lower than that of cow's milk.

MISO

Miso is a fermented soybean paste. The fermenting process eliminates the substance in whole soybeans that causes flatulence. Miso has an extremely rich flavor and is an excellent salt substitute. Miso has an advantage over salt in that it is a high-protein seasoning. The average salt content of miso is 12 percent salt. The following amounts of miso give the same amount of saltiness to your food as ½ teaspoon (2.5 ml) salt: 1 tablespoon (15 ml) salty miso, 2 teaspoons (10 ml) shoyu, 1 ½ to 2 tablespoons (22.5 to 30 ml) mellow miso, or 2 ½ to 3 tablespoons (37.5 to 45 ml) sweet miso.

Miso is a living food containing lactobacillus microorganisms (lactic and bacteria). It has the unique ability to aid in the digestion and assimilation of foods by creating a living digestive culture. This quality is available only in unpasteurized miso. Koji, spores of the mold aspergillus oryzae, is used in making miso and adds healthful microorganisms to miso.

The nutritional advantages to miso are as follows:

- Five percent oil, primarily soy oil and mostly unsaturated oil.

- No cholesterol.

- Rich in lecithin and linoleic acid, which dispel cholesterol and fatty acids from the circulatory system in the body.

- Carbohydrates in the configuration of simple sugars, making them easy to digest and making miso an excellent energy source.

- Very small amounts of fiber and cellulose.

- A very good source of vitamins B12 and B1 (niacin).

- Can be kept for long periods unrefrigerated and for months refrigerated. (An exception are the sweet misos. Due to the fermentation of natural sugars, they spoil quickly and must be refrigerated.)

- Contains calcium and iron.

Miso and other soy products have the amino acids lacking in grains. Thus miso is an excellent complementary protein—raising its quality as much as 30 to 40 percent—to rice, whole wheat bread, and noodles and in grain-based diets.

Miso is available in a wide variety of colors: tan, chocolate brown, amber, claret, cinnamon red, black, yellow, and beige.

Regular miso, which is the most popular, is not pasteurized and is available as follows: red (subtle sweetness), mellow red (slightly sweet), and sweet red; barley (heavy earthy flavor and dark color); and Hatcho (see below). Most rice miso is considered Hatcho or red. It is extremely nutritious if made with brown rice. It is saltier than the other miso and perferred over the others in cooking and soups. The above varieties can be smooth or can have chunks of soy beans or koji grains visible.

Special miso (natto) is sweet and is rarely used in cooking. Use it as a topping for tofu or with grains and spreads.

Mellow white (shiro white) is sweet.

Sweet white miso, mellow barley (sweet), and Quick miso (mellow beige or light yellow) have smooth consistencies and are sweet complements to fruit, salads, and spreads. Mellow barley is excellent in soups. Quick miso has a salty flavor and can be used in all kinds of cooking.

Hatcho is extremely thick and has an astringent flavor and a unique mellow sweetness. It is usually chunky with rice or soybeans. Purchase miso in sealed bags only; they are not pasteurized. The sealed bags can be bought in 1- or 2-pound weights. Miso can be kept in these bags, but reseal the opening securely with tape or a rubber band each time the product is used.

Read labels carefully to make sure no alcohol or other preservatives have been added. Also, be sure that the product you buy contains no synthetics, bleach, or unnatural sweeteners.

Dehydrated miso is also sold in foiled envelopes. Its is an excellent pick-me-up; it takes very little time to dissolve miso paste in hot water.

Miso that has no preservatives and is kept unrefrigerated can develop mold on the surface. Either blend it into the miso or scrape it off and discard. Sweet miso can darken and develop an alcoholic aroma. Neither is harmful, and light cooking will eliminate the alcohol.

Miso should not be cooked or cooked ever so briefly. Prolonged heat destroys the live micoorganisms. Add miso to food immediately before serving.

TOFU

Tofu, or bean curd, is not fermented, aged, or ripened. Tofu is made similarly to the process of making dairy curds. With tofu, the whey is removed from soymilk curds. The curds are heavily pressed for about 30 minutes, and the result is a solid piece of curds — tofu.

Tofu is an alternative to meat. In any form — fresh, dried, frozen, or yuba — tofu contains more protein than any other food. If the five highest protein sources were chosen, they would all be soybean products. Soy protein is a complete protein containing all eight essential amino acids.

Tofu protein is indistinguishable from chicken protein. An 8-ounce (225 g) serving of tofu is equal to 3¼ ounces (90 g) of steak or 5½ ounces (150 g) of hamburger and provides 11.5 grams of protein.

Tofu complements grains, for tofu is high in lysine, which is less abundant in grains. Grains, however, are high in methionine and cystine, the limiting amino acids in soybeans. Also, the carbohydrate in grain supplies energy, and the protein in tofu repairs and enhances tissue growth.

The advantages to tofu, nutritional and otherwise, are as follows:

- Highly digestible.
- Inexpensive.
- Low in calories (8 ounces (225 g) contains 147 calories).
- Free of cholesterol.
- Low in saturated fats (unlike animal food).
- Eight ounces (225 g) provides 30 percent of the daily requirement of protein.
- Contains iron, phosphorous, potassium, sodium, B vitamins, choline, and vitamin E.
- Comparatively low in chemical toxins.
- Contains the essential fatty acids, linoleic and lecithin. Both help remove cholesterol and other fatty acids from the blood stream and vital organs in the body.

Tofu can be purchased in water-packed containers. The water should be drained and replaced daily to keep it fresh. If the tofu is to be served the same day, it can be stored without any water. This gives the tofu a firmer texture and helps prevent loss of flavor.

Tofu must be kept refrigerated. It loses flavor and texture the longer it is kept. It can be refrigerated for up to ten days.

Tofu can be used directly from the container, but the preferred way is to press it before use. The structure and form of the cake or slices should not be lost during pressing. The length of time to press depends on what the tofu will be used for. The texture will be soft with a light pressing; a softer tofu is excellent in salads. Heavy pressing gives a firmer texture that is used for cooking and deep-frying.

Pressing
Using the whole cake or slices, wrap the tofu in a cloth, towel, or paper towels. Set on a dish or in a bowl or colander (with a bowl underneath), and refrigerate 60 minutes to overnight. To quicken pressing, place a 2- to 3-pound weight (1 to 1.5 kg) on top of the tofu. (I usually prop a storage jar with rice or beans on top of it if I'm using the tofu within an hour.) Replace the cloth occasionally.

Crumbling

For use in salads, egg and grain dishes, and casseroles, well-pressed tofu need only be broken up with the fingers into very small pieces.

Scrambling

Crumble pressed tofu into a cold frying pan. Using low heat, cook for about 5 minutes, stirring constantly, until you see the whey separating from the curd (30 seconds for a soft texture, 35 seconds for a firm texture). Drain the tofu and spread it on a plate until it cools. This produces a firmer textured tofu than heavily pressed tofu.

Add scrambled or deep-fried tofu to soups 1 or 2 minutes before the soup is completed. Tofu will give the following soups an added flavor: lentil, split pea, bean, mushroom, onion, cabbage, tomato, squash, and miso.

DEEP-FRYING TOFU

Deep-frying will add the necessary fatty acids to your diet and reduce your intake of saturated fats. Use pressed tofu, cut however you like. Use any of the following coatings (or none at all):

- Roll in cornstarch or arrowroot
- Roll in bread crumbs, flour, or cornmeal
- Dip in beaten egg and roll in breadcrumbs and flour
- Roll in flour and dip in egg
- Dip in a thick batter of cornstarch and egg whites
- Dust with flour, dip into beaten egg, and roll in bread crumbs.
- A tempura batter.

BEANS AND OTHER LEGUMES

There are more than 10,000 varieties of beans including dried peas, peanuts, and lentils. They are the fruit of leguminous plants. The bean grows in the pod that suspends from the stem of the plant. Leguminous plants have a symbiotic relationship with bacteria. This process is called rhizobia; nodules form at the roots of the plant, capturing nitrogen from the air that settles in the soil, thereby making the soil naturally fertilized for future crops. This nitrogen is utilized completely, compared to 50 percent utilization when chemical fertilizers such as anhydrous ammonia or ammonium nitrate are used. The other 50 percent is lost through seepage and runoff, polluting waterways and streams. Nitrogen is the essential element in all protein.

Some of the nutrient value of beans is lost during the drying process; compared to other produce in the supermarkets, however, beans are the most lightly processed food. No preservatives or chemicals are used in the low-heat processing. Beans are protected by their thick pods, which prevent contamination from pesticide residue; however, unless there is a distinct pest problem, pesticides are not used on beans.

Beans are good sources of the B vitamins and minerals including iron. Unlike many foods, beans do not lose their vitamin content during cooking. Beans contain phytic acid and are low in saturated fats.

Buy beans packaged in plastic or cellophane packages or boxes with windows. Make sure beans are of the same size and have an even coloring and few pebbles. Store beans in airtight containers in a dry, cool location; poor storage facilities can add to cooking time. Cooked beans can be frozen easily.

Dried beans should be partially rehydrated by soaking in the refrigerator for 6 hours or overnight to decrease cooking time. If they are not refrigerated during soaking, the beans may ferment. You can cook beans in the liquid they have soaked in, although some say the liquid should be discarded to get rid of the oligosaccharides, which may cause flatulence. The cooking liquid should be 3 cups (750 ml) of water to every cup (200 g) of beans. (If making soup, the liquid should be 4 cups (1 l) of water to 1 cup (200 g) of beans.) Add water to the soaking water, if necessary.

Bring liquid to a boil, boil for 2 minutes, turn off the heat, and let the beans sit in the liquid for 60 minutes or longer. The boiling will break the shell, and rehydration will take place in a shorter time. Then continue to cook at a simmer, with the cover not completely covering the pot.

Cooking time is determined by the type of bean and the combination of foods used with the bean. Acid foods, fats, salts, and molasses harden bean skins, causing an increase in cooking time by hampering the pectic substances that cause the cells to adhere to each other, delaying cellulose softening.

Beans will not soften in hard water, no matter how long you cook them. Hard water leaves a deposit of mineral salts, which prevents the cellulose from softening. The normal cooking time for lentils is 1 ½ hours; for limas, ½ to 1 hour, and for navy beans, 3 hours.

Tomatoes, salt, and fats can be added right before the cooking process is completed or after the beans are tender. Adding baking soda to quicken the cooking process destroys the thiamin content of the bean. Add more water rather than baking soda.

Many foods go well with beans: tomato, onion, corn, green beans, peppers, celery, molasses, honey, mustard, soy sauce, savory, and thyme. Chick peas (garbanzos), soybeans, and white beans are excellent in salads, mixed with crunchy vegetables like carrots, celery, lettuce, cucumber, and onion. Kidney beans and green beans blend well together in salads. Combine several beans, add a sliced tomato, and garnish with egg. Beans are best marinated in dressing before adding the other vegetables.

The other most common beans are red, black-eyed peas or, pinto beans, strawberry, cow peas or mexican frijoles, flageolets, white beans or navy beans, limas, Great Northern and aduki.

SOYBEANS

Like peas, lentils, and other beans, soybeans are the seeds of a leguminous plant. Whole soybeans are rich in vitamin B1, vitamin B2, and iron.

Soybeans contain one and one-half times the high-quality useable proteins of any other legume. Soybeans are very low in carbohydrates. When soybeans are made into tofu however, the complex protein, carbohydrate, and lipid (oil or fat) molecules are transformed into digestible amino acids, simple sugars, and fatty acids.

Soybeans, unlike other beans, must be cooked a long time, until they are very soft. (If you are pressure-cooking them, add 1 ½ teaspoons oil for every cup of beans to prevent clogging of the steam escape valves.)

This lengthy cooking will help digestibility and deactivates the trypsin inhibitor, which impedes the activity of the pancreas-secreted trysin enzyme important for protein digestion and proper growth. Seventy to 80 percent must be destroyed to allow the body to make use of the nutrients in the bean.

Dry-roasted soybeans have 47 percent protein, only a portion of what is available in the whole cooked bean. Dry-roasted soybeans are crunchy with a nut like flavor. They can be purchased salted or unsalted and can be eaten as snacks (like peanuts) or served in salads and casseroles.

After the beans are completely cooked, add any of the following ingredients and simmer for 15 minutes. Add ¼ cup (60 ml) more water, if necessary. The amounts are for 1 cup (200 g) dry soybeans.

- 3 to 4 (45 to 60 ml) tablespoons honey and 1 tablespoon (15 ml) tamari.
- 1 cup (approximately 120 to 150 g) of chopped vegetables, separately or combined: tomatoes, onions, carrots, celery, mushrooms and ½ teaspoon (2.5 ml) salt

Soybeans are great sauteed in a small amount of oil for a few minutes after they are cooked.

SPROUTS

Sprouts contain large quantities of protein, minerals, oil, and lecithin. Vitamin content increases two days after germination; vitamin quantity increases until the fourth day, making seeds a good source of vitamins.

Seeds can be sprouted at any season. The easiest bean or seed to sprout is mung, but any of the following can be used to sprout: alfalfa, garbanzo, millet, lentil, barley, rye, buckwheat, wheat, fava, lima, soybean, pinto, corn, cress, kale, clover, lettuce, caraway, celery, dill, flax, parsley, fenugreek, peanut, onion, oat, pumpkin, radish, red beet, safflower, and sunflower. Sprouts from all of them are edible, both in the raw state and cooked. Sprouts from soybeans contain less calories per gram of protein than from any other vegetable food. Soybean sprouts contain both the sprout and the bean.

SPROUTING

When purchasing beans or seeds for sprouting, make sure they can be used for cooking, sprouting, or planting. Seeds used for feed may be treated with fungicides or insecticides.

1. Soak beans in warm water for 8 hours. Allow 1 cup (200 g) of beans to 4 cups (1 l) of water. Keep them in a warm place; do not refrigerate.
2. Rinse beans with cool water. Put beans in a container made of an opaque material with a wide opening. Avoid containers that are metal or wood.
3. Cover loosely, and let the damp beans remain at room temperatures.
4. Every 8 hours or so, rinse beans in cool water. Drain, and put wet beans back in the container.

The beans will take 3 to 6 days for complete sprouting and will produce sprouts ½ to 4 inches (1.5 to 10 cm) long.

NUTS AND SEEDS

Nuts and seeds are 50 percent fat; an exception is chestnuts, which are 4 percent fat. Nuts and seeds become rancid quickly because of the high fat content; the shell does not prevent this rancidity. The majority of nuts and seeds contain essential fatty acids, B vitamins, a few minerals, and incomplete protein.

Peanuts and chestnuts are often purchased roasted in their shells. The flavor of most nuts improves when they are roasted; however, the heat can destroy thiamin and protein. Chestnut shells should be slashed with a knife before roasting to allow steam to escape and to prevent them from exploding.

When nuts and seeds are used in cooking, add them right before serving so that they stay crunchy.

GRAINS

Half the food consumed by humans is made from seeds that grow on bladelike leaves called grasses. When these seeds are harvested, they are called cereal grains. The most significant grains in this country are wheat, corn, oats, rye, and rice. Less important grains are millet, buckwheat groats (kasha), barley, and sunflower and sesame seeds. Buckwheat is not a seed from the grass family, but from a herbaceous plant, but because of its similarity in structure to other grains, it is added to our list of grains. Grains are good sources of energy because of their starch and fat content.

The seed, before it is processed, consists of the germ, endosperm, aleurone, and bran. The germ, or embryo, is located at one end of the seed and makes up 3 percent of the grain. This is the element of the seed that sprouts when the seed is given a chance to germinate. The germ is the richest part of the grain; it contains carbohydrate, fat, sugar (mainly sucrose), protein, thiamin, vitamin E, iron, riboflavin, and niacin. The germ is usually removed in the milling process because it deteriorates and spoils rapidly. The germ can be purchased as wheat germ, which is sold separately.

The endosperm is the large center part of the seed and constititutes 83 percent of the grain. The endosperm is a reserve food supply for the plant as it matures; it contains gluten-forming proteins, glutenin, and starch. This part of the seed is high in carbohydrate and protein and contains small amounts of cellulose. The endosperm remains in highly refined grain products.

The aleurone (a protein) is a layer of very little nutrient value between the endosperm and the bran. The bran, or pericarp, is the outer covering around the seed; it consists of more than one layer and makes up 14 percent of the grain. The bran is rich in carbohydrate, cellulose, thiamin, riboflavin, niacin, iron, protein, phosphorus, and small amounts of minerals.

Grains are low sources of vitamins A, D, and C (ascorbic acid); however, vitamin C can be found in seeds that are sprouted. Milling and processing greatly reduces the nutrient content of grain, especially thiamin (unstable when heated). Unmilled grain contains calcium, phosphorus, and iron but they are greatly reduced due to binding by the fiber and the high phytic content present, making the minerals unavailable to our bodies.

Cereals are lacking in lysine and threonine (amino acids) but, combined with beans, nuts, or dairy products, cereals give you a complete protein with all eight essential amino acids necessary for life, growth, and health. The protein quality is as good as that in meat, fish, or poultry.

Grains are not edible in the raw state. Once cooked, the starch granules absorb liquid and are digestible. Rice and buckwheat triple in quantity when cooked; the quantity of millet and barley quadruples when cooked.

COOKING GRAINS

What follows are the basic cooking methods for all grains:

Raw grain must be rinsed well in cold water and then drained well, using a strainer or colander. This removes any grit and excess starch. Pick out any small stones by hand.

Most processed rice, enriched rice, buckwheat, and bulgar wheat need not be washed. These products have been cleaned before packaging. If you feel it is necessary to wash them, do so quickly.

Before cooking, grains can be roasted by sauteeing in a dry skillet or a small amount of oil, stirring constantly, until there is a nutlike fragrance. When using oil, try sauteeing chopped onion with the grain. Be careful not to burn your grains.

Buckwheat groats, millet, and sesame seeds are extremely tasteful when roasted. Rice appears white and other grains turn a darker color. The roasting process can destroy one-half to two-thirds of the thiamin and large amounts of protein.

To cook the grain, bring the correct amount of water to a boil. The more seasoned the cooking liquid, the more flavorful will be the taste of the grain. Salt should be added to the grain after it is cooked, however, as salt will prolong the cooking time. Add the grain. (The grain can also be put in the water before boiling, brought to a boil, covered, and simmered.) Lower the flame to simmer, cover, and cook until done. No stirring is necessary, (but never stir more than once, or your grain will have a sticky consistency). When completed, the grains should separate easily and should be well cooked.

Grain should be tasted to see that it is chewy but not hard. If the grain is not done, add a small amount of water, cover, and continue cooking. If the grain is burned on the bottom, the flame was too high. If the grain is too wet, the flame was too low. Not using enough water will give you dry, hard grain; too much water makes the rice sticky and mushy.

After the grain is cooked, keep it covered until ready to use. This will keep the grain warm and it will dry out slightly, to a perfect consistency.

To be properly digested, grains should be chewed extremely well.

RICE

Brown Rice

Virtually all the nutrients are preserved in brown rice because of the mild processing needed to remove the hull. There are hundreds of varieties of brown rice in the world, but long-, medium-, and short-grain rice are the most popular in the United States.

Brown rice needs to be kept in covered containers in a cool place. Because of its high oil content, it becomes rancid easily.

Long-grain rice has thin and slender grains that cook up fluffy and dry. The grains separate easily with no stickiness. Short-grain rice is a short, plump grain that cooks up more firm than the long-grain variety and has a chewy taste. The grains separate if cooked properly but are slightly sticky after they are cooked. Medium-grain rice cooks somewhere between long- and short-grain rice.

When buying brown rice, never buy rice with too many green grains; green grain is not mature and does not have the nutritional quality that mature grain contains. The nutritional balance is disrupted if the grains are broken or chipped during improper milling.

Wild Rice

Wild rice grows wild in swamps and mudflats in the northeastern United States. Wild rice is not a true rice but actually the seeds of a reedlike water plant.

The high price of wild rice reflects the hand harvesting of the rice in flat-bottomed boats. After harvesting, the seeds are dried, parched, or heated for several days to remove the husks. Wild rice is not milled. The grains are long with light and dark brown coloring. The flavor is nutty. Serve wild rice with brown rice, half and half, or alone.

White Rice (Refined Rice)

White rice is rice that has been processed, removing the bran and germ. These by-products are used mostly for animal feed, but germ and bran can also be purchased in a health food store.

After processing, white rice is enriched with thiamine, niacin, and iron. Nevertheless, more than a dozen other valuable nutrients are lost in the processing. The FDA allows riboflavin to be added to white rice, but is not usually used because it turns the rice yellow. Efforts have been made to enrich rice with all nutrients, but as yet none has been successful.

Polished rice is white rice coated with glucose and talc to improve its sheen.

Converted Rice

Brown rice is parboiled with nutrients from the bran absorbed into the endosperm. When dried, the bran is removed, and the end result is converted rice. Converted rice is nutritionally healthier than white rice but not as good as brown rice. After cooking, converted rice is less fluffy than white rice and not as chewy as brown rice.

Instant Rice

Instant rice is white rice precooked and dried. Only a short period of cooking in water is necessary to rehydrate.

Quick-cooking Rice

Quick-cooking rice is small kernels of white rice partially pre-cooked. A short period of cooking in water will rehydrate.

Cracked and Broken Rice

This rice is used for rice grits and, by law, they are enriched. They are mainly used for breakfast cereals.

BUCKWHEAT (GROATS, KASHA)

Buckwheat comes from chopped whole buckwheat kernels. It is high in calcium, vitamin B, iron, and minerals. Buckwheat has the amino acids tryptophan and lysine, making it a good complementary protein with corn.

Buckwheat can be purchased either roasted or unroasted. Roasted buckwheat should be roasted at home for at least 3 minutes to enhance the nutlike flavor.

BARLEY

The protein in barley is found in the aleurone, but milling removes the aleurone and bran. The grain is then polished, resulting in the pearly barley purchased in the store. Barley is used as animal feed and as malt for making beer.

Barley malt is used in many sweets found in health food stores. Barley malt is made by saturating barley with water until it begins to sprout. An enzyme results, which changes the starch in the barley to maltose, a sugar. The malt is then dried and roasted to produce flavor. In beer, the malt is fermented.

CORN (MAIZE)

Corn can be yellow, white, or a mixture of yellow and white. The difference between the two colors is due to pigment; the white has virtually no vitamins.

Cornmeal

Cornmeal and corn flour, which is a more finely milled cornmeal, are milled the same as wheat; however, the nutrient value is much less than wheat, rye, oats, and other grains. When the germ and pericarp are removed to prevent rancidity and spoilage, the meal is labeled degerminated. If the pericarp is the only part removed in milling, the germ and endosperm are ground and labeled decorticated cornmeal. Bolted cornmeal can be found milled to a very fine grind but not degerminated.

When buying cornmeal, check the label for ground whole cornmeal. It contains the germ oil, but must be refrigerated and lasts for only a few weeks.

Corn on the Cob

Corn can be cut away from the cob and sold canned or frozen. If this process is not done carefully, the embryo containing the only complete protein can be removed. The rest of the kernel is deficient in the amino acids tryptophan and lysine.

Corn on the cob is an ideal substitute for potatoes.

Hominy

Hominy is the whole corn kernel with the germ and pericarp removed and then soaked. When hominy is dried, it is called grits.

Masa

To produce masa, which is used for making tortillas, whole kernel corn is soaked or boiled in dilute alkalies (lime, calcium hydroxide), wood ashes (potassium hydroxide), or lye (sodium hydroxide) for 30 minutes. The kernels are drained, washed, and ground into paste, or masa. The masa is shaped into balls, flattened, and cooked on a hot griddle like a pancake.

MILLET

Millet is not a popular grain in the United States and is used mainly as poultry feed and birdseed. The small round yellow or white grains are the seeds commonly available, although there are many different colors, sizes, and shapes.

Millet is the richest grain, closely resembling the amino acid proportions of eggs. It is very high in minerals and very digestible. It can be purchased as whole grain, meal, and groats.

The cooked grain has a stronger flavor than other grains and is very tender and slightly chewy. It complements legumes and dairy products, which are high in lysine and low in methionine. It is great with wheat and baked breads.

OATS

The whole oat has the husk intact. The husk has no nutritional value, and the whole oat is used for sprouting.

Oats have two very tough outer husks. The oats are usually cleaned, dried, and roasted to remove these husks more easily. After hulling, the grain left (groat) is scrubbed to remove some of the outer skin. The groat contains the germ, bran, and endosperm, and the nutritive value is equivalent to the whole grain.

Oats are higher than wheat in minerals, vitamin B, and protein. They have low levels of lysine and methionine. Mixing oats with milk (the most popular way of eating oats), which is also low in methionine, does not increase the nutritive value of either.

Oats can be purchased in three forms: whole oats, steel-cut oats, and rolled oats.

Rolled Oats

Rolled oats have been flattened between heated rollers, and the groats have been flaked for breakfast cereals. Regular rolled oats and quick-cooking rolled oats (rolled into tiny flakes to quicken water absorption) have similar protein and nutritive value.

Steel-Cut Oats (Scotch Oats)

Steel rollers and steaming are used to reduce the size of the groats to granular pieces. The cooking time is longer than for rolled oats; the nutritive value is similar to rolled oats.

Oat Flour

The germ and bran of the groat remains in the flour, making the nutritive value of oat flour similar to that of whole groats or rolled oats.

RYE

The milling of rye is so mild that dark rye flour is nutritionally superior to whole wheat flour. The high level of minerals in rye are more available to the human body than in whole wheat because almost all the phytic acid is expelled during baking.

One problem with fresh rye bread is the possible growth of a poisonous mold called ergot. Commercial rye bread uses calcium propionate or sodium propionate to prevent its growth or that of any other mold. Fresh rye bread should be consumed within a few days of baking and should be kept refrigerated.

The gluten content is low in rye, making rye bread heavier than wheat bread because its ability to rise is not as great.

WHEAT

Wheat can be grown in almost all temperature zones. Each grain is protected by a yellow leaf (glume) and grows on a stalk. When wheat is harvested, the grain, stalk, and glumes are separated into grain, straw, and chaff. The grain is oblong and pointed at one end. The pointed end has a small bunch of hairs called the beard. The other end is the embryo, which was origninally attached to the stalk.

The aim of modern milling is to remove as much pure endosperm as possible. When the endosperm is crushed and sifted, the result is white flour; the nutritious bran and germ become animal food. Two-thirds of the thiamine (B1), riboflavin (B2), niacin, vitamin B6, folacin, vitamin E, iron, phosphorus, magnesium, potassium, copper, manganese, and zinc are lost in the milling process to produce white flour. Approximately 50 percent of the pantothenic acid, calcium, molybdenum, and chromium are lost. Only 2 percent of selenium is lost. Flour is enriched with vitamins B1, B2, niacin, and iron. Vitamin D, calcium, and wheat germ can be added according to FDA regulations, but they are rarely used.

Wheat Grains (Wheat Berries)

The whole grain is called a berry or cracked wheat, which is berries crushed for faster cooking. When you buy wheat berries that are not pre-packaged, make sure you do not purchase wheat for planting. These berries are sometimes coated with a mercury-based fumicide, which is highly toxic.

Varieties of grain to purchase and grind at home are as follows:

- Hard red spring wheat. Used for making bread.
- Hard red winter wheat. Used for making bread.
- Soft red winter wheat. Used for pastry products because of its high starch and low protein content.
- White wheat. Used in pastries and breakfast foods. White wheat is soft, starchy grain, low in protein and gluten. It has no pigment and can be found in spring and winter varieties.
- Bulgar wheat. The wheat is steamed; the husks and very little bran are removed. It is then dried. The nutritional value is similar to that of whole wheat. Only water need be added to make it edible. The flavor is nutty and mild.
- Red durum. Used as livestock feed.
- Durum wheat. Used primarily for macaroni products. The product is obtained from the endosperm of durum wheat and is called semolina. Sometimes semolina is mixed with the wheat flour, making a poor-quality product that becomes too soft when cooked and has barely any nutritive value.

Macaroni products are enriched with iron, niacin, thiamine, and riboflavin, but the nutritive value of the bran and germ are not replaced. Macaroni products are very low in lysine (an amino acid), making the protein quality inferior to whole grains; however, macaroni products made with eggs have protein value equal to that of whole grains. Whole wheat macaroni and regular or egg macaroni have a long storage life.

Wheat germ

Wheat germ has more nutrition value than any other cereal product. The germ (or embryo) is removed in the milling process of white flour, mainly to prevent spoilage of the wheat due to the high oil content of the germ. The germ is only 3 percent of the grain, but it contains more vitamins and minerals than the rest of the grain. The protein quality is very close to animal protein.

Toasting wheat germ increases its nutritional levels. Adding wheat germ to salads, fruits, yogurts, cereals, or cookies will increase the nutritional quality of food.

Wheat germ becomes rancid quickly. Only buy it in stores where it is refrigerated, and keep it refrigerated at home.

READY-TO-EAT CEREALS

Ready-to-eat cereals have been cooked during the processing and need no further cooking. One grain or a combination of grains and other ingredients (sugar, vitamins, minerals) are ground to a paste. The paste is then made into different shapes and sizes and roasted. This produces your puffs, flakes, crunches, and so on.

SORGHUM

Sorghum is a grain added to many crackers and snack foods. It is also used for syrup, by brewing companies, and in animal food.

TRITICALE

Triticale is a new grain acquired by crossbreeding rye and wheat. It is being bred to obtain a protein level and may replace rye and wheat.

VEGETABLES

The word vegetable describes various parts of a plant system: leaves, roots, tubers, seeds, bulbs, stems, fruits, and flowers.

ARTICHOKE (GLOBE OR FRENCH)

The artichoke is the unopened flower bud of a plant belonging to the thistle family. The bud is green and globular, and the leaves grow tight.

The heart and the soft fleshy base of the leaves (peteles), called scales, are the edible parts. Carbohydrates are reserved in this part of the plant in the form of inulin, making them starchless.

When purchasing artichokes, watch for brown or spreading leaves; they are a sign of an overmature or damaged vegetable. Buy only artichokes with an even green color. They should feel heavy when picked up. Quality is not influenced by size. Artichokes spoil in a few days, so they should be kept refrigerated.

To prepare an artichoke for cooking, first cut off the top. Run water over the artichoke, spreading the leaves apart to remove any grit. It is not necessary to remove the thorns from the lower leaves. To cook, put the artichoke, base down, in enough water to half cover it. The water can be seasoned with olive oil and garlic. Cover and simmer for approximately 45 minutes or until a leaf is easily removed.

To eat, peel the leaves off individually and dip into a sauce, butter, mayonnaise, French dressing, or hollandaise sauce, scrape the leaf between the teeth to remove the soft portions at the base of the leaf. Throw the remains away.

JERUSALEM ARTICHOKE (SUNCHOKES)
The Jerusalem artichoke is not a true artichoke. It is the tuberous root, about 2 inches (5 cm) in length, of a sunflower plant. When raw, its texture is crisp, and it has a sweet, nutty flavor. It looks like a small potato. There are two varieties: round and white, or long with red skin. Carbohydrates are stored in a form called inulin, making them starchless. Sugar is stored in a form called levulose. Jerusalem artichokes are high in calcium, phosphorus, iron, and vitamins B1 and B2.

They can be purchased in late winter. They should be firm and without wrinkles.

ASPARAGUS
The word asparagus comes from the early Persian practice of eating the delicious young spears of asparaj, meaning "sprout."

The stalk is the edible portion. The stalks are green, erect, firm stems with tight, small, scalelike tips or leaves. They are harvested while still young. Mature plants become hard and fibrous.

Buy asparagus with tightly closed tips; spreading indicates overmaturity. The green should cover the complete stalk, and vertical ridges should not be visible. Asparagus is a good source of potassium, sodium, iron, calcium, iodine, silicon, sulfur, chlorine, and vitamins A, B1, B2 and C.

White asparagus is grown in Europe. These chlorophyll-free plants are grown without any light. Some brands, found canned in this country, are not from Europe but are bleached white.

Asparagus has to be prepared before cooking. Take each end of the asparagus in each hand and slowly bend the stalk. Asparagus stems will break at their most tender and freshest point. They are best steamed or boiled. They can be seasoned with lemon butter, vinaigrette sauce, or hollandaise sauce, then sprinkled with a pinch of mustard seed, sesame seed, tarragon, or parmesan cheese.

LIMA BEANS (DWARF AND FORDHOOK)

A lima bean is a flat seed enclosed in a flat, dark green pod. There are small (dwarf) and large (fordhook) varieties of lima beans. When purchasing fresh pods, choose those that are not discolored or hard but are well filled and completely green in color. They are well complemented with marjoram, oregano, sage, savory, tarragon, and thyme.

SNAP BEANS, GREEN BEANS, AND STRINGBEANS

These beans are all long and slender. But some are flat and some are round and their green color may be spotted with a lighter color. Buy beans that are young, firm, free of decay and blemishes, and feel like velvet. Snap a bean before buying to check for crispness and immaturity of the seeds. The seeds within the pod should be immature and very tiny.

Most varieties of beans on the market have no strings; however, to be sure, break the tip at one end of the bean, and if there is a string attached to the end, draw it down the side of the bean to remove it. Do the same with the opposite end. If the beans have no strings, the tips should be broken off before cooking.

Cook beans by steaming or boiling. Herbs that go well with beans are basil, dill, marjoram, mint, mustard seed, oregano, savory, tarragon, and thyme. Beans can be served buttered, topped with toasted sliced almonds or with a pinch of nutmeg or with sauteed mushrooms.

BEETS

In ancient days beets were used as medicine; only the tops were used as a vegetable. Two types of garden beets are early beets (Egyptian, Early Wonder), which grow in cool weather and are very sweet in flavor. Late beets (Detroit dark red, Winter Keeper) are grown in warm weather and are slightly less sweet than early beets. There is a sugar beet variety with a very high sucrose content. It is harvested for sugar manufacturing only.

Fresh beets are purchased in bunches, with or without leaf tops. The tops should be a reddish green with no visible wilting. Beets should be smooth, globular, and firm. The color should be a deep red, and they should have slender roots. Some beets can have a yellow color; their flavor is not as sweet as that of red beets. Buy bunches of beets that have a uniform size, for more even cooking. Avoid large beets; they contain strings that do not soften during cooking.

The carbohydrate content of beets is in the form of glucose, fructose, sucrose, and raffinose. The pigment is betaine. Beets have large amounts of calcium, sodium, potassium, chlorine, and vitamins A, B1, B2, and C. Beet tops are high in potassium, calcium phosphorus, iron, sodium, and vitamins A, B1, B2, and C.

Beets should be cooked whole, unpeeled, with a small portion of the stem and roots left on. They must be boiled in water. The skins are easily removed after cooking.

Herbs and spices that go well with beets are bay leaves, dill, savory, thyme, allspice, cloves, ginger, chervil, and caraway and mustard seed.

BROCCOLI

Broccoli is a member of the cabbage family; it is related to Brussels sprouts and cauliflower. Fresh broccoli, grown mostly in California, is available year round. The vegetable is harvested before the buds are open. Both the bud clusters and the stalk are green. Any other color indicates poor quality, and the color will be lost during the cooking process.

Purchase broccoli with tightly closed buds that are firm and that have a dark green flower head. Do not purchase broccoli with open yellow blossoms.

Broccoli is high in chlorophyll, malic and citric acids. Oxalic acid can be found in small qualities. Broccoli is high in calcium, phosphorus, iron, sodium, and vitamins A, B1, B2, and C.

Broccoli should be steamed or boiled. Season with caraway seed, dill, mustard seed, tarragon, lemon butter sauce, hollandaise sauce, or thyme.

BRUSSELS SPROUTS

Brussels sprouts are a member of the cabbage family. The sprouts or buds are small — about the size of walnuts — firm, and bright green. They resemble tiny cabbages in structure, odor, and flavor. The nutritional content is potassium, iron, iodine, sulfur, calcium, phosphorus, sodium, and vitamins A, B1, and C.

When purchasing Brussels sprouts, choose heads all the same size for proper cooking; pick those that are bright green and unwrinkled. Avoid yellow leaves or wilted heads; these are overripened. Fresh sprouts are available from September to December.

Before cooking, trim the bottom of each sprout and cut a cross in it to help cut down on the cooking time; cut large sprouts in half. Remove any discolored and wilted leaves. Wash by immersing in cold water. Sprouts can be cooked whole, either steamed or boiled. Cook only until tender. Overcooked sprouts turn yellow and mushy, and taste like stale cabbage.

Brussels sprouts can be seasoned with lemon butter and mustard sauce, or cooked with chestnuts. Basil, poppy seeds, caraway seeds, dill, mustard seed, sage, and thyme accent their flavor.

CABBAGE

The cabbage family incorporates thousands of varieties. Next to potatoes, cabbage is eaten more than any other vegetable. The most popular cabbage is the head cabbage. Cabbage can be either round or flat. It can be green, red, or white. Cabbage leaves can be either smooth or wrinkled, with tight compact heads.

When purchasing cabbage, pick a head that is firm to the touch, crisp, and with no wilting or blemished leaves. The color is important: too white is overripe, too green is immature. Red leaves should not have a puffy appearance; these are overripe.

Dark green varieties of cabbage have a higher nutritional content than the lighter colors. They contain sulfur, chlorine, iodine, calcium, sodium, and vitamins A, B1, B2, and C.

Cabbage keeps for several weeks in the refrigerator. Cabbage should never be overcooked; excessive cooking causes the sulfur to give off an obnoxious aroma and flavor.

There are two ways to cook cabbage: (1) quarter the head and cook either steamed or in boiling water for 15 minutes; or (2) shred by cutting the head in half, placing the cut side down on a cutting board, and slicing thin. Shredded cabbage cooks in only 7 minutes.

Bok Choy Cabbage
Bok choy cabbage resembles celery when first seen, except that the stalks are very thick and round. The leaves are a dark green, and the stem is either green or white. To cook, cut in pieces and saute or steam.

Chinese Cabbage
Chinese cabbage is a salad vegetable.

Savoy Cabbage
Savoy is a loose-leaved variety of cabbage with crumbled leaves. The leaves are dark green and have a mild taste. Avoid buying savoy with any yellow, flabby leaves, which indicates overripening. Savoy is available only in the fall. Savoy takes as long as 20 minutes to cook, in order to break down the cellulose.

CARROTS
Carrots originated in Europe and western Asia. They are a member of the same family as the hemlock, a deadly poison. Carrots are a taproot available year-round. They have many shapes; they can be short and shaped like a tube or long and narrow. The color can vary from orange to orange-red to yellow. Carrots should be stiff, without any flexibility; softness indicates poor quality. Large carrots can have a very fibrous center; smaller carrots usually have a better flavor. The more mature, the deeper the color and the sweeter the taste. The fiber content remains the same throughout maturity.

The most important nutritional aspect of carrots is the pigment carotene and lycopene. This element changes into vitamin A when used by the intestinal cells. Fructose is the main carbohydrate. Carrots are high in iron, magnesium, sodium, potassium, silicon, sulfur, chlorine, iodine, phosphorus, calcium, and vitamins A, B1, B2, and C.

If the storage condition is ideal, 32 to 40 degrees F (0 to 5 degrees C), carrots will keep in the refrigerator for up to 6 months without any decrease in flavor or texture. Remove the tops before refrigerating because the tops drain the carrot of its moisture content.

Unless they are organic, carrots should be peeled. Carrots can be prepared in many ways: thinly sliced, thickly sliced, diced, shredded, or cooked whole. They can be steamed, boiled, or sauteed. If sauteed, they need to be stirred often due to the high sugar content. Carrots do not lose the ability to change pigment into vitamin A during cooking. Whatever way of cooking is preferred, keep the pan covered to prevent moisture loss in the steam.

Carrots can be seasoned with butter, minced parsley, bay leaves, caraway seed, dill, allspice, ginger, mace, marjoram, mint, nutmeg, thyme, and fennel. Vegetables that complement carrots are onions, celery, mushrooms, green peppers, and peas.

CAULIFLOWER

A member of the cabbage family, cauliflower has creamy white curds, compacted flowers, and upper stems surrounded by green leaves. Purchase only firm heads with large curds, closed, smooth, and white. The leaves should be fresh and green. Avoid heads that are turning brown, or have yellowing flowers or separating curds; these indicate overmaturity. A slight granular curd texture can be purchased in heads that are too compact. A green color on the jacket leaves is a sign of freshness.

Fresh cauliflower is available throughout the year and should be refrigerated in plastic bags or stored in the plastic wrap it came in. Cauliflower is high in calcium and potassium; it also contains citric and ascorbic acids.

To clean and prepare cauliflower, the flowerets need to be removed from the stem. Remove the leaves, and cut the stem off as close as possible to the head. Separate the flowerets from the main stalk by cutting or breaking. Clean the flowerets by rinsing them under cold running water. Cutting small slits in large stems will allow them to cook more rapidly. Steaming or boiling are the best methods of cooking.

Season cauliflower with celery, salt, nutmeg, mace, caraway seed, dill, and tarragon. Serve with melted cheese or cream sauce on top.

CELERIAC (CELERY ROOT)

Celeriac is a variety of celery with a large root (resembles a turnip) rather than stalks and foliage. Its flavor is bitter. Celeriac is a good substitute for potatoes.

The knobby surface should be pared before cooking the root. Chop or cube the root, and boil in a small amount of water or steam.

CELERY

Celery is a fleshy, crisp, tightly packed stalk of the celery plant. The most common varieties are pascal and Utah, which are green in color, and golden hart, which is a bleached white variety. Celery is available throughout the year. Select only the green variety, either light or medium green, rather than the bleached. Avoid celery that is yellowing or that has dry leaves, brown spots, or discolored centers. These are signs of overmaturity.

Use the center stalks for celery sticks; remove any strings. If celery is to be sliced, the strings do not need to be removed. Because of its high moisture content, celery can be stored for several weeks in the refrigerator.

Celery contains sodium chloride, magnesium, iron, potassium, calcium, sulfur, and vitamins A, B1, B2, C, and E. The low solid content is in the form of carbohydrates.

CHICORY, ENDIVE, AND ESCAROLE

Chicory, endive, and escarole are used mainly for salad.

CORN

Fresh sweet corn is a long cob covered with white, yellow and white, or yellow kernels (depending on the variety), enclosed by a leafy husk. Strings of silk hang from the distal end.

When buying corn, look for husks with a fresh cut at the stalk end, and for silk that is fresh-looking and with no signs of wilting or decay. Avoid buying yellow or dry husks; this corn is overmature and will have a tough texture. Corn kernels should be small, plump, bright in color, and show little resistance to pressure. When a kernel is punctured, a milky liquid (starch grains suspended in a liquid) should exude. Large kernels are overripe and will be tough when eaten. The taste of fresh corn is moist and sweet.

Husks should remain covering the cob until the corn is ready to cook. Corn must be refrigerated and should be eaten as soon as possible. If left unrefrigerated, the sugar content of corn rapidly decreases after harvesting, and the starch content increases.

The most popular varieties are Golden Bantam, County Gentlemen, and Towell's Evergreen. Corn has a high oil content within the embryo and endosperm. The color is caused by carotene and cryptoxanthin.

Corn can be steamed or boiled. However, do not boil corn in the water. Bring a pot of water to a boil. Submerge the corn, turn off the heat, and allow the corn to remain in the water, covered, for 5 or 10 minutes.

CUCUMBERS

Cucumber, which is botanically a fruit, is a member of the squash family. The cucumber has a firm, oblong shape, a green skin, and white tender flesh with tiny immature seeds. Cucumbers are generally eaten before they are ripe.

Buy cucumbers that are firm to the touch and completely green. Most cucumbers have tiny bumps on their surface; these should be evenly distributed over the entire cucumber. Buy small cucumbers rather than the large variety. Do not be fooled by the shiny lustrous skin of most cucumbers. This is an artificial wax covering and should not be eaten. Cucumbers can be kept refrigerated for only a few days.

Cucumbers have a high moisture content. The small amount of solids consists of simple carbohydrates, minerals, vitamins, and protein. They are high in silicon and sulfur and contain potassium, iron, magnesium, chlorine, and vitamins A, B1, B2, and C.

Cucumbers can be seasoned with basil, dill, mint, and tarragon.

EGGPLANT (AUBERGINE)

Eggplant, botanically classified as a fruit, can be large or small, but all plants are pear-shaped and feel firm and heavy for their size. Most are a rich purple color; but there are varieties that are yellow, brown, and ash-colored.

Buy only smooth, heavy plants. Other than the small varieties, eggplant should be 3 to 6 inches (7.5 to 15 cm) in diameter at the large end. Avoid soft plants and those with irregular brown spots. They can be stored refrigerated for one or two weeks.

Eggplant becomes dark when exposed to the air. This is due to the contact of eggplant and the iron in the air. Sprinkle or rub with lemon juice to prevent discoloration; cooking in pottery, glass, or stainless steel also helps prevent this discoloration.

Eggplant has a very high moisture content, and moisture should be removed before cooking. There are a few different ways to do this: Either sprinkle with salt and place on a rack; before using, wipe away the dots of moisture that come to the surface. Or place a heavy weight on top of the slices and let stand until moisture is gone.

Eggplant absorbs oil and butter very quickly. The best way to prevent the plant from eating too much oil or butter is to fry it with a coating of bread crumbs or flour. Eggplant can also be used in casseroles.

GARLIC

Garlic grows in bulbs divided into sections called cloves. The bulbs vary in size and number of cloves. Each clove is surrounded by a thin skin. Garlic color can be white, purple, rose, or mauve. The best garlic comes from warm climates.

The strong flavor of garlic comes from a sulfur compound found in the volatile oil of the garlic. The odor transfers easily to the hands during peeling. When this happens, scrub your hands with salt and then wash them with soap.

Garlic cloves can be separated easily by pulling them off the bulb one at a time or by removing the outer loose parts of the sheath and trimming the roots close to the base.

Buy young, plump bulbs. The cloves should be dry and the outer skin intact. Avoid buying soft, sprouting garlic. Garlic, unpeeled, can be stored for many months.

Garlic is used as a flavoring ingredient in cooked dishes and salad oils.

GREENS (CHARD, COLLARDS, KALE, SORREL, SPINACH)

Always buy greens that are fresh, young, and tender, and that have green leaves. Avoid yellowing, flabby, wilted leaves; these are signs of over-maturity. The taste will be strong and bitter, and the greens will have a tough, stringy texture. Unwashed, all greens can be kept refrigerated for about a week.

Greens such as mustard, kale, and collards must be chopped crosswise in 1-inch (2.5 cm) strips before cooking, or they will have a stringy texture. Seasoning greens with vinegar or a mustard sauce helps modify their slightly bitter flavor.

Swiss Chard

Swiss chard is a variety of the beet family that has bright yellow-green leaves and thick stalks. It is usually available in the fall. Chard is high in potassium. It also contains calcium, iodine, iron, and vitamins A, B1, B2, and C. It is excellent seasoned with grated swiss cheese.

Spinach

Spinach has green, arrow-shaped leaves. They can be wrinkled or smooth and can vary in color from dark green to pale green. The color pigments are chlorophyll and carotene. Spinach is in season from spring to autumn.

Buy spinach that has wide thick leaves. Wash well under cold running water to remove any grit. After cooking, season with basil, mace, marjoram, nutmeg, oregano, sesame seeds, onions, or garlic.

Spinach contains the soluble acids: citric, malic, and oxalic. It is a good source of potassium, sodium, calcium, iodine, magnesium, iron and vitamins A, B1, B2, and C.

Sorrel

Sorrel (dock) is a perennial vegetable and should be prevented from flowering. Sorrel has large, thick, red-root leaves that are similar to spinach leaves. Cultivated varieties have large leaves and are more tender than wild plants. The varieties found in the United States are spinach, dock, Belleville sorrel, and fresh sorrel. Sorrel is rich in potassium, iron, and magnesium. It also has substantial amounts of phosphorus, sulfur, and silicon.

Buy sorrel with large, thick root leaves. The acid in sorrel is oxalic and varies from plant to plant. The bitter taste also varies. If used in salads, the leaves should be young and tender. When served alone, chop, cook, puree, and combine with melted butter. To preserve the flavor, sorrel must be cooked very briefly. Do not cook sorrel in an iron pan; not only will the sorrel turn black but it will acquire a metallic taste.

Sorrel is best served combined with other greens, such as spinach or chard. Sorrel is excellent in lentil, tomato, and cucumber soup.

Collard Greens

Collards are an important vegetable in the South. The collard is a variety of the cabbage family. Collards are picked when they are young and tender and have a very strong flavor. They are high in iron, potassium chlorine, and vitamins A, B1, B2, and C.

Dandelion Greens

Dandelions are members of the daisy family and are found in abundance in meadows. While the plant is usually considered a nuisance, it is actually of great value because of the vitamin content of the root. Dandelion greens are available in large bunches during the early spring months. Choose the youngest greens, for they are the most tender. The older they get, the more fibrous they become.

Dandelions are rich in magnesium and iron and high in potassium, calcium, silicon, iron, and vitamins A, B1, B2, and C. They are cooked like spinach and are best mixed with sorrel.

Mustard greens

Mustard greens are the young leaves of the mustard plant. The leaves of the white variety are milder than those of the black. Mustard greens are high in sulfur, potassium, phosphorus, iron, magnesium, silicon, and vitamins A, B1, B2, and C.

Kale

Kale is a variety of cabbage with finely cut loose leaves of diverse forms and a color range from green to brownish purple; the leaves contain the color pigments chlorophyll and carotene. Younger leaves have the most delicate, pleasing flavor, but unfortunately the markets usually sell only the older kale.

Buy kale that is firm and not yellowed. Use the greens as soon after purchase as possible. Tear off the leaves and discard the stalks.

Kale leaves are rich in iron, phosphorus, sulphur, potassium, calcium, and vitamins A, B1, B2, and C.

Lettuce

Lettuce is used mainly as a salad ingredient.

MUSHROOMS

Edible mushrooms are a group of fungi, called saprophytes, that have no chlorophyll. The gill mushroom is the most popular. Buy small to medium size; choose those with a creamy white color, smooth surface, and fresh smell.

Some varieties, however are light brown in color. The gill, the underside of the mushroom, is not visible on fresh mushrooms. As the mushroom ages the cap enlarges, and the gills become visible. Avoid buying mushrooms with discolored or decayed gills or caps. Like any other spoiled vegetation, they can harbor ptomaines and toxins that can cause illness.

The nutritional content of mushrooms is mostly vitamin D. They have to be refrigerated if not used immediately and can be kept for only a couple of days.

Clean gently by rubbing with the fingers under cold running water. The best flavor lies within the skin, so it is best not to peel mushrooms. Stems do not need to be removed, but if you wish to remove them, cut the stem even with the mushroom cap; do not dig out the stem from the gills.

OKRA

Okra is classified botanically as a fruit. Okra is a small to medium-size pod-shaped vegetable, two to three inches in length. The seeds are contained in five or more sections. The okra you buy should feel velvety and soft. Hard, large, or discolored pods are overripe and can be stringy in texture.

Okra has a unique taste and texture, which are caused by a mucilaginous material which also makes it useful for thickening soup and sauces. When cooked, especially when cut or overcooked, it imparts a pasty substance. Okra tastes best when coated with cornmeal and sauteed.

ONIONS

There are many varieties of onion available in this country, ranging from the white and yellow to the large yellow Spanish or Bermuda type to the sweet red Italian to the tiny white onions. The bulbous part of the plant, which can be round, flattened, or spindle-shaped, is the edible portion, consisting of easily separated layers with a strong, sharp smell and taste,

THE NATURAL FOODS PANTRY

which come from an oil rich in volatile sulfur compounds. Onions are also available in a powder or dried flakes; these products are not equal in flavor to the fresh onion.

Onions should be stored in a cool, dry location and do not need refrigeration. Their flavor becomes stronger with storage. Sweet Spanish and Bermuda onions have a milder flavor than yellow onions. The less sweet, the less moisture, however, and the longer the onions will keep in storage.

Onions are high in sulfur, potassium, phosphorus, calcium, chlorine, magnesium, iron, iodine and vitamins A, B1, B2, and C. (Up to 65 percent of the vitamin C can be lost during cooking.) The smaller onions of a particular variety contain more ascorbic acid than the larger of the same variety.

Buy onions that are hard, firm, well-shaped globes with dry skins and small necks. Avoid soft necks that are thick or tough. These are of poor quality and overripe.

The flavor of an onion varies depending on the degree to which it is cooked. If the onions are cooked in large amounts of water, the sulfur compounds are released and dissolved in water or are driven off in the steam, leaving the onions with a mild flavor. Onions should not be allowed to brown or blacken during sauteeing. The flavor becomes bitter. Also, chop onions right before use; once exposed to the air, the onions acquire a stale flavor.

Season onions with caraway seed, mustard seed, nutmeg, oregano, sage, and thyme.

Leeks

Leeks are a member of the lily family and a biennial herb related to the onion and garlic. Leeks resemble scallions, although leeks are about 12 inches (30 cm) long, with stems up to 3 inches (7.5 cm) thick. Some leeks have a bulbous base, while others are straight. Only the white portion is used for cooking.

Sometimes the underground stalks have to be split apart carefully lengthwise to get at the grit for cleaning . Open each leaf, and rub the grit away with the fingers under cold running water.

Purchase leeks with 2 or 3 inches (5 to 7.5 cm) of the white portion extending from the roots. The green tops should be crisp without any

91

yellowing. Leeks contain iron, potassium, sulfur, phosphorus, calcium, and vitamins A, B1, and C.

Scallions (green onions)

The scallion usually has a marble-size bulb with a long, narrow green top. Many scallions in supermarkets are bulbless. Both the green tops and white bottoms are edible. Scallions have more calcium, potassium, and vitamin C than raw onions, but half sodium and little vitamin A.

Buy scallions with at least 2 or 3 inches (5 to 7.5 cm) of white. The tops should be crisp without any yellowing or wilting visible.

Shallots

Shallots are similar to garlic in that they form several pieces in a cluster. They also have a thin skin, although it is the color of a yellow onion skin. Shallots have a mild taste, similar to both onion and garlic. When shallots are sauteed, they acquire a bitter flavor if allowed to brown.

PARSLEY

Parsley is a member of the carrot family. There are a number of varieties; all have bright, fresh green tops. All varieties have a delicous flavor and aroma. Parsley is rich in potassium, calcium, sodium, magnesium, phosphorus, sulfur, chlorine, iron, and vitamins A, B1, B2, and C.

Buy only very fresh, crisp, bright green parsley without any yellowing. Parsley should be washed before storage. After washing drain well and refrigerate in a covered glass jar.

PARSNIPS

The parsnip is a taproot and a member of the carrot family with a delicate and unique sweet flavor and the texture of a soft carrot. Parsnips are white. They are used both as a table vegetable and in soups. Never use the wild variety of parsnip; it contains poisonous elements.

Parsnips are rich in potassium, phosphorus, sulfur, chlorine, calcium, and vitamins B and C.

Buy firm parsnips that are free from blemishes. Avoid large parsnips; their texture can be woody. Also avoid soft or shriveled parsnips which are overripe. Parsnips can be cooked like carrots and are excellent mashed.

PEAS

Fresh garden peas are round in shape and grow in bright green pods that are velvety to the touch. The garden pea is wrinkled and has a sweet taste. Field peas have smooth skins. As peas mature and become larger and tougher, they lose their sweetness and their starch content increases. The best-quality pea is high in sugar and low in starch. Peas are rich in potassium, folic acid, and vitamins B1, B3, C, and E.

Peas are best stored in their pods in plastic bags in the refrigerator. They should be eaten as soon as possible after purchase.

Season peas with basil, dill, marjoram, mint, oregano, poppy seed, rosemary, sage, savory, or curry. Or serve with grated lemon peel, sauteed mushrooms, chopped chives, pearl onions, carrots, or cream sauce.

SWEET GREEN PEPPERS
(CAPSICUM OR RED PEPPERS, BELL)

Classified botanically as a fruit, peppers belong to the same family as the potato, the tomato, and the eggplant. They have little or no pungency. Peppers, which are both green and red, are large bell-shaped vegetables with a hollow center containing many seeds. They are available throughout the year.

Red peppers (can be orange or yellow) are a mature pepper. They are extremely sweet. They contain significant amounts of vitamins A and C. Green peppers are high in silicon and in vitamins A, B1, B2, and C.

Buy red or dark green peppers that are glossy and heavy for their size. They should be firm with no wrinkles. Peppers must be stored in the refrigerator. Discard the inner pulp and seeds before use.

Fresh Ripe Chilies

These chilies are a pungent variety of the Capsicum. They are usually red in color, but can be orange, yellow, cream, or deep purple. When used in cooking, they are removed before the dish is completed and discarded.

Fresh Green Chilies

The flavor of these peppers can vary from very pungent to mild. They are usually used in pickling and in chutney.

POTATOES

The potato is the most popular vegetable in the world. It is a primary source of starch which makes up to 80 percent of the dry weight of the white potato. There are dozens of varieties of potatoes marketed in the United States. The flavor of the potato is from the nonvolatile organic acids (oxalic, malic, tartaric, and citric).

The potato tuber is a part of a stem that grows underground. The outer skin prevents moisture loss and attack by fungi. Freshly harvested potatoes have very little sugar. The sugar content increases if potatoes are stored at cool temperatures (below 45 degrees F or 7 degrees C). Returned to room temperature, the potato's sugar will change back to starch.

Potatoes with too much sugar cannot be used for frying because they become too brown. They also cannot be used for mashing or baking because they lack mealiness and will have a sticky texture.

The nutritional content of potatoes is riboflavin, vitamin B2, thiamine, ascorbic acid, vitamin G, potassium, sulfur, phosphorus, chlorine, and many other minerals and protein. The nutritional quality can vary within the same plant.

Buy potatoes that are firm and crisp. Avoid those with bruises, decay spots, cuts, cracks, and green coloring (indicates exposure to artificial light). A black ring noticed when a potato is cut indicates that it was frost-bitten. Remove the black ring and any green sections before cooking.

Potato skins should be completely intact, except for skins on new potatoes, which may look as if they are peeling. This does not affect their quality. Beware of potatoes that are artificially colored or waxed.

Potatoes are classified into three categories: mealy, new, or waxy potatoes.

Mealy (Russet, Bake-king, White Rose, and Idaho)

Mealy potatoes are high in starch. The starch cells swell and burst during cooking, causing cells to separate. They are best used for frying, baking, and mashing because they will not brown as quickly as other types.

Waxy (Maine)

Waxy potatoes are low in starch and high in sugar, which causes the potato to become translucent during cooking. Waxy potatoes are best boiled, sliced for salads, or scalloped.

New Potatoes

New potatoes are harvested before they become mature. They are small and have thick skins. The skins are extremely easy to remove. New potatoes are used in stews, boiled, and creamed. Some red new potatoes have been inflicted with artificial coloring.

RADISHES

Radishes are tender roots. Buy radishes that are firm, plump, round, medium in size, and with a bright red color. Soft radishes are overmature. Radishes are high in potassium, iron, and magnesium and contain sodium, sulfur, chlorine, phosphorus, and vitamins A, B1, B2, and C.

Daikon

Daikon is a large white radish grown in Japan. It is used, grated, as a flavoring in soups and stews.

RHUBARB

Rhubarb is a spring plant used as both a fruit and a vegetable. The fleshy part of the stem is eaten. These stalks are 12 to 18 inches (30 to 45 cm) long. The leaves should never be eaten; they contain toxic levels of oxalic acid. Rhubarb contains calcium, potassium, sulfur, and vitamins A, B1, and C.

Buy only the tender young stalks. They should be firm, crisp, and tender and be a bright red or pink with a glossy appearance. (There is a variety of very good quality that is a light green.) Avoid either very slender or very thick stems. These are overmature and will have a fibrous texture.

SQUASH

Summer Squash (Cymlings)

Classified botanically as a fruit, summer squash is harvested before it matures. It is high in vitamin C. The seeds and skin are tender, and the whole squash is edible. Buy those that are small and firm, have a glossy skin, and feel heavy for their size.

Pattypan squash is round with scalloped edges. The skin is smooth and tough but edible.

Straightneck and crookneck squash are narrow at the neck and full at the blossom end. The color is usually yellow, and the skin is extremely tender.

Zucchini is long and narrow with dark green tender skin. It is similar in looks to a cucumber.

Do not store summer squash for more than a couple of days. Cook by removing the ends and cut as desired. Steam, bake, or boil squash in a very small amount of water.

Season summer squash with allspice, basil, cinnamon, cloves, fennel, ginger, mustard seed, nutmeg, rosemary, sage, chervil, or oregano.

Winter Squash
All winter squash except butternut has a hard rind, is brightly colored, and is very heavy for its size. Neither the skin nor seeds of winter squash are edible. Winter squash is high in vitamin A and potassium.

Avoid buying squash with watery spots; they indicate overmaturity. Uncut winter squash (hard rind) can be stored for several months in a cool, dry, dark location; with longer storage, the starch content turns to sugar.

Winter squash can be baked whole. If you cut squash in half, remove the seed and stringy portions and either cook as is or cut into smaller pieces. Cut pieces can take anywhere from 10 to 60 minutes to cook, depending on the squash.

Squash has a rather bland taste. It can be seasoned while cooking with honey or brown sugar mixed with butter. Or you can cook and mash the squash and blend in nutmeg, mace, cardamom, honey, sugar, or butter.

SWEET POTATOES
There are two varieties of sweet potatoes in the United States; one has yellow flesh and a dry, mealy texture; the other, called a yam (the true yam is not available in the United States), has a moist, deep orange flesh and a high sugar content. Both varieties have brown skins, high starch content, and large amounts of carotene. The raw potato contains glucose, fructose, and sucrose.

Sweet potatoes are much higher in potassium, sulfur, phosphorus, and chlorine than white potatoes. Both varieties of sweet potatoes are extremely high in vitamin A. They also contain vitamins B1, B2, and C.

Buy sweet potatoes that are firm and are free from worm holes, decay spots, and scars. Store them in a cool, dry, dark location. They spoil easily and should be used within a couple days of purchase.

Baking or boiling sweet potatoes in their skins prevents enzymatic browning. Season them with allspice, cardamom, cinnamon, cloves, and nutmeg.

TOMATOES
Tomatoes, classifed botanically as fruit, can be round with flattened ends or long and pear- or plum-shaped. Small cherry tomatoes are perfect spheres. Tomatoes are usually a uniform red color, but some are yellow and purple. As tomatoes age, the solid content decreases, and sugar, acids, and moisture increase. The color pigments are carotene, lycopene, and chlorophyll; the organic acids are citric and malic.

Tomatoes contain large amounts of sodium, calcium, potassium, and magnesium. They are high in amino acids and in vitamins A and C; they also contain vitamins B1 and B2.

Tomatoes cannot be stored at low temperatures. Store them at 65 to 75 degrees F (18 to 24 degrees C) in good light, avoiding sunlight. Green tomatoes will ripen slowly at 50 degrees F (10 degrees C) temperature.

Season tomatoes with basil, bay leaves, celery seed, oregano, sage, sesame seeds, tarragon, and thyme.

Peeling tomatoes
Drop firm, ripe, red tomatoes one at a time into boiling water for 10 seconds. Remove them from the water. Remove the stem and peel off the skin starting from the stem area.

Tomato Seeds and Juice
Tomatoes can be squeezed either peeled or unpeeled. Cut the tomato in half crosswise. Squeeze each half cautiously to remove the seeds and juice. If the tomatoes are to be stuffed, sprinkle them with salt, which will draw out more liquid, and then turn them upside down to drain.

TURNIPS
Turnips are a hearty-flavored root vegetable. The root comes in different sizes and can be flat, round, or cylindrical. Most varieties are white fleshed with a purple tinge.

Turnips provide the highest percentage of calcium of all vegetables. They are also high in potassium, sodium, iron, sulfur, phosphorus, magnesium, chlorine, and vitmains A, B1,B2, C, and E.

Buy turnips that are small or medium in size, smooth, firm to the touch, and have the leaves intact. Avoid a soft-textured turnip; it is over-ripe. Turnips are usually cooked; raw turnips have a bitter taste.

Rutabaga (Swedish turnip)

Rutabagas, a root vegetable, is a hybrid of cabbage and turnip. Rutabagas have thick yellow or buff flesh and crisp, firm roots. They are pear-shaped and heavy for their size. They contain larger amounts of carbohydrate, calories, calcium, and vitamin A than normal turnips.

Choose those that are small or medium in size; avoid large rutabagas or those with blemishes or signs of decay. They can be boiled or steamed in their skins, peeled and chopped. They are best combined with peas and carrots or any other desired vegetable. They can be fried or served raw.

Rutabagas do not keep very long. Because the moisture content is lost rapidly, they should be eaten soon after purchasing.

Kohlrabi

This cabbage variety is so often mistaken for a turnip. There are two varieties: white (to light green) and purple. The flavor is somewhat like that of a delicate turnip. Because kohlrabi becomes bitter as it ages, buy only young roots. Cook and prepare as you would celeriac.

WATERCRESS

Watercress is used mainly as a salad vegetable.

COOKING VEGETABLES

If you want to be a better cook and to cook more naturally, you will have to spend more time in the kitchen, doing all the chopping, grinding, and slicing that is necessary. Cooking properly can determine a healthy or unhealthy life. It begins in the kitchen. All food nutrients—the amounts vary with the vegetable—are available in vegetables, especially minerals and vitamins.

The grading of vegetables is not compulsory in most states, and little of the produce in your supermarkets is graded. The highest vegetable grade is U.S. Fancy; U.S. 1 is second grade, and U.S. 2 is third grade. U.S. 1 is the wholesale grade most commonly given to fresh vegetables found in supermarkets. Alphabetical grades, U.S. grades A and B, are found on potatoes, broccoli, parsnips, spinach, and turnips.

After vegetables are picked, life remains but the process of respiration begins to take place, causing a loss of nutrition and vitality. To prevent decay, vegetables must continue to use oxygen to metabolize cell food substances, and to release carbon dioxide, water, and energy (heat). This process can be slowed down considerably by the proper storing and refrigerating of vegetables, which prevents loss of moisture and changes in the fibers and pectins.

Choose vegetables that have a bright, natural color. There should be no signs of wilting or shriveling. Avoid plastic-coated produce.

Store vegetables in moistureproof plastic bags. Different varieties of vegetables should be kept in separate bags. Combining vegetables may cause spoilage. Vegetables should not be washed before storing. The excess water can cause mildew and a loss of water-soluble vitamins. There is usually enough moisture in the vegetable to keep it fresh, but there are a couple of exceptions:

1. Succulent vegetables should be stored in well-ventilated, covered containers.
2. Roots and tubers should be stored in a well-ventilated area at 55 to 60 degrees F (12.5 to 15 degrees C). Remove tops (the leaves) from radishes, beets, turnips, and carrots to prevent moisture loss. Again, some fruits and vegetables will spoil others if stored in the same area. Apples expel ethylene gas that gives carrots a bitter taste. Onions shorten the spoilage time of potatoes.

When some vegetables, such as greens, begin to deteriorate, they can be freshened by rinsing them under cold running water. Shake off the excess water, drying them if possible, and store back in the plastic bag, and replace in the refrigerator. Vegetables prepared to be eaten raw can be placed in a cold area of the refrigerator for a few hours or kept on ice to restore their crisp texture.

It is necessary to wash vegetables carefully just before cooking. Spinach, cauliflower, broccoli, and cabbage sometimes need to be soaked to remove grit, sand, and worms. There is, however, a nutritional loss that increases with long soaking.

Depending on the thickness of the skin, some vegetables need to be pared or scraped. This is also true of vegetables that are not organic and have been sprayed with insecticides that do not completely wash off. Pare carefully, for many vitamins lie next to the skin and can be lost in discarded peels. If the produce is organic, it needs only to be heavily scrubbed. This applies to potatoes, squash, carrots, parsnips, and beets.

Remove any damaged areas before cooking. These areas can give a disagreeable flavor to the cooked vegetable and show up as discolorations after cooking.

When cooking vegetables whole, if possible, first cook the vegetable and then remove the skin later. This prevents excessive vitamin loss.

Home cooking can destroy more nutrients than commercial processing. Here are some good cooking techniques for vegetables:

- After bruised areas have been removed, cover the spots with a small amount of oil to seal in nutrients.
- Cook just as long as needed for vegetables to be tender and crisp. Overcooking softens the cellulose, causing nutritional loss.
- Cook vegetables unpeeled to prevent oxidation of vitamin C.
- Steam—this is a superior method of cooking for retention of nutrients.
- Use a minimum amount of water in cooking. Water depletes nutrients.
- If vegetables are cooked in liquid, save the liquid. Many nutrients are water-soluble and leak from the vegetable into the liquid. Serve this liquid at the same meal, however, for these water-soluble vitamins are now in an unstable form.
- Serve cooked food immediately after cooking.
- Frying at low temperatures can retain up to 100 percent of the nutrients. Frying at high temperatures can destroy up to 80 percent of the nutrients. The same principle of low and high temperature cooking applies to baking.

Each vegetable has its own distinctive flavor. This structure is formed by plant acids, sugar, cannins, and volatile oils. There is no one way to cook all vegetables. A cooking method must be used to minimize loss of nutritive value and changes in color, texture, and flavor.

The nutrients that suffer most through cooking are simple sugars, manganese, sodium, potassium, calcium, magnesium, phosphorus, sulfur, iron, copper, and ascorbic acid (vitamin C). The B complex vitamins, thiamine, mineral salts, and fatty acids are slightly affected, and proteins are affected very little. Nutrients are lost because the heat causes the cell membranes to become tender, and the nutrients escape into the cooking liquid or escape in the steam.

Nutrient loss is increased by high cooking temperatures and by the amount of acidity or alkalinity in the cooking liquid. Also, soaking in cold water can cause a loss of vitamin C and B complex vitamins. The degree of loss is also determined by the size of the cut surface, so reduce the amount of cut surface exposed to water. If possible, cook the vegetable whole with the skin on. If cutting is necessary, always slice the vegetable diagonally. This prevents a great many nutrients from being lost.

Whether you cook vegetables whole or sliced, make sure they are about the same size so that all pieces are cooked in the same amount of time. This prevents partial overcooking.

Green vegetables should be cooked quickly. Cook in small amounts of boiling water or in a steamer. Cook uncovered for the first 3 minutes to free the volatile organic acids, then cover until tender.

Red vegetables should be cooked in a small amount of boiling water or steamed. The cooking pot should be covered. Add a small amount of lemon juice or vinegar to the water to prevent any color loss.

Yellow vegetables (carrots, tomatoes) are practically unaffected by cooking conditions. Cook in a covered saucepan, either by steaming or in a small amount of water.

With white vegetables (cabbage, cauliflower), care must be taken not to overcook or the color will become dark and look unappetizing. Cook in a small amount of water or steam with the cover on, cooking only until tender. Vinegar or lemon juice in the water helps prevent color change but causes the vegetable to toughen. Never use baking soda for color retention. Baking soda destroys nutritional value and causes a soft texture in the vegetable.

Starchy vegetables (potatoes) must be cooked until mealy to be palatable. Avoid overcooking.

Flavor changes can occur when some vegetables are overcooked. Onions and the cabbage family (Brussels sprouts, broccoli, turnips, kale) have sulfur compounds that can be freed by improper cooking or overcooking. These flavors can be unpleasant. Bitterness can occur in eggplant and cucumbers. These vegetables should be sliced, sprinked with salt, and allowed to stand at room temperatures for about 20 minutes. The salt draws out the liquid containing the bitter flavor, forming beads of liquid on the surface of the vegetables. Wipe this liquid off before cooking.

Organic acids can cause health problems if they are eaten cooked in large amounts. Raw, they are harmless. Vegetables that are so affected are spinach, chard, beet greens, and rhubarb.

There are similarities and differences between vegetables and fruits. Protein and water content is higher in vegetables, but fat content is similar for the two. Fruits have a higher calorie content than vegetables and contain more organic acids than vegetables. Both fruits and vegetables contain starch and sugars; however, during the ripening process, sugar turns to starch in vegetables. For example, corn and peas are extremely sweet and tender when young, but as they mature they become more starchy, less sweet, and less tender .

CUTTING VEGETABLES

As we have discussed, cooking vegetables whole or cutting them on the diagonal prevents a good deal of nutrition loss. There are different methods of cutting vegetables. First, all cutting should be done on a wooden board or chopping block. To prevent the board from assimilating juices from different vegetables, wipe it with a wet sponge. The board will soak in the water, preventing absorption from any other source. Occasionally wipe the board with sesame oil to prevent it from warping or drying out but avoid using soap. Soap absorbs into the wood of the board and the taste can never be removed.

Chopping

Hold the chopping knife firmly at both ends. You will chop with the cutting edge of the knife in quick up-and-down movements, pushing the vegetables in a pile, and chopping until the desired amount is chopped.

102

Julienne (matchsticks)

Use this method on carrots and other root vegetables. Slice the carrot in long strips lengthwise. Cut the sliced pieces crosswise, 1 to 2 inches (2.5 to 5 cm) in length. Then cut lengthwise into slices 1 ⅓-inch (.3 cm) thick.

Half Moons

Use this method on long root or tuber vegetables such as carrots and turnips. Cut the vegetable in half lengthwise, then cut each half crosswise into pieces ½ to ¼-inch thick (.5 to 1.5 cm).

Small Rectangles

Use this method with thick vegetables such as carrots and turnips. Cut vegetable crosswise into 1 ½-inch (1.5 cm) pieces. Then cut these sections into thirds, vertically. Place each piece on the largest surface and cut lengthwise, ⅛-inch (.3 cm) thick, into rectangles.

COOKING METHODS

Baking Vegetables

Bake at low temperatures to prevent loss of vitamins underneath the skin. Baked vegetables have a distinctive flavor that is worth a small loss of nutrition. There are four good baking methods, the fourth usually reserved for baking squash.

1. Use whole vegetables or large chunks. Put ¼ inch (.5 cm) of water in a baking pan, add vegetables, and cover. It is important to cover the dish to lock in the natural juices and prevent the vegetables from drying out through evaporation. Bake for 20 to 45 minutes in a preheated 350 degrees F (180 degrees C) oven.
2. Brush the baking dish lightly with oil, place the vegetables in the pan, and sprinkle with salt. Bake as in Method 1.
3. Put Kombu (seaweed) in a baking dish and place the vegetables on top. Add ¼ inch (.5 cm) of water. Bake as in Method 1.
4. To bake summer or winter squash, remove the stem and cut the squash in half. Remove the seeds from winter squash. Place the squash on an oiled baking pan or cookie sheet and lightly brush the

tops with oil. Bake in a preheated 375 degrees F (190 degrees C) oven for 30 to 60 minutes, depending on whether it is summer or winter squash. To test for doneness, prick squash with a fork. If the fork penetrates easily, the squash is done. If it is still hard, continue to bake until cooked completely.

Steaming

Steaming is the quickest and most efficient way to cook vegetables. Less nutrients are lost because there is no contact with water. Special pots can be purchased for steaming. More than one vegetable can be cooked at the same time in a steamer if both require the same amount of heat.

Put about 1 inch (2.5 cm) of water in a saucepan. Insert the steamer. Place the vegetables in the steamer. Sprinkle with a pinch of salt (optional) and cover. Bring the water to a boil. Lower flame to medium and cook for 5 to 25 minutes, depending on the vegetables and how they have been prepared for cooking.

If a vegetable steamer is not available, vegetables may be steamed in the following method: Put ¼ inch (.5 cm) of water in a pot. Add the vegetables and add a pinch of salt (optional). Bring the water to a boil. Cover, lid slightly ajar. Lower flame and simmer for 5 to 25 minutes or until done. The length of cooking time depends on how the vegetables have been prepared for cooking.

Boiling

Beets and other root vegetables should be boiled covered with water. The skins should not be removed. (This prevents excessive loss of nutrition in cooking.) Cook only until tender.

All other vegetables should be cooked in water no deeper than ⅛ inch (.3 cm). Bring water to a boil; add a pinch of salt if desired. Add the prepared vegetables, then cover and bring to a boil. Remove the cover to mix the vegetables and reduce the heat to simmer. Repeat this process frequently with green vegetables to free the acids released from the vegetables while cooking and ensure no color change. Cover and simmer until just tender.

To prevent burning, more water will be needed with vegetables that take a longer time to cook (kale) or that have a very low water content (beans, potatoes, peas).

Parboiling

Bring a pot of water to a boil. Drop the vegetables into the water and cook very briefly. If the vegetable is to be cooked in another liquid, a casserole, or another food dish, parboil for 30 to 60 seconds. If the vegetable is not to be recooked, boil for 1 to 2 minutes for root vegetables. Large pieces of vegetables take 3 to 4 minutes. If the vegetables being parboiled have a tendency to overcook, quickly plunge them into cold water as soon as they are cooked.

Add ¼ teaspoon (1.5 ml) of salt for each 2 cups (500 ml) of water when parboiling green vegetables, to maintain their green color.

Deep-Fat Frying

The vegetables must be very dry before frying; if you have coated the vegetables in bread crumbs or flour, allow the coating to dry for 10 minutes before frying. Always fry right before serving or keep warm in a 250 degrees F (130 degrees C) oven.

Bring the fat to 350 degrees and maintain the temperature by using a deep-frying thermometer. It is extremely important to keep the temperature stable. The oil is too hot if it smokes.

Before submerging the vegetables in the hot oil, test it with a little of your batter on one piece of vegetable. If the batter rises quickly to the surface of the oil and browns in about 45 seconds, the temperature is perfect. If it submerges and rises slowly, the oil is not hot enough. If it does not submerge but sizzles on the top, the oil is too hot. Oil that is too hot will burn the batter; oil that is too cold will not give the crisp texture desired.

Remove any floating pieces of batter with a perforated utensil. Cook the vegetables until the coating is a golden brown.

Stir-Frying

Stir-frying is used mainly for vegetables with a high water content that require very little cooking time. A wok is the pan normally used for stir-frying, but a heavy skillet or electric frypan will suffice. Vegetables cooked in this manner remain crisp and tender and do not lose color.

The complete process of stir-frying lasts about 4 minutes if all vegetables are cut alike. Longer-cooking vegetables should be put in the wok first and the tender ones added afterwards.

Use 2 teaspoons (10 ml) of oil (not olive oil) to every pound of vegetables. Heat the pan until very hot, add the oil, and heat until a piece of vegetable sizzles when put in the oil. Reduce the heat to moderate. Garlic or fresh ginger root can be cooked briefly and removed before adding the vegetables.

As you add the vegetables, you must stir quickly to coat all the vegetables with oil, or they will stick to the sides of the wok and burn. Stir constantly until the vegetables are tender and crisp. You can cover the wok, but then you will have a texture that resembles steamed vegetables rather than fried.

Watch your vegetables closely. You may need to add more oil if they begin to stick. After vegetables are tender, you can add a sauce, cover, and cook only long enough to bring your sauce to a boil.

If you want to stir-fry beans and root vegetables, you will need ¾ cup (175 ml) of water or stock added for each pound (450 g). They take about 8 minutes to cook.

Pressure Cooking
Pressure cooking retains food nutrients better than any other method. Steaming and boiling are combined, and the steam becomes heated to very high temperatures. Timing is difficult. Vegetables can be overcooked in seconds.

Microwave
Microwave cooking is equivalent to boiling but takes far less time, thus conserving more nutrients, flavor, and color. Timing is extremely important to prevent overcooking and drying out vegetables that are high in cellulose.

Canned Vegetables
Separate vegetables from their liquid. Cook and reduce liquid to about one-third its volume. Add the vegetables and heat thoroughly.

SALADS

PREPARING SALADS
Preparing salads is easy to do, and the combinations of vegetables to prepare salads are endless. The nutritional content of dark green leaves is

usually higher than that of lighter leaves, for the dark leaves contain more vitamins A and C than the inner leaves. This holds true for all types of lettuce, cabbage, and vegetables. The calorie content is almost identical in all of them.

Lettuce does not brown as quickly as other salad vegetables. It browns more rapidly once the leaves are cut, broken, or crushed, so you should prepare a lettuce salad shortly before eating.

Lettuce should be cleaned thoroughly. Leaves must be separated and cleaned under cold running water. Place the leaves in a colander to drain the liquid.

The solid core of iceberg lettuce must be removed before cleaning by using a knife. Hold the head of lettuce upside down under cold running water. The water will separate the leaves and clean them without any damage. Boston, field, and wild lettuce are filled with grit and sand; extra care must be taken in cleaning them. Bibb lettuce can be cleaned while remaining in the head form. Spread the leaves gently while running the lettuce under cold running water. The leaves should be torn into bite-size pieces, rather than cut. The pieces should not be so large that they have to be cut nor so small that they are unrecognizable.

Spread lettuce pieces on an absorbent towel or paper towel to dry. Then wrap them and chill them in the refrigerator until ready to use. This not only chills the leaves but makes them crisp. Bibb lettuce, if left whole, also should be wrapped in a towel and chilled for several hours before use.

Dry ingredients enable salad dressings to adhere to all surfaces; even slightly damp ingredients prevent dressings from clinging. All salad ingredients must be dried thoroughly: tomatoes, water chestnuts, bamboo shoots, sliced or grated carrots, onions, avocados, sweet peppers, mushrooms, broccoli or cauliflower flowerets, scallions, radishes, cucumber slices, bean sprouts, sliced or chopped squash, artichoke hearts. Cooked vegetables are great. Marinate them in oil and vinegar dressing before adding to the salad. Cooked and raw vegetables can be combined in salads.

Tomatoes, unless they are cherry tomatoes, should be served separately as a side dish. The juice can prevent salad dressing from clinging to your vegetables. Water chestnuts and bamboo shoots add crunch to a salad, but water chestunuts are very perishable and should be frozen after you remove them from the can. Adding cooked macaroni, bulgar wheat, or wheat germ to salads increases their nutritional value.

SALAD DRESSINGS

Salad dressings should coat all ingredients. There should never be any dressing left on the bottom of the salad bowl or plate.

The proportions of a salad dressing should be 3 tablespoons (45 ml) of oil (olive or vegetable oil or a combination) to 1 tablespoon (15 ml) of vinegar or lemon juice. A pinch of herbs can be added for flavor right before serving, or add ⅛ teaspoon (.5 ml) of dry mustard and a pinch of salt to the oil and vinegar. Shake all ingredients well for 30 seconds. Refrigerate until you are ready to use.

Salt is the most important seasoning in the salad. Add approximately ⅛ teaspoon (.5 ml) to every 6 tablespoons (90 ml) of oil. A clove of garlic can be added to the dressing mixture and removed before serving. Rub the garlic onto the salad bowl before mixing the dressing into your lettuce. Or rub the garlic onto a piece of dry crust of bread; toss the bread with the salad and remove it before serving. This is called a chapon.

Adding fresh tarragon, a pinch of cumin, or a few drops of rosewater to an oil mixture will give the oil an extremely fine taste. A pinch of sugar will reduce the acidity of the vinegar or lemon juice. You can also add to your dressing a pinch of dry or fresh herbs: dill, tarragon, basil, oregano, chervil, rosemary, parsley, thyme, sage, or a combination of any of them.

The dressing for a tossed salad should be added at the table just before serving. Salad dressing draws out moisture and vitamins from the salad ingredients, and so the salad loses crispness almost immediately.

To make salad dressing, put all salad ingredients in a large bowl. Start with 1 tablespoon (15 ml) of oil and toss the ingredients well, lifting them with a fork and spoon until they are coated with the oil. Add more oil if necessary and then add vinegar or lemon juice. Add the remaining ingredients you choose. Toss well.

SALAD GREENS

Belgian Endive, French Endive, and Witloof

Belgian endive is imported; the leaves are the bleached center of the leafy endive. The yellow-white leaves are elongated and 6 to 8 inches (15 to 20 cm) in length. They look like corn on the cob before it has been shucked. The flavor of endive is bitter, but it perks up blander lettuce.

Bibb, Boston, and Butterhead Lettuce
The leaves of bibb, Boston, or butterhead lettuce are a succulent dark green on the outside and light yellow inside. The leaves are held loosely in a small head and have a velvety texture. The taste is tender and mild.

Chinese or Celery Cabbage
Chinese or celery cabbage resembles in size and appearance a bunch of celery. The leaves are a light green. They are crisp and firm and have a milder flavor than cabbage.

Head Cabbage
Cabbage (red or green) is usually shredded and adds crunch to a salad.

Curly Endive, Chicory, and Escarole
Often thought of as the same plant, curly endive, chicory, and escarole are all different. Curly endive has loose fringed-edged leaves growing in a bunch and a yellowish stem. It has a slight prickly texture and a very bitter flavor. Escarole is an endive that grows in a loose head; the leaves are broader than curly endive leaves and without any curl (or very little curl) at the tips. The bunch is slightly flattened in shape and has a yellowish center. The color is darker than that of curly endive and the taste is less bitter. Escarole is also known as Batavian endive. Chicory can be found in curly leaved bunches. The leaves range in color from white to yellow to green and red. It has a very bitter flavor.

Dandelion Greens
Dandelions are found in most fields and lawns. The greens should be picked before they flower. After flowering, the greens are tough and bitter. The taste goes well with beetroot leaves.

Iceberg (Head) Lettuce
True iceberg lettuce is not sold commercially. The lettuce we eat is the New York or imperial strain. Iceberg must be grown in cool climates and resists mildew and brown blight. The leaves are very crisp and grow in a firm head with tightly packed leaves; but avoid heads that are too firm.

The outer leaves are darker than the crisper inner leaves. Avoid lettuce with brown edges, which indicates poor quality.

Leaf Lettuce

Leaf lettuce leaves grow from a single stalk and can be all shades of green. The texture is crisp. Leaf lettuce must be picked young, or the leaves will be tough. It is rarely sold commercially because it is highly perishable.

Oakleaf Lettuce.

Oakleaf lettuce is a leaf lettuce that has the shape of an oakleaf and is a green or bronze color.

Red Leaf Lettuce

Red leaf is a variety of romaine with a bunching head. The red-tipped leaves have a mild flavor.

Romaine, Cos, or Dark Green Lettuce

Romaine, cos, or dark green lettuce has an elongated head. The leaves are rather firm and are medium to dark green in color on the outside; the inner leaves are very crisp and light green in color. The flavor is stronger than that of iceberg lettuce.

Sorrel

Sorrel grows in fields and grasslands and has an acid taste. There are many varieties. Cooked and pureed, sorrel is excellent with fish.

OTHER GREENS USED FOR SALADS

Garden Cress

Garden cress is similar to watercress except that its leaves are very thin and tiny. It has a pungent taste.

Mustard, Turnip Greens, Kale, and Collards

Raw, mustard, turnip greens, kale, and collards have a very sharp, bitter taste. The young leaves should be combined with milder-flavored lettuce.

Spinach

The tender leaves of spinach are excellent as salad greens.

Watercress

Watercress is cultivated in huge ponds. The dark green leaves are dime to quarter size. The leaves grow on sprigs from a main stem; they are smooth and have a peppery flavor.

To keep cress for a long time, set it in a container that does not fit too snugly with 1 inch (2.5 cm) of cold water, cover, and place in the refrigerator. Wash right before using. Watercress is beginning to decay when the leaves start to yellow.

Wintercress (American Cress, springcress)

Wintercress is a wild cress. Only use the young rosette of root leaves for salads. The leaves are much smaller than watercress and have a stronger flavor.

FRUITS

Most fruits have a high water content. Except for avocados, coconuts, and olives, fruits are very low in fat, making them low in calories. They are also very low in protein, with only enough protein to keep the plant alive. But they have a very high carbohydrate content, which includes starch, nondigestible carbohydrates (cellulose, hemicellulose, lignin and pectic, used for structure the same way as we use bones), and sugar. Some fruits increase their sugar content as they ripen. The nondigestible carbohydrates change as the fruit ripens and when it is cooked. Fruits are good sources of vitamins A, B, C, and some minerals.

The fresh fruits that come to market have been violated with chemicals (to increase their size) and herbicides (to develop fruit before the flowers are pollinated). This is especially true for grapes, strawberries, figs, blueberries, cranberries, apricots, peaches, pears, apples, guavas, and cherries. Sulfur dioxide and sodium bisulfite is used in processing fruits. Ascorbic acid is used in most frozen fruits.

Fruits have been handled frequently by the time they reach the consumer. Wash them well before use. Some fruits need to be cored, pitted, or trimmed before using. Fruits are fragile and need to be handled gently.

Fruits such as apples, apricots, avocados, bananas, papayas, cherries, peaches, pears, and persimmons become brown on the surface when cut or broken. This is called enzymatic browning; it is caused by a reaction between tannins inside the fruit cells and oygen. This browning is not harmful to eat, but you can prevent it in either of two ways:

1. Rub acidic juice (lemon, pineapple) over the cut surfaces. Do not soak the fruit in the juice, or a loss of nutrients will occur.
2. Salt can be used instead of acidic juice, but it gives the fruit a salty taste.

Cooking softens fruit and causes texture and flavor to be lost. This is so because heat softens the cellulose and hemicellulose within the cells of the fruit. Starch becomes like gelatine, and there is also a loss of liquid and air—all causing softness. Adding sugar to fruit during cooking helps prevent the softening effect of heat, especially for berries and peaches. Too much sugar can make apples and pears tough.

APPLES
Apples not only have a delicious flavor but are available year round. Stored properly, they can last for weeks refrigerated at temperatures as close as possible to 32 degrees F (0 degrees C). When keeping apples for a long time, check them occasionally to remove any that develop brown spots.

If you buy apples prepackaged in the supermarket, open them to check for mold, overripeness, wilting, decay spots, and shriveling. Try to buy apples that are firm; those that have soft areas or are in general soft or yield to a small amount of pressure will have a dry, mealy texture. Avoid shriveled skins or bruised apples.

Winter apples are usually sweeter than the tart summer varieties; also, the redder the apple, the sweeter the flavor. Apples are rich in magnesium, iron, and silicon. They contain malic acid, an organic element involved in the digestive processes. They also contain vitamins A, B1, B2, and C.

APRICOTS
Apricots are available in July and August. They are grown in California, Washington, and Utah. Apricots are harvested when green which results

in a product with poor flavor. If you purchase immature fruit, place it in a paper bag at room temperature; it will ripen in a couple of days. The best known varieties are Alexander, Blenheim, and early golden.

Buy apricots with a reddish or golden orange color. They should be plump, juicy-looking and firm; but avoid very firm fruit with a greenish or pale yellow coloring or that is small in size. These apricots are immature. Soft apricots are beginning to decay.

Apricots are good sources of calcium, phosphorus, iron, sulfur, and potassium. They are high in vitamin A and also contain vitamins B1, B2, and C.

AVOCADOS

The avocado originally was grown only in Mexico and other parts of Latin America, but is now also grown in Florida and California. Avocados come in many varieties. The Florida avocado is available from late winter to late spring and has an excellent flavor. California varieties are available during the fall. Avocados are very high in protein and oil.

An avocado has a large nut in the center surrounded by a green flesh that is in turn surrounded by a green skin. The fruit is picked when immature; it will ripen at room temperature in a few days. A ripe avocado is slightly soft, and the skin gives slightly to the touch. Avoid avocados with dark, sunken spots; these are overripe.

Avocado flesh turns dark when it is exposed to air. This can be delayed by sprinkling lemon juice on the exposed surface.

BANANAS

Bananas are picked immature, which helps them to keep better for the long distances they must travel. Also, allowed to tree ripen, bananas acquire a bitter taste. Bananas are a good source of potassium and vitamins A and C.

Buy firm bananas with green at the tip and yellow in the middle that are free of bruises. They will ripen at room temperatures, but will not ripen properly below 55 degrees F (13 degrees C). They are at their best eating when the yellow develops brown flecks; the starch in the banana turns to sugar. Ripe bananas can be refrigerated, but the skin will turn brown or black. This does not affect the flavor in any way.

A bluish-green chalky appearance to bananas results from a copper-sulfate insecticide spray. Wash the fruit well to avoid contamination of your hands and of the edible portion of the fruit.

CHERRIES

The cherry is a member of the drupe family, meaning it is a fruit containing a single seed inside a hard stone. Cherry pits have been found in Stone Age caves, which indicates the long history of the cherry.

The most popular cherry, the Bing, is large and heart-shaped and almost black in color. The Bing is grown on the West Coast. Bing cherries are high in calcium, phosphorus, iron, sodium, potassium, and vitamins A, B1, and C. A smaller variety grown on the East Coast is even darker in color and is called the Schmidt. Both are available from May to August. There are sweet cherries for eating and sour cherries for use in preserving and baking.

Buy plump, firm, glossy cherries with fresh-looking stems. Avoid cherries that have a leaking flesh or brown discoloration; they are damaged fruit.

BLUEBERRIES

The blueberry shrub, or cockatoo bush, grows in all parts of the world. Blueberries are available from June to August. The small berry, smaller than a marble, is dark blue. It appears to be coated with a waxy substance, but this is a natural coating to protect the berry. The fruit is high in potassium, calcium, phosphorus, iron, sodium, and vitamins A, B, B2, and C.

Buy plump berries that are uniform in color and size. Stem caps should not be attached to the berry. Blueberries do not store well but will keep briefly refrigerated.

COCONUTS

The coconut grows on a palm tree. It consists of an outer husk and a large nut containing the thick edible meat and the fluid called coconut milk. The husk is usually removed before the cocunut reaches the consumer. The outside skin of the nut is green until it reaches maturity.

Coconut is high in potassium, chlorine, phosphorus, sodium, sulfur, calcium, magnesium, iron, and vitamins B1, B2, and C.

DATES

The date is the oblong fleshy fruit of the date palm, which is grown in California and Arizona. Dates have a very high sugar content and contain significant amounts of calcium, phosphorus, and potassium. They are a relatively weak source of vitamins A, B, and C. Look for plump shiny fruits with a waxy, but not sticky, surface.

FIGS

The fig is a small fruit that contains a seedy pulp with a sweet flavor. Fresh figs, which are available in September, constitute only about one-quarter of all figs sold. Due to their perishability, most figs are dried. Figs are a good source of calcium, phosphorus, potassium, and vitamins A, B, and C.

When buying fresh figs, look for fruits that are soft to the touch, indicating ripeness, and that have bright colors ranging from green to deep purple. Ripe black figs are best for eating. Avoid those that have a sour smell which indicates overripeness. The skin of black figs is not edible; the skin of green figs is edible.

GRAPEFRUIT

Unlike many other fruits, grapefruit is picked ripe. The best ones are heavy for their size, firm, and thin-skinned; they produce more juice. Puffy-looking, ridged, rough, or wrinkled specimens may have thick skins but are usually low in juice. The fruit should be somewhat flattened at each end; pointed ends indicate a thick skin, thus more pulp and less juice. Grapefruit is high in potassium, calcium, phosphorus, and vitamin B1, B2, and C.

Ripeness is important as grapefruit contains an element called naringin that supplies the bitterness and is reduced as the fruit ripens and the flavor is balanced by fruit sugar and citric acid. Skin blemishes have no effect on quality or flavor. The best buying season for grapefruit is from mid-December to mid-May.

The pink variety is a natural color. The coloring comes from the pigment carotene, a vitamin A precursor. This variety is more nutritional and many prefer the pink grapefruit because it is generally considered to have a better flavor.

GRAPES

No other fruit has as many flavors as the grape. Grapes should be picked when ripe. They do not improve in sweetness, flavor, or color after harvesting. Grapes are high in sulfur, iron, calcium, potassium, magnesium, and vitamins A, B1, B2, and C.

There are certain qualities to look for when buying any kind of grapes. The color should be rich, and the fruit should be plump with a waxy feel and no evidence of leakage. The sweetest grapes are the white or green grapes that have a slight trace of amber or straw coloring and the red varieties where the red coloring predominates. Avoid buying grapes that have a white coloring close to the stem. Shake the bunch; if the grapes come loose easily, they have been stored too long and are no longer fresh. Store in the refrigerator in plastic bags.

LEMONS

Lemons are harvested in America while still green and are ripened off the tree. This method causes lemon to have a strong acidic taste. Lemons provide calcium, magnesium, potassium, and vitamins B1, B2, and C. The lemon is the richest food in bioflavanoids, which regulate the temperature of the body. Lemon juice can be an effective antacid if taken in small quantities.

Buy plump, heavy, unblemished lemons. Look for lemons that are free from any green coloring because they are less acidic. Thin-skinned lemons have more juice than the thick-skinned varieties. Those with leathery or hard skins or with dark yellow coloring are overly mature and should not be purchased.

LIMES

The lime is a green or greenish yellow globular fruit with a very acid pulp. Limes are harvested before they are ripe and are also consumed green. Ripe limes are orange-yellow or lemon yellow in color.

Limes contain calcium, potassium, phosphorus, and vitamin C. They are similar to lemons in acidity, but less tart. The majority of limes sold in this country are imported from either the Middle East or the South Pacific.

Buy limes that have glossy skins, are bright green in color, and are heavy for their size.

116

MANGOES

Mangoes are picked unripe and ripened at room temperature. It is not advisable to eat green mangoes or unchilled mangoes; the flavor is like turpentine. Mangoes have large amounts of vitamin A and C.

A ripe mango is yellow-orange with a rose-colored spot at one end. The skin can be removed with a floating blade peeler and the flesh cut away from the large pit. Green mangoes are used in making chutney.

MELONS

Melons last longer if they are refrigerated. And avoid keeping melons in humid areas, because humidity promotes decay. An extremely soft area around the stem is a sign of overmaturity. There is no sure method for determining the best-quality melon, but the following subsections give you a guide to buying melons.

Cantaloupes

The cantaloupe is a hard-rind variety of the muskmelon; it has a gray-green ridged skin that ripens into yellow. The two most popular varieties of cantaloupe have deep orange flesh and light green flesh; both have a delicate aroma. Cantaloupes are high in potassium and vitamin A.

Look for cantaloupes that have a smooth green indentation at the skin end, where the melon was removed from the vine, with no trace of a stem or a jagged stem scar. The netting, or ribs, should thickly cover the whole cantaloupe. The color, under the netting, should be either light green with a gray cast or a pale gold. Avoid melons with a dull, dark green coloring underneath the netting.

When they are ripe, they give off a sweet aroma. (If there is no sign of a stem, it means the melon was allowed to ripen on the vine.) Cantaloupes are best when picked immature and allowed to ripen at room temperature.

If the melon yields to a slight touch, it is already ripe, possibly overripe, and should be avoided. Cantaloupes should be completely firm. After it is ripened, the melons should be refrigerated. It should be kept in a plastic bag to prevent the strong aroma from permeating other foods.

Honeydews

The honeydew is another member of the muskmelon family. Honeydew is a winter melon with a smooth skin; some may have slight traces of netting. The pale green to white flesh is sweet and tasty. Honeydews contain the same amounts of minerals and vitamin B as canteloupes, but have less vitamin C and much less vitamin A.

Look for melons that weigh about 5 to 6 (2.25 to 2.5 kg) pounds and are 6 inches (15 cm) in diameter. To test for ripeness, squeeze the blossom end, which should yield to the touch. Also, check for a pleasant aroma. If the melons you buy are the correct size and color but are hard to the touch, they can be ripened at room temperatures, kept away from any sunlight. Avoid small honeydews that are white or greenish white. They are immature and will lack flavor.

Honeydew melons should be refrigerated when ripe. They should be kept in plastic bags to prevent the strong aroma from permeating other foods.

Watermelons

The best way to tell the quality of a watermelon is to cut it in half or in quarters. The flesh should be a rich red and the seeds brown or black. Avoid grainy-looking flesh, pink flesh, and white seeds. When buying a whole melon, look for a dull surface. And the underside should be turning yellowish. Avoid melons with hard white streaks running lengthwise. Keep melons in the warmest part of the refrigerator.

Watermelon contains vitamins A, B1, B2, and C.

Persian Melon

Persian melons resemble cantaloupes in color and netting, although the Persian's netting is finer. Persians are larger than cantaloupes, about the size of honeydew melons.

Casaba Melon

Casaba melons have a pumpkin-like appearance. The rind is hard and is either yellow or green; bright yellow indicates overmaturity. The surface is covered with shallow furrows running lengthwise. There is usually a scar where the stem was removed. The stem does not separate from a ripe casaba when it is harvested, and so it must be cut off later.

Casaba melon has the same mineral and vitamin content as honeydews.

Casaba melons can be purchased green and ripened at room temperatures. When ripe, the stem end should be slightly soft. Avoid melons with dark, soft spots.

NECTARINES

Nectarines are a smooth-skinned variety of the peach. The flesh of the nectarine is firmer and more aromatic than that of the peach. Most of the major varieties are clingstone. They are usually harvested unripe. They contain iron, phosphorus, sodium, postassium, and vitamins A and C.

Buy nectarines that have no trace of green at the stem and allow them to ripen at room temperature. Avoid buying hard or shriveled fruit, which may be immature. When ripe, nectarines will yield slightly to pressure, with a slight softness at the stem end, and will be a rich orange-yellow with red speckles. Refrigerate after ripening.

A nectarine will brown after being cut. Like apples, cut nectarines right before using.

ORANGES

The orange is technically a berry with a reddish-yellow, leathery, aromatic rind. It is grown domestically in California, Texas, and Florida and is available year round. State laws require oranges to be harvested when ripe.

As a rule, the California varieties are a deeper orange, have thicker skins, and give less juice than the Florida varieties. Most California varieties are the navel, a seedless fruit; they are easiest to peel and are the best for eating out of hand. Valencia oranges are harder to peel and are best for juice or slicing. The best Florida varieties are Parson Brown, the pineapple orange, and the temple. The best Florida oranges are small, heavy, and thin-skinned. Some Florida and Texas temples, tangelos, and others are dyed with Citrus Red No. 2. This is not stamped on the orange and rarely is a sign posted saying the fruit has been colored artificially.

Choose smaller varieties; they usually provide more juice and flavor than the large sizes. They should feel firm and heavy and have a bright color. Avoid buying oranges with a rough surface; this indicates a thick skin and little juice. Green spots, a greenish cast, or a lacy, brownish blemish (russeting) are not signs of immaturity or poor quality.

Orange juice contains magnesium and sulfur, and is very high in calcium, phosphorus and vitamins A, B1, B2, and C.

PAPAYAS

In their natural habitat in the tropics, papayas are called melons that grow on trees. The oblong papaya weighs from 2 to 20 pounds (1 to 9 kg).

It is yellow to orange with a minimum amount of green at the stem end; when ripe, it has a soft texture and black seeds in the middle. The flavor compares with that of the peach or the cantaloupe. The papaya contains potassium, silicon, and vitamins A, B1, B2, and C.

Papaya contains papain, which is excellent for the digestive system. The greenish fruit contains more active enzymes than the ripe fruit and can be eaten. Green fruit can be ripened at room temperatures. Also, choose round, rather than oblong, papayas, and ones that are plump and free of decay.

Papayas are extremely perishable, do not store well, and therefore are not widely available in this country. Papayas often reach us in a milky juice form, which has become a popular commercial item.

Papayas can be difficult to peel. They can be submerged in boiling water for 1 minute, then dipped in cold water. The skin can then be removed easily.

PEACHES
Peaches have a single seed enclosed in a hard outer casing. The pulp is yellow to white with red areas; the skin is smooth and downy. White varieties have the more delicate flavor. The two major varieties are cling-stone and freestone. Freestones have a bitter flavor for raw eating and are good for freezing. Clings are good for canning. Both varieties can be purchased canned. Peaches contain magnesium, sulfur, potassium, and vitamins A, B1, and C.

Peaches should ripen on the tree. Their season runs from July through September. The test for ripeness is an increasing yield when squeezed. A ripe peach will be tender. Avoid those that are green and are either very hard or very soft. Peaches brown after being peeled or cut, so cut the fruit right before serving.

PEARS
Soft, juicy pears supply very little protein and fat. Pears are high in iron, magnesium, potassium, and vitamins A, B1, B2, and C. Favorite varieties are Bartlett, pale to rich yellow, and Winter Nelis, medium to light green. Most pears should be greenish yellow to brownish. Pears are harvested while slightly green and can be ripened in a warm place, out of the sun.

120

Buy pears that are firm, beginning to soften slightly, plump, and free of signs of bruising, shriveling, and cuts on the skin. Pears show their decay beginning near the stem; avoid pears with soft spots or bruising at this end. Because pears brown when cut open, don't prepare pears until ready to serve.

PINEAPPLES

A native of Hawaii, the pineapple is a solid mass of succulent fleshy fruit surrounded by a tough outer skin and crowned with small, tough, spiky leaves. Pineapples are rich in potassium, chlorine, sodium, phosphorus, magnesium, sulfur, calcium, iron, iodine, and vitamins A, B1, B2, and C. Among the varieties are red Spanish, yellow to orange, with white flesh; and cayenne, smoother-edged leaves, yellow to green when ripe.

Most pineapples are harvested green; they lose some acid and lack some sweetness as they mature to yellow. If a pineapple is not ripe when purchased, allow it to stand at room temperature until it is. At this time, it will give off a delightful fragrance. The best test of the freshness of a pineapple is the aroma. Another test is that, when ripe, the quilted flesh "gives" under the skin, and the leaves readily fall off when pulled.

Buy pineapples that are firm and heavy for the size. Avoid pineapples that are a dull yellowish green or have brown areas. Brown leaves indicate the fruit was harvested while immature; fresh green leaves on a completely yellow fruit indicate harvesting after the fruit ripened.

PLUMS

There are four major varieties of plum: American, damson, European, and Japanese, the latter two being the most common worldwide. Colors range from dark red to royal purple to golden. Europeans, which are blue or purple, have firm flesh and are mild in flavor. Japanese are very juicy; they are never blue or purple and come in many shapes. The American variety is basically yellow, but sometimes reddish yellow, even red. Damsons are small, of a deep purple color and have a somewhat bitter taste. Plums are rich in iron, calcium, magnesium, potassium, and vitamins A, B1, B2, and C.

Buy full, plump plums. Ripe plums have a softening at the top as well as a delightful aroma. The firmness should be midway between soft and hard. Avoid plums with any brown discolorations.

POMEGRANATES

The pomegranate is about the size of an orange. It contains multiple seeds in a reddish pulp. The membrane between the seed sections is white and bitter and is surrounded by a leathery, ruby red skin. The pulp is sweet. Pomegranates contain magnesium, sodium, and vitamin C.

Pomegranates should be ripe when eaten. Ripeness is indicated by a slight cracking of the skin. The pulp around the seed is what is eaten. The seeds may be swallowed or discarded, or the juice may be separated from the seeds by crushing the kernels in a food mill and straining to separate the seeds from the juice.

RASPBERRIES, BLACKBERRIES

The blackberry and the raspberry are members of the same family; the rose family. Blackberries are picked when fully ripe; their flavor runs from sweet to bittersweet. They ship well and retain their freshness until they reach the consumer. Blackberries are high in calcium, phosphorus, iron, sodium, potassium, sulfur, and vitamins A, B1, B2, and C.

Ripe berries are black; a red color indicates immaturity. The individual cells of the berry should be plump. When purchased, blackberries should not have their stem caps attached. Avoid buying berries with stains on the container. Keep blackberries cool and dry. Raspberries are high in potassium, calcium, phosphorus, sulfur, and vitamins A, B1, and C. They are considered the best tasting of all berries. Buy plump, firm fruits, bright in color and dry on the outside.

STRAWBERRIES

The strawberry is a member of the rose family. There are thousands of varieties of strawberry in different shapes, sizes, and shades of red. Strawberries contain iodine, sodium and silicon and are high in iron and vitamin C.

Buy plump, bright red strawberries with dry flesh. Beware of white patches, which indicate that the fruit was picked unripe. The stem caps should be intact and appear fresh without any noticeable wilting. Avoid poorly shaped strawberries and buy during the peak of the season, which is May and June.

Always examine the berries at the bottom of the container; strawberries are usually packaged with the ripe berries on top. The strawberry bruises easily and should be used as soon as possible.

TANGERINES

The tangerine is a variety of orange, although it is usually considered a separate fruit. Tangerines contain magnesium, calcium, potassium, and vitamins A, B1, B2, and C. Buy tangerines that are orange-red with tight skins. Avoid very soft fruits and greenish or pale yellow fruit.

HERBS

SWEET BASIL

Basil is an herbaceous plant that grows to 2 feet (61 cm) in height. Basil must be sown, 12 inches (30 cm) apart, in light, rich soil in a sunny location. Basil needs to be protected from wind and cannot withstand frost. It can be grown successfully under glass.

Basil leaves are light green with a smooth texture. The best quality leaves are the tender, very young leaves; older leaves are tough. Young leaves have a sweet, strong scent with a flavor similar to cloves. Basil can be purchased in a dried form and the flavor resembles that of curry.

When you are using basil for cooking, crumble the leaves between your fingers instead of chopping them. Basil is used in stews, egg dishes, and soups; it is also an excellent addition to seafoods, spinach, eggplant, squash, peas, and onions. Cheese and basil have a tremendous affinity with tomatoes.

BAY LEAF

The bay is a small, bushy laurel tree grown in the United States and Mediterranean countries. It has tough, aromatic, shiny leaves and produces berries in warm climates. Bay needs a very rich soil with equal portions of loam, peat, sand, and compost. It is difficult to grow, especially in a home garden, because the soil can never dry out.

The fresh leaves have a slightly bitter taste; the bitterness dissipates if the leaves are allowed to wilt for a few days. The scent and flavor will not be lost. The dried form is suitable only if it is freshly dried. Most purchased dried bay leaves lose their flavor so quickly that they are really not worth using.

Bay leaves are used in stews, chowders, and soups; with pot roasts, carrots, custards, fish, tomatoes, and pickles.

BORAGE

An annual plant that grows to 3 feet (1 m) in height, borage needs a well-drained calcareous, or chalky, soil, warm temperatures, and sun. The leaves and stems are covered with rough hairs that can be irritating to the touch.

Borage is always used fresh and has the flavor of cucumber. Use it with yogurt or cream cheese.

FINES HERBES

Fines herbes is a combination of three or more delicate herbs. The ones used most commonly are parsley, tarragon, chervil, and chives.

BURNET

A perennial plant that grows to 12 inches (30 cm) in height and has small leaves growing in pairs. Burnet (garden burnet, salad burnet) is a sturdy plant that grows easily in any soil. It is raised from seed or by division of bunches. Burnet can be purchased in dry form. Like all fresh herbs, the leaves should be crumbled between the fingers rather than chopped. Once crushed, burnet smells somewhat like cucumber. Burnet is used in butter sauces; the fresh, tender young leaves can be used in mixed green salads.

CAMOMILE

Sweet and wild camomile (chamonile) are very easy to grow. Camomile tea is made from drying the flower buds of the camomile plant.

CHERVIL, GARDEN

Chervil is an annual plant that grows to 18 inches (46 cm) in height and has curly leaves similar to parsley. The plant is very easy to grow in the garden or window box, but it needs slightly humid conditions. It goes to seed quickly. Seeds must be sown at intervals or cut back to root level to encourage new leaf growth in order to carry a supply through the summer. It can be grown during the winter in a terrarium or greenhouse. Chervil can also be purchased in dry form.

The flavor is similar to parsley but is not as strong. The herb is used in cooking, usually after the dish has been taken off the heat, and never for long cooking. It is used in omelets, souffles, eggs, and salads; with lamb, veal, pork, and seafood; and in Bechamel, verte, vinaigrette, remoulade, and Bearnaise sauces.

CHIVES

Chives are perennials and members of the onion family. The thick stems look like grass. There is hardly any bulb and the plants grow in bunches. They are bright green. Chives are easily grown in any garden soil; they can be raised by seed or by dividing the bunches. The flavor of chives is like that of onion, only extremely delicate. Chives can be purchased dried, usually freeze-dried.

Chives are used in potato salads, soups, and sauces; and with eggs, cream cheese, and baked potatoes.

MARJORAM

Marjoram is a strongly aromatic perennial herb of the mint family that grows to 2 feet (61 cm) in height. It will not survive cold weather, needs to be sown in light soil, and must have a sunny location. It is sweeter when grown in ideal conditions.

Marjoram, both fresh and dried, is used extensively in the kitchen. Marjoram should never be cooked for a long time; it should be added to cooking shortly before completion. Fresh, it is used in salads. Dried and fresh marjoram is used with meat, seafood, poultry, mushrooms, carrots, zucchini, peas, and spinach; and in soups, egg dishes, and sauces.

MINT

There are many species of mint, which is the leaf of the perennial spearmint plant. Mint is easily grown in average soil in partial shade and prefers to have its soil moist at all times. Mint can be used both fresh and dried and is rarely mixed with other herbs.

Mint is used in beverages and fruit salads; and with potatoes, peas, beans, lentils, tomatoes, mushrooms, carrots, cucumbers, apples, and stewed fruit. It is also used in sauces for lamb and veal.

OREGANO

Oregano (origan) is a perennial herb of the mint family. There are many varieties and as many types of soil and climate to grow it in. Oregano is

125

sold fresh in bunches or can be purchased dry; the dried form has a strong flavor. Oregano has a strong odor with a slightly bitter flavor.

Oregano is used in tomato sauces, salads, stuffings, meat loaves, and stews; and with zucchini, eggplant, cheese, beans, and pork. It is also an ingredient in chili powder.

PARSLEY

Parsley is a biennial. There are many varieties from curly-leaved to a hardy plain-leaved. Planted in the spring, it will take 2 months to germinate. Plant parsley far enough apart so that the leaves never come in contact with one another. The soil should be fairly rich; and parsley likes partial shade. In the fall, parsley can be transplanted into pots and brought indoors for a winter supply.

Parsley is used in fresh and dried forms. Drying parsley at home is almost impossible, but it is dried successfully in the commercial variety. Rinse fresh parsley well, and squeeze to remove as much water as possible before use.

Parsley is used in bouquet garni, sauces, butters, soups, eggs, garnishes, and in endless ways.

ROSEMARY

Rosemary is a 6-foot (2 m) evergreen bush with sharp leathery leaves. It is best grown in calcareous soil and needs plenty of sun. The oil in rosemary contains camphor, and the flavor is very aromatic.

Rosemary is used fresh in the whole sprig form, dried, or powdered. It is used in bouquet garni, split pea and minestrone soups, and stews; and with vegetables, salmon, meats, stewed fruit, and poultry.

SAGE

Sage is a perennial plant of the mint family. There are many varieties, but for kitchen use the narrow-leaved variety is most suitable. The leaves are covered with fine, satiny hairs. Sage is an easily grown herb as long as the weather does not get too cold or too wet. The soil should be porous.

The fresh leaves dry easily and can be purchased commercially either fresh or dried. The flavor is strong and should be used sparingly. Sage is used in sausage or fowl stuffings, cream soups, chowders, and vegetable dishes; and with seafood, eggplant, onions, tomatoes, and lima beans.

SAVORY

Savory (summer savory) is a hardy annual herb growing to 12 inches (30 cm). Savory needs a light soil and plenty of sun, but it grows easily and usually self-sows. For the best-flavored leaves, wait until after flowering.

Savory is used, fresh or dried, in stuffings, dressings, and lentil soup; and with beans, peas, rice, cauliflower, zucchini, poultry, and pork.

Winter savory is a perennial herb that can be grown in poor soil but needs plenty of sun. Its flavor resembles that of summer savory. Its uses are the same as for summer savory.

TARRAGON

Tarragon is a perennial bush native to Siberia. The leaves are narrow. Tarragon needs porous soil and will grow in partial shade but prefers full sun. Tarragon is used both fresh and dried. The flavor of tarragon becomes very strong in cooking.

Tarragon is used in vinegars, sauces, omelets, cream soups, salads, and egg dishes; and with chicken, mushrooms, sweetbreads, fish, veal, and lamb.

THYME

Thyme (garden thyme) is a perennial plant grown best in calcareous soil with sun and conditions that are fairly dry. Thyme grows easily from seed or from root-stem separations. Thyme has a potent flavor and contains an essential oil called thymol, which is a disinfectant; hence thyme is used in preserving. Thyme is used both fresh and dried.

Thyme is used in tomato dishes, clam dishes, stuffings, soups, and bouquet garni; and with seafood, potatoes, sweet peppers, onions, carrots, beets, and cheese. It is often combined with marjoram.

VERBENA

Verbena (lemon verbena) is easily grown from seeds or cuttings. It prefers garden soil and a warm, sunny location. Verbena is easily grown indoors, again in a sunny location.

SPICES

Most spices are grown in the hot, sunny, humid climate of tropical countries. When spices reach full maturity, they are harvested by hand and dried in the sun. This method has not changed for hundreds of years.

Some spices are ground before they are exported; others are left whole and milled at their destination. Factory-ground spices undergo analytical testing during processing to assure that all spice blends have a balance of ingredients, giving you value for the price you pay.

When buying spices in the ground form, buy small amounts to avoid any decrease in freshness. Store spices in airtight containers in a dark, cool place; both light and heat will cause flavor changes.

When possible, buy spices in their whole form. Most spices can be easily ground at home. Use either a pepper mill or an electric or manual coffee grinder for most seeds. A special grinder will have to be purchased to grind the tiny poppy seeds. Also, cinnamon and mace cannot be ground in a pepper mill. There are also special graters for nutmeg, although an ordinary kitchen grater can be used. Grate on the area with the smallest mesh. Always grind only the amount you need, no more.

To get a more powdery grind, sift the ground spice through a strainer or a piece of rough cheesecloth. A powder can also be achieved by using a mortar and pestle. For a coarser grind, use a mortar and pestle.

The flavor is enhanced in fenugreek, cumin, poppy, and coriander if these spices are heated slightly before being ground. Heat a non-stick pan over a very low flame. Put the seeds in the pan, constantly moving the pan to keep the seeds from burning. The seeds will begin to pop when heated sufficiently. Then use them as desired.

Because of the small amount of spice ingested, the trace minerals available in spices, except for chromium and manganese, are of no signficance nutritionally.

ALLSPICE
Allspice has an aroma and flavor similar to a mixture of nutmeg, cloves, and cinnamon. The small pea-size berry turns brown when dried. Allspice berries resemble large peppercorns. Ground allspice is used in cakes, puddings, preserves, and Middle Eastern cooking.

ANISE

Anise is the small, dried ripe fruit of an annual herb. The flavor is that of licorice. Anise is used in cakes, breads, cookies, candies, sauces for seafood, and fruit and vegetable salads.

CAPER

The caper is the small flower bud (size of a wild rose) from the caper bush. After the buds are left to wilt in the air for a day or two, they are marinated in salted white vinegar or dry-salted. The price you pay is determined by the grade of caper.

Capers are purchased bottled in a vinegar solution. When removing capers from the bottle, leave as much liquid behind as possible to cover the remaining capers. Capers must never dry out; however, adding more vinegar will spoil them.

Capers are used in salad and fish sauces, butters, salads, and vinaigrette sauces.

CARAWAY

Caraway is a biennial plant that can grow more than 2 feet (61 cm) high. The flowers are creamy white; the leaves are fernlike. The plant is very easy to grow in a semishaded location in fairly heavy soil. The plant will self-sow if the seed is not collected.

The young, tender green leaves have a bland flavor rather like that of parsley or dill. The leaf can be sown at any time during the summer. Germination of the fruit is slow. The fruits split into two seeds, which are the spice. The taste is sharp and peppery and changes as the plant ages.

Seeds are used in cakes, bread, rolls, cheese, coleslaw, salads, cookies, tomato, and potato or cucumber salads; or with cooked cabbage, carrots, sauerkraut, turnips, onions, noodles, and rice.

Note that many books on Eastern cooking give caraway as an ingredient in curry. The ingredient should be cumin.

CARDAMOM

Cardamom is a perennial plant of the ginger family and grows 8 feet (2.5 m) high. The leaves are large and lance-shaped. The flowers are white, edged with yellow and blue. The stalks bearing the small seed pods, which contain 15 to 20 dark, hard seeds, grow out from the base of the plant.

Many species of related plants that resemble cardamom are sold as cardamom. They are inferior plants. Cardamom is expensive, so make sure you buy the real thing.

Because the aroma is lost almost instantly when the seeds are exposed to the air, dried seed pods are purchased in the store. Never buy cardamom in the ground state; it loses its essential oils rapidly.

The seeds are very hard and should be pounded before use. The seeds have a bittersweet taste with a slight lemony flavor. Cardamom is used in cakes, pies, cookies, curries, pilafs, preserves, beverages, pickles, marinades, puddings, stewed fruits, and for barbecue sauces.

CAYENNE

Cayenne peppers are small, hot red chili peppers, ground fine. They came originally from Cayenne in French Guiana. They are used in meats, stews, sauces, and salad dressings. Cayenne can also be used like black pepper.

CELERY SEED

The celery seed is an herb of the parsley family. The seedlike fruit is dried, and the flavor is similar to that of celery. Celery seed is used in meat and fish dishes, salads, and salad dressings.

Celery salt is a very common condiment. To make it, salt is added to ground celery seed.

CHILI POWDER

Chili powder is ground chili pepper pods blended with other spices—oregano, chocolate, cumin—and other flavorings to give a very hot flavor. It is used in chili con carne and other Mexican dishes.

Homemade chili powder is made by lightly roasting dried chilies in a frying pan over low heat until the color is a deep red. They can then be ground in a blender or mill and strained through a sieve to make a fine powder.

CINNAMON AND CASSIA

Both cinnamon and cassia come from small evergreen trees and bushes. The spices consist of thin inner bark peeled from thin branches. These pieces, or "quills," are dried in the sun and curl up. Sticks that look like a roll of dried paper and are pale in color are the finest quality.

Cinnamon has a delicate flavor. Ground, it is used in sweet dishes, cakes, pies, cookies, and puddings. Sticks are used for fruits, preserves, and beverages.

Cassia is used in curries. Its taste is stronger than that of cinnamon.

CLOVES

Cloves are the tight buds of the clove tree. The tree can grow 30 feet (9 m) high and is native to the East Indies. The buds are dried gently in the sun or over slow heat. Once dried, they turn a red-brown color; these are the cloves we purchase in the store. There is a substantial variety of sizes and flavors, depending on the age of the cloves and environment from which they came. The flavor is due to oils that are a powerful antiseptic.

Choose cloves that are plump, oily, and not shriveled. All cloves have such a strong flavor (sweet and tangy) that it is not necessary to search for a "perfect" clove. They should be purchased whole, not ground.

Stick cloves in onions to make stock or curry. Whole cloves are excellent partners to apple dishes of all kinds. Cloves are also used in pickling and with meat and fish. Ground (at home), they are used in cakes, cookies, and puddings.

CORIANDER

Coriander is a hardy annual plant of the parsley family (Chinese parsley, Japanese parsley). The feathery leaves are fan-shaped with white, pink, or pale mauve flowers set in clusters. Coriander can be grown easily, even in a flower box. The plant grows to 2 feet (61 cm) in height. To prevent seeds from dropping, they must be sown in spring and harvested when the seeds ripen in August and September.

The round seed is easily split in two. When ripe, the color varies from green to cream or brown. Use immediately after grinding; coriander loses flavor quickly. The taste is aromatic, sweet; it is somewhat like that of an orange peel.

131

Coriander leaves are used in Indian dishes, soups, and stews. The seeds are used in baking, condiments, pickling, chutneys, sweets, puddings, egg dishes, and lentil and bean soups.

CUMIN

Cumin is a delicate annual plant of the parsley family that grows best in hot climates. Originally from the East, cumin is now popular in both Mexico and North Africa. The plant is grown primarily for the seeds. They are dried and made available in both whole and ground forms. The seed has a unique, strong, and highly aromatic flavor. Cumin is a powerful spice, and, if not used sparingly, will dominate any dish in which it is included. Heat the seeds slightly before use to increase the aroma.

Cumin is used whole in soups, cheese spreads, stuffed eggs, stews, and sausage. It is used ground in curries, chili powder, rye bread, cheese dishes, and tomato sauces; and with carrots, beets, potatoes, and legumes. Note that in Indian recipes, when caraway is mentioned, cumin is actually meant.

CURRY POWDER

Curry powder was invented for Europeans. To make it, the following spices are ground and combined: black pepper, chili, cloves, cinnamon, cardamom, coriander, cumin, curry leaves, fenugreek, ginger, mace, mustard seed, poppy seed, and turmeric.

DILL

Dill is a hardy annual plant of the parsley family with feathery, stringlike leaves. The plant grows to about 3 feet (1 m) in height. Dill is extremely easy to grow, although the plant prefers a warm position out of the wind. It is grown from seed sown in the spring. It grows in any soil and usually self-seeds.

The dill plant is important for both its leaves and seeds; however, in most cooking it is the leaves that are used. Dill leaves have a distinctive flavor. The seed has a sharp taste similar to that of caraway, due to the presence of the essential oil, carvone.

Dill leaves can be dried, but they lose most of their flavor. Occasionally dill is added to the food at the beginning of cooking. Dill loses its flavor when cooked, however, and is best added just before the cooking process is completed.

Dill seed is mainly used as a condiment in making dill pickles. The leaves are used in pickling, dill vinegar; and with cucumbers, yogurt, sour cream, spinach, and fish.

GINGER

Grown in India, the ginger plant resembles the iris with its long leaves and fat creeping rhizomes. The plant grows 2 to 4 feet (61 to 122 cm) high and has spotted yellow flowers. The knotty ginger rhizomes keep for a long time.

The appearance of fresh ginger is dried, plump, firm to the touch, not shriveled, and slightly fibrous. Ground ginger suffers all the defects of other ground spices by being dried, scraped, boiled, peeled, and ground to extract the flavor, which is lost in the air. The fresh root is more pungent than the ground. Ginger can also be purchased canned, crystallized in sugar, or preserved in syrup. Stem is the name for the finest grade of preserved ginger; it has a very low fiber content.

The ginger root is used in chutneys, pickles, preserves, and dried fruit. Shaved, it is used in Oriental cooking and with vegetables. Ground ginger is used in sweets, cakes, breads, and curries.

FENNEL

The fennel plant is a hardy perennial that will last for several years. The seeds are sown in April, and the plant is not fussy about the soil it grows in. It is a large plant, growing to 6 feet (2 m), with bright green leaves and yellow flowers. Both fennel leaves and seed are used.

There are many varieties of fennel in the leaf form, from slightly bitter with no anise flavoring to varieties with a strong anise flavoring. The leaf can be used fresh or dried.

The herb is used in vinaigrette sauces, salads, stuffings, mayonnaise, tomato sauce, potato or crab salads, and macaroni dishes; and with lentils, legumes, and artichokes. The aromatic seeds are most often used as a breath sweetener to be chewed after meals.

Florence fennel, or finnochio, is a vegetable variety of fennel that has a bulb formation at the end of the stalk. In the raw state, it is popular in salads. The flavor of anise is very delicate.

FENUGREEK

A leguminous plant of the pea family, fenugreek looks similar to a clover with a small flower. The reddish yellow seeds are slightly bitter with a distinctive smell. The seed is rich in vitamins and protein.

The green leaf of the fenugreek plant is curried in Indian vegetable dishes. Fenugreek is an ingredient in curry powders and a significant ingredient in Oriental vegetarian cooking.

MACE, NUTMEG

Mace is the bright scarlet flesh, or aril, surrounding the kernel, or "nutmeg," a hard wrinkled seed of the nutmeg fruit from the nutmeg tree grown in Indonesia. The ripe fruit resembles a yellow plum. After the fruit ripens, it dries and splits open. The covering (mace) is removed, pressed, and dried; it has the appearance of a yellow-brown seaweed. Mace in this state is called the "blades of mace." Mace is also available in ground form.

The flavor of mace resembles that of nutmeg with a more subtle, exotic, slightly bittersweet flavor. Mace is very expensive.

In the blade state mace is used in soups, stews, fish sauces, pickling, and preserving. Ground, it is used in cakes, cookies, pies, and chocloate dishes, Bechamel sauce, and egg, cheese, and vegetable dishes.

Nutmeg is sold whole and ground and can be dark or white. The best way to purchase nutmeg is whole. Grate it fresh, as needed. The powder form loses its aromatic flavor quickly. Nutmeg enhances the flavor of spinach, string beans, cheese, and onion sauce. It is also used in sausage, cakes, doughnuts, pudding, and eggnog.

Mace and nutmeg are interchangeable in most recipes.

MUSTARD

Mustard seeds come from an annual herb plant. The seeds and the dry powder forms do not have the strong mustard taste; however, once crushed and mixed with water, the essential oils, mixed with an enzyme, causes a glucoside (a substance related to sugar) to react with water to give the pungent taste of mustard.

The condiment we use for eating and cooking requires seeds of three plants of the cabbage family to acquire the taste we know as mustard. To maintain the pungency in cooking, add right before the dish is completed and simmer gently.

Mustard is used in sauces, gravies, salad dressings, and casseroles; and with creamed and other vegetables.

PAPRIKA
Paprika is made from special varieties of ripe red peppers that do not have the pungent flavor of chili peppers. The seeds and septae are removed to further destroy any strong, hot flavors. The peppers are grown in Chili, the United States, and parts of Europe. The pepper is dried and purchased in its ground state and has a mild, sweet flavor. If the color is anything but bright red, it has deteriorated and is stale.

Paprika is used on shellfish, chicken salads, salad dressings, canapes, and spreads. It is an excellent source of vitamin C.

PEPPER
Grown in India, the peppercorn is a dried, small, round berry of a vine. Peppercorns can be purchased whole and ground. Whole pepper is used in pickling meats and stews. Ground pepper is used as a seasoning on foods.

White pepper has the black covering of the mature berry removed; it is found mostly in the ground form. White pepper is used in cooking when the strong flavor of black pepper is not desirable.

POPPY SEEDS
These are the small, dark gray or black seeds of the poppy plant, which is grown in the United States and Turkey. Poppy seeds are used whole for toppings on rolls or in fillings for buns; in cheese and egg dishes and in salads; and with noodles and rice, carrots, celery root, peas, spinach, turnips, cauliflower, and potatoes. It is also used in oils for salads.

SAFFRON
Saffron is the dried stigma of a perennial plant grown in Spain, France, and Italy. To make one pound (450 g) of saffron takes 250,000 stigmas from 76,000 flowers, and so it is a very expensive spice.

Saffron is sold in the bright orange stigma form (it looks like tiny threads) in small tubes or packets. Saffron can be purchased in ground form, but because of the expense, is often mixed with additives. It is used mainly to add a yellow color to food; in stews, soups, gravies, and meat sauces; and with rice, poultry, and veal.

SESAME SEEDS

The small, white, flat seeds of the sesame plant, sesame seeds are extremely oily (oil content is 60%) with a sweet, nutty flavor. Sesame seeds can be purchased as whole seeds, raw or roasted, in a paste called tahini, as a ground meal, and as an almost tasteless cooking oil that is high in protein. The smell is light, and the oil does not go rancid easily.

Sesame seeds are used on rolls, breads, cookies, candies, chicken, fish, meat loaves, cabbage, spinach, green beans, carrots, noodles, rice, salads—almost on anything.

SUNFLOWER SEEDS

Sunflower seeds come from the tall sunflower plant. The huge flower, with hundreds of seeds, resembles a gigantic daisy.

The seeds are roasted in their husks and can be purchased in their husks or with husks removed, salted or unsalted. They are eaten like nuts.

The seeds are used for a cooking oil that is highly unsaturated. The oil has very little taste and is a very light yellow color. It is an excellent oil for cooking and for salad dressings. The buds of the sunflower can be used in salads.

TURMERIC

A perennial plant of the ginger family, turmeric is grown in the tropics and the Orient. The bright orange rhizomes of the plant are boiled, the skins removed and ground, supplying the form that we use in cooking. Turmeric powder is yellow and has a slightly bitter flavor. It is used in meat and egg dishes, curries, rice dishes, and pilafs.

TEA

Tea is an infusion of dried leaves or roots from a wide variety of aromatic evergreen shrubs and trees of the camellia family; it is prepared by extraction of substances in leaves or roots soaked in water. Tea is called an infusion because the temperature of the water used for extraction is below that of boiling. The flavor, odor, and color of tea depend on the leaves or roots extracted, their processing, and the method of preparing the infusion.

The two top leaves and bud of each stem of the shrub are pinched off and processed to make the tea. These tender young leaves, designated by such names as flowering pekoe, flowery orange pekoe, broken orange pekoe, and orange pekoe, are the highest grade of tea. The less desirable (older and larger) leaves farther down the stem are used to make pekoe or souchong teas. Special blends of tea are available with added spices and flowers; jasmine tea, for instance, contains jasmine flowers.

After the tea leaves have been pinched, they may or may not be fermented. Leaves that are not fermented are dried at high temperatures to inactivate the enzymes. Green tea consists of the unfermented leaves of the plant. A short fermentation period produces oolong tea, a longer fermentation produces black tea. Tannins, which are bitter and stringent, become less so after fermentation.

Most tea sold in the United States is black tea made from a mixture of orange pekoe and pekoe. Tea bags contain broken or crushed leaves, a smaller amount of which are necessary to produce a given amount of infusion than with whole leaves because crushed leaves expose more surface area, pack down more, and occupy less space. Use tea leaves in loose form, as the paper in tea bags can subtly alter the delicate flavor.

Instant tea is a spray-dried or drum-dried tea infusion. Some instant teas have lemon and sugar added for flavor and maltodextrin to improve stability. Infusions for instant tea are usually made from black tea. Instant tea lacks the full flavor of the leaves in a freshly prepared infusion.

Tea should be brewed in ceramic pots, china, or earthenware. Metal pots either react directly with the tannins in tea or contain metal oxides that react, forming a scum on the surface of the tea. If a metal pot is used for tea, it should be thoroughly scoured to remove the mineral deposits.

Any pot used to brew tea should be preheated. Preheat by rinsing the pot out with scalding hot water. Always use fresh cold water for boiling. Water should be brought to a boil and poured immediately onto the leaves. The usual ratio is 1 rounded teasoonful (5 to 10 ml) of tea per 8-ounce cup (250 ml) of water.

Tea leaves may be placed loose in the pot or in a tea ball or tea bags used for easy removal. Tea leaves should be steeped no longer than 3 to 4 minutes. This infusion time permits maximum extraction of desirable flavors and stimulants with minimal extraction of bitter components. Loose leaves should be strained out after this time. For a weaker tea, add hot water to a full-strength brew after the full brewing period.

Stir the tea before pouring to make it uniformly strong. Circulating the brew agitates the oils that add to the flavor of the tea. If the tea has to stand for any length of time, strain the liquid from the leaves (or remove the tea ball or bags). Do not reheat tea after it is brewed. Serve immediately.

Don't judge the strength of the tea by its color. Some teas brew light, some dark. Brew by the clock.

Lemon lightens the color of tea because its acid bleaches the tannins. Always use milk, at room termperature, instead of cream in order to let the true flavor come out.

COFFEE

Coffee is grown on a tree or shrub that produces a fruit known as the berry. Inside the berry are two beans, each surrounded by a silvery skin which in turn is enclosed in a cherrylike pulpy substance.

It takes about five years for the coffee tree to produce its first full crop, at which time white blossoms appear. The berries that appear after the flowers have fallen are picked by hand and transported to nearby processing plants. At the plant, the beans are separated from the berries by one of two methods: wet or dry. In either case, the first step is to wash the berries and separate them from twigs, leaves and other debris.

The dry method is used in Brazil and in countries where water is scarce. The berries are spread out on dry ground for a few weeks, raked daily to ensure even drying, and then heaped and covered at night for protection against moisture. When dry, they are processed through a milling machine to remove both the dried husk and the inner silver skin.

The wet method is used in countries where the water supply is plentiful. The berries are put into machines that remove the outside pulp and expose a sticky material surrounding the beans; they are transferred to concrete tanks to remove this material, then poured into washing machines that cleanse them with constantly changing clear water. They are then drained, dried, and finally processed through a hulling machine to extricate the beans. At this stage the beans are graded for size, type, and quality and packed in 132-pound bags for export.

The finished coffee that reaches its destination is "green coffee," which consists of beans that are green or blue-green and can be stored for a long period. Most coffee imported into the United States is green coffee.

The different grades of coffee fall into two general categories: arabica, which is not grown in Arabia but comes from Central and South America and has a rich, mellow flavor; and robusta, a less flavorsome, less expensive variety that comes from the lowlands of Africa. About 58 percent of the world's green coffee is from Central and South America; 37 percent comes from the African continent. More than half of the total is imported by the United States. The green beans arrive in this country and are blended, roasted, and packed for shipment to wholesale and retail outlets.

When the beans arrive in this country, they go through a process of controlled heating called roasting, which develops the distinctive coffee aroma and taste. During this process, the beans expand to about twice their orignial size and turn from green to brown. The longer the beans are roasted, the deeper their color. The darker roast has absolutely no effect on the strength or stimulation of the brew; it merely creates a darker-colored beverage.

There are over a hundred different coffee growths from twenty-odd countries throughout the world. The bag of coffee purchased in the specialty store or supermarket is not the product of one or even two of these growths, but contains a blend of eight to ten varieties. Flavor, aroma, and price are the considerations going into a particular coffee blend.

Coffee tasters sample from a vast combination of the different varieties and grades within these varieties. The taster considers the acidity (in coffee terms, the brightness of the flavor accent), body, color, aroma, and flavor. A typical blend might include the following: 40 percent high-grade Santos from Brazil, 40 percent Medellins from Colombia, and 20 percent Maracaibos from Venezuela. While blends for whole roasted beans are rather simple, commercially ground coffees, which are sold by major packagers in vacuum cans, are much more complicated, sometimes combining 40 to 50 different coffees. Here are some typical coffees:

African Arabica: highly flavorful and aromatic.

African Robusta: mildest and lightest.

Brazilian Santos: robust, somewhat "sweet," heavy-bodied.

Central American: flavorful, grand bouquet.

Colombian Medellin: full-bodied, rich, "winy."

Ethiopian Djimmah: full-bodied, aromatic.

French Roast (dark): the darkest and most bitter blend. Used in espresso blends, to build strength as mixer for regular coffees, and for demitasse.

French Roast (light): slightly overroasted blend with oily surface (for demitasse), which brings out nutlike flavor when mixed with regular coffees.

Italian Roast: medium-strong.

Jamaican Blue Mountain: rich, mellow.

Java: mild, but rich.

Kenya: medium-strength African.

Kona: mild Hawaiian.

Mexican: slightly smoky flavor.

Mocha: unique, sharp flavor, from Aden.

Mocha Java: heavier than mocha, more aromatic and smoother.

Peaberry: medium-strength African.

Spanish Roast: a demitasse blend lighter than the French roasts.

Tanganyikan: medium to mild African.

Turkish Blend: full-bodied, extremely strong.

Each of the above blends has its own distinctive flavor. The differences among them can be considerable. The best approach is to sample them until you find the blend that best suits you.

Many areas of the country do not have coffee stores or specialty shops that carry whole-bean roasted coffee. In such areas, whole-bean coffee is sometimes available in the food departments of large department stores. Also, some of the chain supermarkets carry this product.

Grind refers to the size of particles produced from coffee beans. The more surface area exposed to water when an infusion is made, that is, the finer the grind, the more substance will be extracted from the ground coffee. The size of the grind must always be related to the method of making the infusion. If grounds are subjected to very hot water for a long period of time, a coarse grind is recommended. Conversely, if they are subjected to lower temperatures and shorter times, the finer grinds can be used.

Coffee cannot be brewed from the whole roasted bean and still provide a delicious taste. The particular grind adapts the bean for one of a number of preparation processes so that the maximum flavor will be extracted through contact with hot water. If the grind is too coarse, the water passes through too quickly. If it is too fine or powdery, the coffee will taste bitter. The grind relates directly to the amount of time the coffee should be in contact with the hot water:

fine grind (vacuum),	1-4 minutes
medium grind (drip),	4-6 minutes
coarse or "regular" (percolator),	6-8 minutes

Coffee can be ground at home in hand or electric grinders. Some of the more expensive models have exact-timing devices to ensure that the grind will be as desired.

Coffee beans have a fairly high fat content. Once the bean is ground, the fat is subject to oxidation because of the greater surface area exposed. This oxidation is a type of rancidity that produces undesirable flavors and odors. Therefore, exclusion of air and moisture is essential to maintain freshness in ground coffee.

The ideal cup of coffee is a myth. It is strictly a matter of personal taste. But there are a number of important steps to follow in order to get the best brew out of the coffee beans.

GETTING THE BEST BREW

Storing Coffee

Fresh-roasted beans are usually sold in bags. They should be transferred to a container with a sealable lid and kept in the refrigerator until they are to be used. If more than one bag of beans is purchased at a time, the extra beans should be transferred to storage containers and kept in the freezer where they will stay fresh for months.

Allow coffee beans to stand at room temperature for about 30 minutes before grinding or brewing; otherwise, the temperature of the coffee will be too low. Never prepare a brew from beans just removed from the freezer; always use beans that are at room temperature. Your best bet is to have one "ready" jar in the regrigerator. Remember to keep the container securely sealed, for coffee, once widely used as a room deodorant, quickly assimilates odors from other foods.

Water

The compositon of the water (hard or soft) has an effect on coffee. Hard water flows through the coffee grounds faster than soft water. Thus, slightly more coffee is needed for hard water than soft water. Cold water should always be used because hot-water pipes accumulate mineral deposits than can affect the taste of the brew. In all methods of preparation, the water temperature should be near 200 degrees F (93 degrees C) or just under the boiling point as the water comes in contact with the coffee grounds. At higher temperatures, the chemical components tend to break down; and at lower temperatures the beverage is too cool for best drinking. Take into account the temperature of cold cups as well as the addition of milk or cream and sugar as elements that will lower the temperature of the coffee.

Measuring Coffee

The method of brewing and the proportions of coffee to water, as well as the brand of coffee, determine the flavor and strength of a coffee infusion. The more grounds that are present in relation to water, the stronger the infusion becomes; this is the preferred way to obtain strong coffee infusion. If brewing time is extended to obtain a stronger infusion, the infusion will contain a high proportion of undesirable flavors and bitterness.

For each 6-ounce cup (180 ml) of water, 1, 2, or 3 level tablespoons (15 to 45 ml) of ground coffee should be used. This produces mild, average, or strong infusions. Note that the markings on coffee pots and measurements for preparing coffee are based on 6-ounce (180 ml) coffee cups.

Timing

Percolator method: 6 to 8 minutes; drip method: 4 to 6 minutes; vacuum method: 1 to 4 minutes. Too little time and the coffee will be weak, too long and it will be bitter. Always make coffee full-strength and use the coffee maker to as near capacity as possible.

Serving Coffee

Coffee is brewed, not boiled. Boiling coffee ruins its flavor. Always serve coffee immediately after brewing. Coffee can be held for up to one hour (but not much longer) at 185 degrees-190 degrees F (85 to 88 degrees C). Never reheat coffee that has been allowed to cool. This breaks down the chemical components and results in an undesirable flavor.

METHODS OF PREPARATION

The Drip Method

The drip method (and the vacuum method) are superior to percolation because the water passes through the ground coffee with the greatest efficiency. In the drip method, boiling water is poured into an upper container and trickles slowly through coffee grounds, extracting the coffee brew as it drips into a lower bowl. There are three types of drip makers: regular, filter cone, and electric filter cone.

Regular Drip Coffee Maker

1. Preheat the pot by rinsing with boiling water.

2. Measure drip-grind coffee into coffee basket and replace upper section.

3. Bring water to a boil and let it cool for about 4 minutes. The water should not be more than 200 degrees F (93 degrees C) when it makes contact with the coffee. Boiling water extracts bitter elements from the coffee. A slightly lower temperature improves the brew. Pour the correct amount of water into the upper section. Cover. When dripping is complete, remove upper section and stir coffee.

Filter-Cone Drip Pot

A very desirable method of coffee preparation, the filter-cone drip pot uses specially treated filter paper to extract sediments and oils that can negatively affect the brew.

1. Preheat the pot by rinsing in hot water.

2. Place proper filter in upper cone and add regular grind coffee (this method requires a coarser grind than the regular drip coffee maker).

143

3. The first portion of water that hits the coffee should be a small amount that wets through the coffee but does not float in it. Filter manufacturers claim that "this portion of water is to disturb the air and to blast the cells of the woody structure of the coffee."

4. Allow to stand for 1 minute. Continue by slowly adding water in small amounts, never allowing the liquid level in the filter cone to rise much above that of the dry coffee. This ensures that all the water is in contact with all the coffee and that the brew is emitted through the very tip of the cone. When adding the water, use a circular motion.

5. Remove filter cone and serve.

Electric Filter-Cone Drip Pot

A relatively new item on the market is the electric filter-cone drip pot. It is a nearly foolproof, as well as convenient, method of coffee preparation. The principle is the same as in the preceding manual filter method except that the water is poured into a separate compartment, heated electrically, and forced up through a spout in even amounts to trickle through the coffee grounds, which are held in either a chemically treated paper filter cone or a nylon filter. The brew seeps through into a waiting pot, which stands on a hot plate, maintaining the coffee at a temperature of 185 to 190 degrees F (85 to 88 degrees C). Some models have a high-speed heating element that allows for the complete brewing of eight cups of coffee in as little as 2 to 3 minutes.

The Vacuum Method

With the vacuum method, steam from boiling water in a lower bowl creates pressure that forces water into an upper bowl, where it gently bubbles through the coffee grounds. As the lower bowl cools, a vacuum is created that pulls the brew through a filter into the lower bowl.

1. Remove upper bowl and insert filter. Add fine-grind coffee.

2. Bring cold water to boil in lower bowl. Remove from heat.

3. Insert upper bowl, twisting slightly for tight fit. Return to reduced heat.

4. Let water rise into upper bowl and mix with coffee for 1 minute, starring with a zigzag motion for 20 minutes.

5. Remove from heat. When brew returns to lower bowl (2 minutes), remove upper bowl and serve.

The Percolator Method

Percolating coffee is a poor method for brewing. Household coffee percolation spoils the coffee aroma by steam distillation and leaves strong-tasting soluble residues. In this method, the water bubbles up through a tube and sprays over the coffee in a basket at the top of the tube. As it trickles through the grounds, the coffee is extracted. However, the brew has actually been boiled, and this spoils its taste. Boiling brings out the tannic acid in the coffee bean and makes the brew bitter as well as cloudy.

Be careful to check out the water-level markings on a percolator; they are often inaccurate.

RANGE-TOP PERCOLATOR

1. Remove coffee basket and stem. Fill basket with regular-grind coffee.
2. Bring measured water to a boil in percolator. Remove from heat.
3. Insert coffee basket. Cover. Return to low heat. Water level should always be below bottom of basket.
4. Percolate for 6 to 8 minutes. Remove coffee basket and stem before serving.

AUTOMATIC PERCOLATOR Follow the manufacturer's instructions when using an automatic percolator. In many such models, the brewing time takes up to 20 minutes, resulting in overbrewed coffee. End manually, if necessary, after 8 minutes.

ESPRESSO MACHINES & MACCHINETTAS

Italian espresso uses steam pressure to brew the rich, nut-flavored coffee. Small electric models are available for home use. The Italian version of the drip coffee maker is the macchinetta. Use it like any drip coffee maker.

HOBO ("COWBOY") COFFEE

Use only a pot or pan and some water for hobo coffee.

1. Warm an ordinary pot or pan in hot water.

2. Measure into pot 4 tablespoons (60 ml) of coffee for each pint (500 ml) of boiling water.

3. Pour on water, place lid on pot, and keep hot.

4. After 4 minutes, lift lid and touch coffee, which is floating on top, with a spoon. After a moment, it will settle to the bottom. Serve.

INSTANT COFFEE

Instant coffees are water soluble. They are not really special grinds but are composed of tiny crystals of very strongly brewed fresh coffee that has been dehydrated, obtained by drum-drying, spray-drying, or freeze-drying. The flavor of instant coffee depends largely on the blends it contains. When boiling water is added, the crystals turn into a beverage once again. "Freeze-dried" differs from regular instant coffee in that the brewed coffee is frozen and then dried by vaporization in an effort to preserve more of the freshness, flavor, and aroma of the original brew.

DECAFFEINATED COFFEE

Decaffeinated coffees are available in both instant and ground forms. The caffeine is removed from the green coffee beans by steaming the beans in water, which also removes flavoring components. The caffeine is then separated from the flavor components by extraction of the caffeine solution with methylene chloride. The caffeine-free solution is added back to the coffee beans, which are then dried, roasted, and ground.

CLEANLINESS

It is absolutely essential to maintain a clean coffee maker. Coffee contains oil, which forms an almost invisible film on the inner walls of the pot. Unless completely removed, this oil will turn bad and spoil the taste of subsequent cups of coffee. After making a pot of coffee, wash all the parts of the pot in hot water with a mild detergent. Rinse with clear water. Scald with very hot water before using again. From time to time, it is advisable to take the coffee maker apart and scrub all the parts.

POTS, PANS, AND ELECTRICAL APPLIANCES

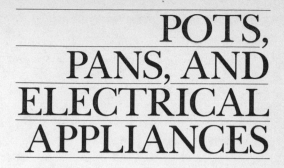

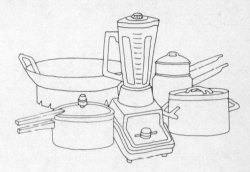

COOKWARE

The material of which pots and pans are made, as well as their size and shape, can often spell success or failure in cooking.

Pots, pans, and casserole cookware should be good conductors of heat to prevent food from burning and sticking. They should also have a heavy bottom to prevent them from tipping. The best cookware is cast iron that is heavily enameled. It is easy to clean, and the enamel will not cause discoloration of food. It must be of very good quality, however, or acid foods will cause enamel deterioration.

Iron cookware without enamel is a low heat conductor. Such cookware also discolors acid foods and rusts easily. Iron cookware must be greased well and baked in a 450 degrees F (230 degrre C) oven for 30 minutes. Scour new cookware with steel wool before use.

Stainless-steel cookery can develop hot spots, and when this happens, food will stick and burn easily. Stainless steel is also a poor conductor of heat; but it is the easiest cookware to clean. Stainless steel cookware with copper bottoms is a bad choice unless the copper is ⅛ inch (.3 cm) thick. This cookware is a poor conductor of heat with the same problems as stainless steel without copper. Stainless steel cookware with a cast-iron bottom is a good conductor of heat; it is the best choice if stainless steel is preferred.

Copper cookery should be lined with stainless steel. Cooking on copper can be poisonous, for copper is affected by acid foods. Copper cookware with a stainless-steel lining is an excellent heat conductor that heats evenly and quickly in heavier gauges.

Properly glazed earthenware holds heat and will not cause food discoloration, but it is a poor heat conductor. Improperly glazed earthenware can have lead in the glaze; if the cookware is chipped, it can cause illness. Care must be taken with earthenware. Breakage can occur with sudden temperature changes; and grease can collect in cracks, become rancid, and seep into foods.

Pyrex and porcelain are poor heat conductors. They also crack and break easily.

Tinware conducts heat well but rusts easily. It also turns a dark color after use, and acid foods affect the metal.

Avoid using cookware of aluminum and teflon. Aluminum is a good heat conductor; but it affects food color, and scratches easily. And oxidation can take place, leaving metal in the food. Aluminum extracts radiation from the air, raising food temperatures, causing premature spoilage, and destroying good taste. Aluminum pots and pans must be cleaned with mild abrasives. To remove the discoloration of the cookery, bring 1 quart (1 l) of water to a boil, add 2 teaspoons (10 ml) of cream of tartar, and boil for 10 minutes.

Teflon scratches easily, and scratched surfaces can add chemicals to your food. The surface deteriorates at 450 degrees F (230 degrees C) and can melt.

UTENSILS
Wooden utensils are best. They will not scratch or leave a metallic taste in your food. Plastic utensils usually can withstand high heat, but some of them are ruined by washing in temperatures over 140 degrees F (60 degrees C). Some retain grease that cannot be washed off, and some are ruined by oil and grease.

CONTAINERS
Some containers made of toxic chemicals can contaminate food. Acids in foods increase the solubility of the metals in the storage containers. Some other problems are:

- Some glazed containers contain lead.
- Galvanized containers contain zinc.
- Chipped enamel containers contain antimony.
- Some ice-cube trays and other containers can contain cadmium.

Baking Containers
Round pans brown more evenly than square ones. Square pans brown in the corners. Dark enamel or glass containers hold heat better than metal ones. The metal deflects the heat.

WOK COOKING
A wok is an Oriental cooking utensil. It is cone-shaped with a very small area at the bottom that is flat. Wok cooking can be better than cooking in

a skillet, especially frying or sauteing in oil, for a number of reasons:

1. Because of the wok's shape, oil heats quickly in it, and regulating the temperature becomes easier.

2. It takes very little water to cover the small bottom of the wok. When steaming vegetables, very few actually touch the water.

3. Less oil is used to cover the cooking surface of a wok.

4. Food can slide down the sides of the wok and into the hot oil without splashing.

5. Most woks have a draining rack that fits on the top of the wok. Using this rack allows you to save on oil because excess oil drips from the food back into the wok.

6. Because of its large cooking area, a wok cooks food quickly, allowing the food to be cooked exactly right, and crisp.

7. Food can be removed easily because of the large surface area.

Clean the wok immediately after cooking. Use water and a brush; soap should not be used.

ELECTRICAL APPLIANCES

Automatic Pulp-Ejector Juicers

Automatic pulp-ejector juicers are similar to centrifugal-force juicers, except that in the automatic the juice is passed through a release spout, while the pulp and fibers go out through an exhaust spout. The advantage of this kind of machine is that it allows continuous operation. It does not have to be stopped and cleaned after a quart of juice has been extracted, although it does have to be cleaned after every use. The disadvantage is that it is less efficient than the centrifugal-force machine and does not extract nearly as much juice.

Electric Juice Extractor

Electric extractors separate the juice from the fibers and pulp of a fruit or vegetable. The advantage of juice extractors is that they get valuable nutrients from vegetables and fruits in a form the body can readily assimilate. These nutrients—vitamins, minerals, trace elements, and enzymes are not found in the pulp and fibers, only in the juices. When the fruit or vegetable is eaten in solid form, some juices remain hidden in the fibers, which often cannot be digested by the body and pass through as waste.

Hydraulic-Pressure Juicers

Hydraulic juicers are the best (and most expensive) machines, although they are better suited to restaurants or institutions than for home use. Fruits and vegetables are chopped, broken and shredded into tiny pieces, then hydraulically pressed. The hydraulic press extracts a higher percentage of juice than from any other machine, leaving behind a very dry "mat" of fibers and pulp. The juice is often so strong that it has to be diluted for drinking.

The Citrus Squeezer

The old-fashioned orange-juice squeezers our mothers used have been updated in modern electric versions that speed and simplify the process. The principle is still the same: cut a citrus fruit in half and squeeze it until every possible drop of juice is removed. Although the electric squeezers are more convenient, somehow the old-fashioned method is still appealing. Squeezers should be used for all citrus fruits. The juice from an extractor is so concentrated that it hardly tastes like the familiar "orange juice" we know.

Centrifugal-Force Juicers

A centrifugal-force juicer is the ideal type of juicing machine for everyday use in the home. Fruits and vegetables are cut up and fed through a slot into a spinning basket, which has sides perforated with very small holes. On the bottom of the basket is a separate cutting blade, a spinning plate with dozens of tiny sharp teeth, which cuts the fruits and vegetables, forcing the pulp and fibers centrifugally against the perforated sides of the basket. The juices run though the holes into an outer bowl surrounding the basket and then down a release spout into a glass or container. The pulp and fibers remain pinned to the sides of the basket in a semidry state.

Blenders

While the juicer extracts, the blender liquifies by cutting or chopping the pulp to an extremely fine, liquid blend. The blender transforms solid food into liquid food; the juicer creates a totally different kind of food (drink), which has a chemical and nutritional composition different from that of the solid from which it has been extracted.

Still, many really delicious drinks can be prepared in a blender. It is best to follow the operating instructions from the manufacturer for the particular model you own.

Blenders are great labor savers; however, they do change the flavor and texture of a sauce. The blender whips in a great deal of air and makes your sauce foamy and less tasty. A brown sauce becomes much lighter in color.

RECIPES

SOUPS

SOUP BASE

Four vegetables, using about ¾ cup (175 ml) of each, plus 8 cups (2 l) of water, make a good base for a soup. Chop vegetables into small pieces, or, if large pieces are used, cook longer.

Saute the vegetables in a small amount of oil before adding the water or stock. Sauteing vegetables before making a soup adds flavor, making a more delicious soup. However, to avoid an intake of too much oil, sauteing is not always necessary, especially for daily use. After sauteing, add the stock or water and bouquet garni. Bring to a boil, lower flame, and add a pinch of salt to bring out the flavor. Cover and simmer for 1 hour to 1 ½ hours; longer cooking makes a tastier soup. Ten minutes before cooking time is up, add more salt, soya or miso to taste. Adding a thickener, if desired, will also increase your cooking time.

Eight cups (2 l) of soup will serve 6 to 8 people.

SOUP THICKENERS

The following ingredients can be added to your soup for a thickening agent. Add any kind of noodles or macaroni 30 minutes before end of cooking. Pre-cooked rice can be added 5-10 minutes before the cooking process is completed.

Add any of the following 1 hour before the end of cooking:

1 ½ teaspoons (7.5 ml) barley for each cup (250 ml) stock.
1 ½ teaspoons (7.5 ml) rice for each cup (250 ml) stock.
1 ½ teaspoons (7.5 ml) oatmeal for each cup (250 ml) stock.

Flour: use 1 ½ teaspoons (7.5 ml) flour for each cup (250 ml) stock or water. Add twice as much stock to the flour, very slowly, blending constantly to make a paste. Ten minutes before the cooking process is completed, add this paste, slowly, to your simmering soup, stirring constantly. Simmer for 10 minutes.

157

For a smooth soup, blend small amounts of the soup at a time until smooth in a blender. In a saucepan combine 1 tablespoon (15 ml) oil or butter with 1 tablespoon (15 ml) flour. Saute flour and butter until it turns a light brown. Add ½ cup (125 ml) water, constantly stirring until the mixture is smooth. Return the blended soup to original saucepan. Add flour mixture to soup slowly. Heat and serve. Cream can also be added to pureed soup instead of a flour and butter mixture.

SOUP STOCKS

Good stocks are still the secret to making excellent soups. They can be simple or complicated.

GRAIN SOUP STOCK

Roast the grain until it is golden brown and gives off a nutty fragrance. Add the grain to boiling water and boil for 5 minutes, then strain, removing the grain from the stock.

BASIC VEGETABLE STOCK

Use leftover vegetable roots, stems, tops, or leaves. Boil them in a few quarts (l) of water for 10 minutes, then remove and discard, saving the liquid. Use for any vegetable, grain, or bean soup or for miso soup. Seasoning is not necessary; or the stock can be seasoned in the soup.

3 tablespoons (45 ml) oil
2 carrots, chopped
2 celery stalks with leaves, sliced thin
2 onions, chopped
2 potatoes, chopped
1 turnip, chopped
2 quarts (2 l) water
   Bouquet garni

Heat the oil in a large saucepan. Saute the vegetables for approximately 15 minutes, stirring frequently. Add the water and bouquet garni. Bring to a boil, cover partially, and simmer for 1 to 2 hours. Strain, saving the liquid.

BARLEY SOUP

- 2 tablespoons (30 ml) oil
- ¼ cup (50 g) pearl barley
- 6 cups (1.5 l) stock
- 1 cup (115 g) peeled and thinly sliced carrots
- ½ cup (100 g) thinly sliced celery
- ¼ cup (40 g) chopped onions
- 2 cups (300 g) peeled and chopped tomatoes
- ½ cup (50 g) fresh peas
    Salt to taste
- 3 tablespoons (45 ml) chopped fresh parsley

Heat oil in a large saucepan. Saute onions until tender; do not brown. Add carrots and celery and saute for 3 minutes. Add barley and roast, stirring constantly, for 3 to 5 minutes or until they begin to turn brown. Add stock, tomatoes, peas, and salt. Bring to a boil, cover, lower flame, and simmer for 1 hour or until the barley is tender. Right before serving, add parsley.

Serves 6 to 8.

CELERY SOUP

- 2 tablespoons (30 ml) butter or margarine
- 1 small onion, chopped
- 4 cups (500 g) chopped celery (use outer stalks plus a few leaves)
- 1 large potato, peeled and chopped
- 4 cups (1 l) vegetable stock or water
- ½ to 1 cup (125 to 250 ml) cream (optional)
- ⅛ teaspoon (1 ml) grated nutmeg
    Salt to taste

Melt the butter in a large saucepan. Saute the onion until transparent; do not let it turn brown. Add the celery and potato and saute for an additional 3 minutes, stirring constantly. Add the stock and bring to a boil. Lower the flame to simmer, cover, and cook for about 30 minutes, until the vegetables are soft.

Puree the mixture in a blender or food processor, adding the nutmeg. Season and add the cream. Reheat before serving.

Serves 6 to 8

MISO SOUP

Use a vegetable stock or the following dashis as your base.

DASHI KOMBU SEAWEED

3 cups (750 ml) water
1 strip kombu, lightly wiped with a damp cloth to remove some salt.

Bring water to a boil, add kombu. Remove from heat and let stand for five minutes. Remove kombu. Kombu can be cut into small pieces and added to your soup.

Bonito flakes can be added to completed kombu stock. Let sit until flakes settle, then drain.

For each cup (250 ml) of stock or dashi, use 1 to 1½ T (15 to 22.5 ml) red, barley, or Hatcho miso; 2 tablespoons (30 ml) mellow miso; or 2 to 3 tablespoons (30 to 45 ml) sweet white or sweet red miso.

Place miso in a small bowl. Remove about ½ cup (125 ml) of stock from your saucepan, adding a little of the liquid at a time to the miso until well blended. Return miso mixture back into the soup. Always add the miso right before serving.

Miso should never be boiled as the enzymes, which aid in digestion, will be destroyed. Miso is added only to the amount of soup you will be using at that meal, to avoid boiling at the next use.

MISO SOUP DASHI (BONITO FLAKES)
(JAPANESE STOCK)

3 cups (750 ml) water
½ cup (25 grams) bonito flakes (fish flakes)

Bring water to a boil and add flakes. Remove from heat and let stand until flakes settle, about 5 minutes. Remove any foam, strain.

BASIC MISO SOUP

2 strips wakame (seaweed)
1 medium onion, sliced thin or ½ large leek cut into thin rounds (no green parts)
4 tablespoons (60 ml) miso, pureed (see dashi kombu, page 160)
1 teaspoon (5 ml) oil (for sauteing vegetables)
4 tablespoons (60 ml) minced scallions
4 cups (1 l) stock, dashi, or water
4 ounces (100 grams) tofu cut into ½-inch cubes

Wash wakame quickly in cold water to remove any dirt, then allow to soak for 10 minutes or until it has softened. Slice into ½ inch (1.25 cm) pieces, discarding tough pieces. Saute onion in oil, if desired. (It will add flavor to the soup.) Place sliced onion and wakame in a saucepan and add the stock or water. Bring to a boil, reduce flame, and simmer for 15-25 minutes, until onions are soft. Turn off heat. Add pureed miso. Stir gently to blend well. Simmer 3 minutes. Avoid boiling. Top with scallions and tofu.

Any of the following ingredients can be added or substituted for onion and wakame. Saute 2-3 minutes each, extending cooking time until vegetables are tender.

Onions and cabbage
Cabbage and carrots
Carrots and onions
Onions and squash
Chinese cabbage and carrots
Watercress
Spinach
Turnips

Cooked rice
Daikon and daikon greens
Wakame, onions, and carrots
Leeks
Cooked beans
Deep-fried tofu
Cooked noodles

POTATO SOUP

2   tablespoons (30 ml) oil
2   medium onions, sliced
4   celery stalks, sliced thin
2   medium potatoes, peeled and chopped
    Boiling water
½   teaspoon (2.5 ml) salt
½   bay leaf
2   tablespoons (30 ml) butter
    Milk
    Paprika to taste
    Chives, chopped

Heat oil in a large saucepan. Saute onions until tender; do not brown.
Add celery and potatoes, and saute for an additional 5 minutes. Add
enough boiling water to cover the vegetables. Add salt and bay leaf. Boil
until potatoes are tender.

Blend mixture in a blender, then return it to pot. Add butter and
blend well. Thin with milk if necessary. Heat, adding more seasoning if
necessary. Add paprika. Serve topped with chives.

Serves 4

VICHYSSOISE

3   cups (525 g) peeled, sliced potatoes
3   cups (450 g) sliced leeks, white only
1½ (1.5 l) quarts stock
    Salt to taste
½   to 1 cup (125 to 250 ml) heavy cream
2   tablespoons (30 ml) minced chives

Combine vegetables with stock and salt. Bring to a boil. Partially cover
and simmer for 45 to 60 minutes, until vegetables are tender.

Puree in a blender and then strain through a sieve to remove any
lumps. Allow to cool. Add the cream and mix well. Season to taste. Add a
little more salt because cold soups lose their flavor. Chill. Serve with
chives sprinkled on top.

Serves 6-8

GAZPACHO

1 garlic clove, put through a garlic press
1 teaspoon (5 ml) salt
1 cup (50 g) soft bread cubes, no crusts
¼ cup (50 ml) wine vinegar
4 medium tomatoes, peeled and diced, keeping one tomato separate
1 cucumber, peeled and diced
1 green pepper, diced
1 small onion, diced
3 tablespoons (45 ml) oil
2 cups (500 ml) cold water
2 cups (500 ml) tomato juice
  Chopped scallions

Combine garlic, salt, bread cubes, and vinegar. Mix until you have the consistency of a paste. Add 3 of the diced tomatoes and ½ of the cucumber. Either mash the cucumber with a fork or in a blender. Mix with remaining diced tomato, cucumber, green pepper, and onion. Put in the refrigerator to chill.

Before serving, add the oil, water, and tomato juice. Mix well. Season with more salt if desired. Garnish with scallions.

Serves 4 to 6

BOUQUET GARNI

Tie all or some of the following ingredients in a piece of cheesecloth and add to the pot while the soup is cooking. Remove bouquet before serving.

- 3 stalks parsley, 1 sprig thyme, 1 small bay leaf
- 2 sprigs parsley, 1 sprig thyme, 1 bay leaf
- 2 sprigs parsley, 1 sweet marjoram, 1 winter savory, 1 lemon thyme
- 1 sprig rosemary; 1 sprig thyme; 1 sprig dill; 2 sprigs parsley; 1 celery stalk, chopped; 1 carrot, chopped

Other ingredients, such as orange peel, garlic, cloves and other spices, ginger, leeks, and chervil can be added to the above combinations.

ONION SOUP WITH MISO

- 3 tablespoons (45 ml) oil
- 3 large onions (at least 4 inches (10 cm) in diameter), sliced thin
- 8 cups (2 l) water
- 3 tablespoons (45 ml) red, barley, or Hatcho miso
- 1 tablespoon (15 ml) butter
- 2 tablespoons (30 ml) grated, mild cheese

Heat oil in a large saucepan. Saute onions until transparent. Add water, bring to a boil, cover, lower flame, and simmer for 4 hours, stirring every 30 minutes. Remove 1 cup (250 ml) liquid. Dissolve miso and butter in the stock and return it to the pot. Return to boil and remove from heat. Allow to cool.

Refrigerate overnight or all day. When ready to serve, stir in the cheese, bring to a boil and lower flame. Simmer until cheese melts. Serve hot or cold.

Serves 4

BLACK BEAN SOUP

- 2 tablespoons (30 ml) oil
- 1 medium onion, minced
- 1 celery stalk, sliced thin
- 1 cup (200 g) black beans (soaked overnight)
- 6 cups (1.5 l) stock
- 1 carrot, peeled and sliced thin
- ½ teaspoon (2.5 ml) salt
  Fresh parsley or scallions, chopped

Heat oil in a large saucepan. Saute onions and celery until onions are tender. Add beans and stock. Bring to a boil, cover, lower flame, and simmer until beans are tender, about 1 hour. Once beans are completely cooked, add carrots and salt and cook for an additonal 15 minutes. If carrots are added too soon, the bean juice will turn them black. Check seasoning and serve. Garnish with parsley or scallions.

This soup can be pureed in a blender. Return to the saucepan, add 1 tablespoon (15 ml) dry sherry, or to taste. Heat. Serve with chopped egg on top.

LENTIL SOUP

  1 tablespoon (15 ml) oil
1½ (225 g) cups chopped onions
1½ (300 g) cups dried lentils
  1 bay leaf
  8 cups (2 l) stock
  2 celery stalks, sliced thin
  1 carrot, peeled and grated
  1 large potato, peeled and chopped
  2 cups (500 ml) tomato juice
  1 tablespoon (15 ml) chopped fresh basil
    Salt to taste

Heat oil in a large saucepan. Saute onions until tender; do not brown. Add lentils, bay leaf, and stock. Bring to a boil, cover, lower flame, and simmer until lentils are tender, approximately 1 hour. Lentils should always be kept covered with stock. Add more stock if necessary. Add celery, carrots, potatoes, tomato juice, basil, and salt. Cover and continue to simmer until vegetables are tender.

Serves 8 to 10

ADZUKI BEAN SOUP

  1 tablespoon (15 ml) oil
  1 medium onion, chopped
  1 large carrot, peeled and sliced thin
 ¼ teaspoon (1.5 ml) nutmeg or cinnamon
  1 cup (200 g) Adzuki beans
  6 cups (1.5 l) stock
    Salt and pepper to taste
    Chopped scallions

Heat oil in a large saucepan. Saute onions until tender; do not brown. Add carrots and saute for about 3 minutes. Add stock and beans. Bring to a boil, cover, lower flame, and simmer until beans are done, approximately 1 ½ to 2 hours. Add nutmeg or cinnamon 15 minutes before completion of cooking.

      Season with salt and pepper. Garnish with chopped scallions.

Serves 6 to 8.

CREAM OF BROCCOLI SOUP

3 tablespoons (45 ml) butter
1 medium onion, minced
4 large stalks of broccoli, peeled and chopped
1 stalk celery with leaves, sliced thin
1 carrot, peeled and sliced very thin
4 cups (1 l) vegetable stock
½ teaspoon (2.5 ml) salt
1 bay leaf
½ teaspoon (2.5 ml) dried oregano
1 cup (250 ml) heavy cream

Melt butter in a large saucepan. Saute onion until transparent; do not let it turn brown. Add broccoli, celery, and carrots. Saute for 5 minutes. Add stock, salt, bay leaf, and oregano. Bring to a boil. Cover, lower flame, and simmer for 45 minutes.

Puree in a blender and pour into a clean saucepan. Add the cream. Add more salt if desired. Heat and serve.

Serves 6

SPLIT PEA SOUP

1 tablespoon (15 ml) oil
1 medium onion, chopped
1 carrot, peeled and chopped
½ celery stalk, sliced thin
6 cups (1.5 l) stock
1 cup (200 g) split peas
2 teaspoons (10 ml) salt
1 bay leaf
⅛ teaspoon (5 ml) thyme

Heat oil in a large saucepan. Saute onion until tender; do not brown. Add carrots and celery and saute for 3 minutes. Add stock, peas, salt, bay leaf, and thyme. Bring to a boil, cover, and lower flame. Simmer until completely cooked, approximately 1 to 2 hours, adding more stock if necessary. Remove bay leaf before serving.

Serves 6 to 8

VEGETABLE SOUP

 2 tablespoons (30 ml) oil
 ½ cup (75 l) chopped onions
 ½ cup (60 g) thinly sliced celery
 ¼ cup (30 g) peeled chopped carrots
 ¼ cup (30 g) peeled chopped turnips
 ¼ cup (45 g) peeled chopped potatoes
 6 to 8 (1.5 to 2 l) cups of stock or water
 ¼ cup (30 g) green beans, cut into ½-inch (1.25 cm) pieces
 ¼ cup (30 g) peas
 ¼ cup (30 g) corn
 1 cup (150 g) peeled and chopped tomatoes
 1 teaspoon (5 ml) chopped fresh parsley
 1 teaspoon (5 ml) salt
    Bouquet garni (optional if stock is used)
 ½ cup (25 g) chopped spinach or watercress

Heat oil in a large saucepan. Saute onion until transparent. Add celery, carrots, turnips, and potatoes. Saute for an additonal 5 minutes. Add all ingredients except spinach. Bring to a boil, cover, lower flame, and simmer for 1 hour or longer. Five minutes before completion, add spinach. Correct seasoning and serve.

Serves 8 to 10

SOUP ADDITIONS

To add some variety to your soups, try the following:

- Just before serving bean, cabbage or vegetable soup, add 1 cup (250 ml) stale beer for every 3 cups (750 ml) of liquid.
- Add miso to soup.
- Add cooked beans before serving. Heat only long enough to heat beans.
- Add greens right before serving.

MAIN DISHES

BAKED STUFFED EGGPLANT

Precook a whole small eggplant in a preheated 400 degrees F (200 degrees C) oven for 20 minutes. Cut lengthwise and scoop out center, leaving a ½-inch (1.25 cm) shell. Save.

Stuffing
    Chopped eggplant center
½ (100 g) cup cooked lentils
½ cup (50 g) grated cheddar cheese
¼ cup (30 g) chopped apple
¼ teaspoon (1.5 ml) cumin
¼ teaspoon (1.5 ml) sage
    Salt to taste

Combine all ingredients. Oil the skin of the eggplant. Place in a baking dish. Put stuffing into eggplant halves. Bake in a preheated 350 degrees F (180 degrees C) oven for 30 minutes.

Serves 2

CORN FRITTERS

2 cups (325 g) cooked corn, fresh or frozen
3 eggs, separated
½ teaspoon (2.5 ml) salt
¼ cup (30 g) flour
    Oil for frying

Cook corn on the cob. Cut kernels from the cob with a sharp knife. Or thaw frozen corn.

Beat egg yolks until well mixed; beat egg whites until very stiff. Combine the egg yolks, corn, salt, and flour. Fold the egg whites into the mixture. Drop by spoonfuls into a hot oiled griddle or frypan. Fry on both sides until brown and cooked through.

Serves 6

POTATO CASSEROLE

2 large potatoes, cooked in their skin
2 large onions, sliced thin
3 large tomatoes, cut in ½-inch slices
   Butter
¾ cup (75 g) Parmesan cheese, grated
2 teaspoons (10 ml) paprika
   Salt to taste

Peel and slice potatoes about ¼ (.5 cm) inch thick. Grease a casserole dish and layer the onions, potatoes, and tomatoes. Dot each layer with butter and sprinkle with salt and cheese. End with potatoes and a final dotting of butter and sprinkling of cheese. Sprinkle paprika over the top. Bake in a preheated 375 degrees F (190 degrees C) oven for about 1 hour.

Serves 4

RATATOUILLE

1 pound (450 g) zucchini, sliced into ½-pieces
1 pound (450 g) eggplant, peeled and cut into 1 to 1 ½-inch pieces
2 medium onions, sliced
1 red pepper, seeded and sliced into ½-inch (125 cm) strips
1 green pepper, seeded and sliced into ½-inch (125 cm) strips
4 large tomatoes, peeled, seeded, and quartered
2 garlic cloves, minced
   Salt to taste
3 tablespoons (45 ml) olive or vegetable oil

Before cutting the eggplant into pieces, slice and salt to remove excess moisture (see Eggplant, page 87). Do the same with the zucchini slices.

Heat oil in a large skillet. Saute the onions and garlic until tender; do not brown. Add the peppers, zucchini, eggplant, and tomatoes in layers, seasoning each layer. Simmer, covered, for 35 minutes. Uncover and continue to cook until the liquid is reduced, about 10 minutes. Serve hot or cold.

Serves 4 to 6

SPINACH SOUFFLE

¼ (40 g) cup minced onions
4 tablespoons (60 ml) butter
2 tablespoons (30 ml) flour
1 cup (250 ml) milk
½ teaspoon (2.5 ml) salt
3 eggs, separated (yolks beaten and whites stiffly beaten)
1 cup (200 g) cooked chopped spinach
½ cup (50 g) grated cheddar cheese

Melt butter in a small saucepan. Saute onion until tender; do not brown. Add flour and cook until smooth. Add milk, very slowly, stirring constantly. Continue to cook and stir until sauce thickens. Blend in salt and beaten egg yolks. Add spinach and cheese. Blend gently. Fold the stiffly beaten egg whites into the spinach mixture. Pour into a well-greased 1-quart baking dish. Set in a pan of hot water and bake in a preheated 350 degrees F (180 degrees C) oven for approximately 50 to 60 minutes. Serve immediately.

Serves 4

STUFFED ZUCCHINI

2 medium zucchini
¾ cup (75 g) bread crumbs, preferably whole wheat
2 tablespoons (30 ml) grated Parmesan cheese
⅛ teaspoon (5 ml) rosemary
⅛ teaspoon (5 ml) marjoram
¼ teaspoon (1.5 ml) oregano
¼ teaspoon (1.5 ml) sage

Choose medium zucchini; larger zucchini has less flavor. Steam zucchini until slightly tender. Cool. Slice in half, lengthwise. Scoop out the centers, leaving a ¼- to ½-inch (.5 to 1.25 cm) shell. Chop the scooped-out zucchini.

Combine all ingredients except the zucchini halves. Stuff the shells with the mixture. Bake in a preheated 350 degrees F (180 degrees C) oven for 15 minutes.

Serves 4 to 6

VEGETABLES OVER RICE

2 tablespoons (30 ml) oil, butter, or margarine
1 medium onion, chopped
1 leek, white part only, sliced thin
½ cup (75 g) thinly sliced scallions and tops
1 cup (50 g) chopped spinach, stems removed
1 cup (120 g) green beans, sliced ½ inch thick
1 small eggplant, peeled and cubed
½ cup (60 g) thinly sliced celery
½ cup (40 g) chopped fresh parsley
1 tablespoon (15 ml) lemon juice
¼ teaspoon (1.5 ml) ground cinnamon
⅛ teaspoon (5 ml) ground nutmeg
   Salt to taste
½ cup (125 ml) water
1 cup (250 ml) plain yogurt

Heat oil in a large saucepan. Saute onion, leeks, and scallions until tender; do not brown. Add all ingredients except the yogurt. Cover and simmer approximately 25 minutes, until all vegetables are just tender; do not overcook. Add more water if necessary. Add yogurt and cook only long enough to heat the yogurt. Serve over hot brown rice.

Serves 4 to 6

WELSH RAREBIT

8 ounces (225 g) sharp cheddar cheese, grated
2 tablespoons (30 ml) butter
¼ cup (50 ml) stale beer
¼ cup (50 ml) heavy cream
1 egg
¼ teaspoon (1.5 ml) Worcestershire sauce
¼ teaspoon (1.5 ml) paprika
   Dash of cayenne pepper
¼ teaspoon (1.5 ml) dry mustard

In the top of a double boiler, heat the cheese, butter, beer, and cream until it has a smooth consistency. Beat in egg and season with remaining ingredients. Serve over toast with slices of tomato.

Serves 4

TEMPURA

  3 inches (7.5 cm) oil heated at 350 degrees F (180 degrees C) or higher.
  1 cup (140 g) whole wheat flour or ½ cup (70 g) whole wheat flour and
      ½ cup (60 g) unbleached flour
1¼ cups (300 ml) ice water
 ¼ teaspoon (1.5 ml) salt

Mix flour and salt. Add water and stir until batter is smooth. Some of the batter will separate from the dipped vegetables (see below) when they are added to the hot oil, but if it separates too much, your batter is too thin (add more flour). If none of the batter separates, it is too heavy (add a little water). If you have time, allow mixture to stand a few minutes in the refrigerator before using.

Warm air can make the batter thick. Add a little water to return to desired consistency.

Vegetables should be cool and dry before using. First salt vegetables, then dip into flour. The batter will adhere to your vegetables if they are floured first, but this is not necessary. Dip into batter and fry. They take about 5 minutes to cook.

Pieces of debris in the oil should be removed with an oil skimmer between cooking vegetables.

Vegetables for Dipping

Asparagus: After snapping the tender end from the tough end, cut the tender portion into 3½-inch (9 cm) pieces.

Broccoli: Use flowerets 3 inches (7.5 cm) long.

Butternut squash: Cut into strips 1 inch (2.5 cm) by 3½-inches (9 cm) by ¼-inch (.5 cm).

Carrots: Cut on diagonal into ¼-inch (.5 cm) rounds or cut into 1—inch—long (2.5 cm) pieces and cut again into matchsticks. Mix spoonful with enough batter to make a tiny dumpling; fry.

Carrot greens: Use leafy section 5 inches (12.5 cm) long. Dip only one side into batter.

Cauliflower: Cut into flowerets.

Celery: Cut into 3-inch (7.5 cm) lengths. Cook leaves in same manner as carrot greens.

Eggplant: Slice into pieces ¼-inch (.5 cm) thick.

Green peppers: Remove seeds and cut into rounds ¼-inch (.5 cm) thick.

Parsley: Hold 2 sprigs together at the bloom and dip into batter, covering stems and half of bloom.

Parsnips and turnips: Prepare as carrots.

Potatoes: Cut as for French fries.

Sweet potatoes: peel and cut into strips ½-inch (1.25 cm) thick and steam. Cook until only slightly tender. Cool. Roll in pastry flour and dip into batter.

Tofu: Should be pressed before frying (see page 64).

Watercress: Prepare as parsley.

Zucchini: Do not peel. Cut into strips ½-inch (1.25 cm) wide and 2 to 3 inches (5 to 7.5 cm) long.

Fruit

Bananas, sliced crosswise or lengthwise

Apples, cored and sliced

Strawberries, whole

DAIKON SAUCE

½ teaspoon (2.5 ml) grated daikon
2 tablespoons (30 ml) tamari
2 tablespoons (30 ml) water

Combine ingredients and serve in individual dishes for each person.

Serves 2

GINGER SAUCE

¼ teaspoon (1.5 ml) grated ginger root
2 tablespoons (30 ml) tamari
2 tablespoons (30 ml) water

Combine ingredients and serve in individual dishes for each person.

Serves 2

FRIED NOODLES WITH VEGETABLES

1 lb (450 g) whole wheat spaghetti, cooked, drained, and chilled
3 scallions, thinly sliced
2 very thin slices fresh ginger, minced
½ cup (60 g) thinly sliced celery
1 thinly sliced carrot
½ cup (50 g) chopped cabbage
½ cup chopped (25 g) fresh mushrooms
3 tablespoons (45 ml) oil

Sauce
3 tablespoons (45 ml) soy sauce
1 tablespoon (15 ml) dry sherry
½ teaspoon (2.5 ml) salt
1 cup (250 ml) stock

Heat oil in a skillet. Add all vegetables and ginger, and saute until tender. Add noodles and saute until tender. Add noodles and saute until noodles are lightly browned. Add sauce ingredients to noodle mixture. Bring to a boil, cover and simmer for about 10 minutes. Liquid should be absorbed. Serve hot.

Serves 4-6

STUFFED CABBAGE

4 large whole cabbage leaves
2 tablespoons (30 ml) oil or butter
1 cup (150 g) chopped onions
½ cup (60 g) very thinly sliced celery
½ cup (60 g) matchstick-cut carrots
¼ cup chopped (15 g) mushrooms
½ cup (75 g) buckwheat groats (kasha)
1 cup (250 ml) vegetable stock for cooking kasha
   Extra vegetable stock for baking the stuffed cabbage
   Pinch of salt
½ cup (125 ml) sour cream
1 tablespoon (15 ml) chopped fresh dill

Boil cabbage leaves until tender but not soft. Save liquid for sauce. Set leaves aside to cool.

Heat oil in a skillet with a cover. Saute onions until tender. Add celery, carrots, and mushrooms and saute for an additional 5 minutes. Add groats. Saute until they have a nutlike fragrance, about 5 minutes, depending on whether grain is preroasted or unroasted. Cool. Add the stock and salt and bring to a boil. Cover and reduce flame to simmer. Simmer for 30 minutes or until all water has evaporated. Remove from flame and allow to cool.

Cut away hard part of the cabbage leaves (the part that was connected to the core). Place groats mixture on cabbage leaves and fold in sides of leaves. Secure with toothpicks or tie with strings. Place leaves in a pot and add enough water or stock to almost cover. Cover and bake in a 350 degrees F (180 degrees C) oven for approximately 45 minutes or until leaves are quite tender. Remove leaves and keep warm.

Make a Bechamel sauce (page 226) with the stock. Add the sour cream and dill and heat through. Pour sauce over stuffed leaves.

Serves 2

CREPES

Basic Batter

The batter can be made from whole wheat flour, unbleached flour, or buckwheat flour, or from a combination of whole wheat flour and unbleached flour. Use 3 cups (750 ml) of water for every 1 cup (125 g) of flour. Combine water and flour, add salt to taste. Let stand, refrigerated, for 2 hours.

Heat the pan until very hot. (The pan must be cast iron, smooth, and even, and the edges must be low. A crepe pan will produce the best results.) Spread oil on pan with a pastry brush or with a piece of cloth. Lower the flame to medium-low.

The amount of batter to use depends on the size of your crepe pan. For a 9-inch (23 cm) pan (diameter of the bottom), use 7 fluid ounces (225 ml) of batter for each crepe. As you pour in the batter with your left hand, keep turning the pan clockwise to spread the batter evenly over the pan. Cook 6 to 10 minutes for the first side, 3 to 6 minutes for the second. Timing depends on how thick you have poured your crepe. Loosen the crepe from the sides of the pan with a spatula before turning.

FILLING FOR CREPES

Soft fillings work best. For example, saute carrots; carrots and onions; scallions, endive, and zucchini; zucchini and onions; onions, dandelion greens, watercress, and asparagus.

As a dessert: Slice baked apples or saute an apple in oil with raisins and toasted almonds, applesauce, or chestnut cream. Three tablespoons (45 ml) of brown sugar can be added to the batter for sweeter crepes.

BUCKWHEAT CREPES

3 cups (750 ml) water for every 1 cup (125 g) fine buckwheat flour
  Salt to taste
1 egg, beaten

Combine well. Allow the batter to stand for 2 hours, refrigerated. Make crepes as above.

STIR–FRIED VEGETABLES

¼ head cabbage, slice
½ cup (60 g) thinly sliced celery
½ cup (60 g) grated carrots
2 small onions, chopped
1 cup (100 g) bean sprouts
1 clove of garlic, mashed
1 small piece of fresh ginger, minced
  Salt to taste
2 tablespoons (30 ml) oil
1 tablespoon (15 ml) cornstarch or arrowroot
3 tablespoons (45 ml) water or stock

Heat oil in a wok or skillet. Add ginger and garlic and saute for a few seconds. Add the vegetables, except the sprouts, to the oil and saute until tender but still slightly crisp. Add the sprouts and saute for only a minute, stirring constantly. Don't allow the sprouts to get soft. Salt to taste. Combine the cornstarch and water. Add to the vegetables. Stir until the liquid becomes thick.

Serves 4

RICE WITH VEGETABLES

 3 tablespoons (45 ml) oil
 1 small onion, chopped
 2 scallions with green part, sliced thin
 1 cup (200 g) brown rice
 3 tomatoes, peeled, seeded, and chopped
 1 small zucchini, chopped
 ½ cup (100 g) cooked pinto beans or any other bean
 1 carrot, peeled and chopped
 2 stalks celery, sliced thin
 ½ cup (125 ml) dry white wine
 3 cups (750 ml) stock
 1 teaspoon (5 ml) dried basil
 ¼ teaspoon (1.5 ml) dried sage
    Salt to taste
 3 tablespoons (45 ml) butter
 ½ cup Parmesan cheese, (50 g) grated

Heat oil in a large saucepan. Saute onions and scallions until tender; do not brown. Add rice and saute until rice begins to turn white. Add tomatoes, zucchini, beans, carrots, celery, and wine. Bring to a simmer. Add the stock, cover, and simmer until the rice is cooked, approximately 30 to 45 minutes. After about 20 minutes, add the herbs and salt. Mix once. When rice is cooked, add the butter and half the cheese. Blend well. Serve with the remaining cheese on the side.

Serves 4 to 6

PIROSHKI

1 to 2 tablespoons (15 to 30 ml) oil
½ cup (75 g) minced onions
¼ cup (25 g) minced cabbage
½ cup (60 g) peeled and grated carrots
¼ cup (15 g) minced watercress
    (or use any vegetable combination you want to use)
1 cup (170 g) cooked rice, cooked in a stock
    Salt or tamari to taste
    Dough for 2 pie crusts
1 egg yolk, beaten

Heat oil in a skillet. Saute onions until transparent; do not brown. Add cabbage and carrots, and saute for 5 minutes more. Add watercress and saute only until it wilts. Add rice and saute for a few minutes. Season with salt or tamari.

Preheat oven to 350 degrees F (180 degrees C). Roll out half the dough on a floured surface, to ¼-inch (.5 cm) thickness or thinner. Roll out the dough on wax paper if you wish. Cut into rounds 4 inches (10 cm) across. Roll out remaining dough and cut into rounds. Form the rice mixture into small balls, one for each round of dough. Place a ball on each round of dough. Fold the dough round over, making a half circle, and press the edges together with a fork. Brush dough with egg yolk. Bake for 30 minutes or until dough turns golden brown.

Serves 4

For pie crust recipe, see page 222-223.

VEGETABLES

GREEN BEANS WITH TOMATOES

1 pound (450 g) green beans, cleaned and dried
1 tablespoon (15 ml) oil
1 tablespoon (15 ml) butter
1 medium onion, minced
1 garlic clove, minced
2 medium tomatoes, peeled, seeded, and chopped
  Salt to taste
1 tablespoon (15 ml) dried basil
2 tablespoons (30 ml) chopped fresh parsley

Heat oil and butter in a skillet. Saute the onion and garlic until onions are tender; do not brown. Add tomatoes, salt, basil, and parsley. Blend well. Add the beans, cover, and simmer until beans are tender, about 5 to 10 minutes.

Serves 4

BAKED ACORN SQUASH

2 large acorn squash
3 tablespoons (45 ml) melted butter
1 teaspoon (5 ml) cinnamon
¼ teaspoon (1.5 ml) nutmeg
½ cup (75 g) chopped nuts (optional)

Wash surface of squash. Cut squash in halves crosswise. Mix all ingredients. Spoon the mixture, evenly, into the four halves. Place in a covered baking dish with the bottom covered with about ½ inch (1.25 cm) of water. Coat edges of squash with oil.

Bake in a preheated 350 degrees F (180 degrees C) oven for approximately 1 hour, removing the cover for the last 30 minutes. The squash is done when it can be pierced easily with a fork.

Serves 6

180

CAULIFLOWER WITH CHEESE I

1 head cauliflower with tough stem removed
¼ (25 g) cup grated Parmesan cheese
¼ teaspoon (1.5 ml) paprika
  Toasted almond slivers

Steam cauliflower until cooked. Remove from steamer. Sprinkle top with cheese and paprika. Place under broiler flame for 5 to 10 minutes. Serve immediately with slivers of almonds stuck into the flowerets.

Serves 6

CAULIFLOWER WITH CHEESE II

1 head cauliflower with tough stem removed
¼ cup (50 ml) melted butter
½ cup (50 g) bread crumbs seasoned with salt to taste
1 tablespoon (15 ml) minced fresh parsley
2 tablespoons (30 ml) grated cheddar cheese

Steam cauliflower until cooked. Keep warm. In a small saucepan, cook bread crumbs in butter until they turn golden brown. Add the parsley and cheese. Place warm cauliflower in a serving dish. Sprinkle the seasoned bread-crumb and cheese mixture over the top.

Serves 6

BEETS WITH CARAWAY SEEDS

2 cups (360 g) cooked, sliced beets
2 tablespoons (30 ml) butter
1 tablespoon (15 ml) fresh lemon juice
½ teaspoon (2.5 ml) salt
¾ teaspoon (3.5 ml) whole caraway seeds

Combine all ingredients in a small saucepan. Heat thoroughly.

Serves 4

SAUTEED BEETS WITH TOPS

2 bunches beets with tops
3 tablespoons (45 ml) butter
   Salt to taste

Remove the tops from the beets. Wash beets, peel with a vegetable peeler, and grate the beets. Remove the stems from the leaves. Wash leaves well. Pat dry with paper towels.

Melt 2 tablespoons (30 ml) butter in a saucepan with a dash of salt. Add grated beets; blend well with the butter. Add leaves, the remaining butter, and more salt if desired. Cook over a low flame, covered, until beets are tender, mixing occasionally. Will take approximately 10 to 15 minutes.

Serve with cooked-down pan juices on top.

Serves 4

RAISIN–GLAZED CARROTS

1 bunch carrots
½ cup (125 ml) water
¼ cup (50 g) brown sugar
2 tablespoons (30 ml) butter or margarine
¼ cup (40 g) raisins

Scrape carrots if not organic. Cut into 1-inch (2.5 cm) pieces and place in a saucepan. Add water, cover, and simmer 10 mintues. Drain and save liquid. If you do not have ¼ cup (50 ml) water left, add some. Combine carrots, sugar, and butter. Return liquid to carrots. Bring to a boil over medium heat. Cover and lower the flame to simmer. Simmer for 15 to 20 minutes or until tender. Add raisins and cook for 5 minutes more.

Serves 3 to 4

CARROT SESAME

3 tablespoons (45 ml) sesame seeds
1 tablespoon (15 ml) oil
2 large carrots, peeled and sliced
½ cup (125 ml) water or stock
Pinch of salt
3 teaspoons (15 ml) tamari

Saute the sesame seeds in oil for a few minutes. Add the carrots and saute for 2 minutes. Add the stock and salt. Cover and simmer until carrots are tender and all the moisture has evaporated. Add tamari to taste and cook, uncovered, for 3 minutes more.

Serves 2

CREAMED CARROTS

1 bunch carrots, peeled, cooked, and cut into 1-inch pieces
1 tablespoon (15 ml) butter
2 tablespoons (30 ml) flour
⅛ teaspoon (5 ml) ground ginger
½ cup (125 ml) milk
1½ tablespoons (22.5 ml) honey
Dash of salt
¼ cup (40 g) slivered almonds

While cooking the carrots, prepare the sauce. Melt butter in a small saucepan. Add the flour and ginger. Cook until the flour begins to have a nutty fragrance. Make sure your flame is low. Add the milk very slowly, stirring constantly until sauce thickens. Add the honey and salt and stir until honey is well blended. Pour sauce over cooked carrots. Sprinkle almonds on top.

Serves 4

BAKED BRUSSELS SPROUTS

1 pint (200 g) fresh Brussels sprouts, cleaned, stems removed, and cooked
2 tablespoons (30 ml) melted butter
½ cup (50 g) grated Parmesan cheese
1 teaspoon (5 ml) fresh lemon juice
  Large pinch of nutmeg

Put the cooked sprouts in a shallow baking dish. Combine rest of ingredients and pour over sprouts. Bake, covered, in a preheated 350 degrees F (180 degrees C) oven for 20 minutes.

Serves 2

BRUSSEL SPROUTS IN BROWN BUTTER WITH ALMONDS

1½ pounds (560 g) Brussels sprouts, cooked, and kept warm
3 tablespoons (45 ml) butter
¼ cup (40 g) blanched almonds, halves or slivers
  Salt

In a skillet, combine the butter and almonds and cook until they turn brown. Season with salt. Pour over cooked Brussels sprouts.

Serves 4 to 6

RUTABAGAS WITH LEMON

4 medium rutabagas, cooked, and cut into thin slices lengthwise
3 tablespoons (45 ml) melted butter
1 teaspoon (5 ml) fresh lemon juice
¼ teaspoon (1.5 ml) minced fresh dill

Combine the butter, lemon juice, and dill. Pour over cooked rutabagas.

Serves 4

RINGS AROUND CABBAGE

1 cup (100 g) shredded cabbage
1 sliced onion, left in rings
1 green pepper, cut into rings
1 chopped tomato, pulp only
   Salt to taste
   Oil

Saute all vegetables, except tomatoes, in a small amount of oil. Add tomatoes and cook only until tomatoes are hot.

Serves 2

SAUTEED CHINESE CABBAGE

2 tablespoons (30 ml) oil or butter
1 head Chinese cabbage, trimmed, cleaned, and shredded
2 teaspoons (10 ml) crushed fennel
   Salt to taste

Heat oil in a skillet. Add the cabbage, mixing well with the oil. Saute for a few minutes until cabbage is tender. Add salt and fennel. Serve hot.

Serves 4

SPICED CABBAGE

½ small cabbage, shredded
   Salt to taste
⅛ teaspoon (5 ml) nutmeg
1 clove garlic, pressed through a garlic press
1 teaspoon (5 ml) crushed coriander seeds
½ teaspoon (2.5 ml) butter

Bring a saucepan filled with ¼ inch water to a boil. Add cabbage, cover, lower flame, and simmer until cabbage is just tender, about 5 to 10 minutes. Drain well. Add all ingredients, mixing thoroughly. Serve hot.

Serves 4

BROCCOLI WITH SESAME SEEDS

1 head broccoli
2 tablespoons (30 ml) butter or margarine
1 small onion, chopped
1 tablespoon (15 ml) sesame seed, not roasted
1 tablespoon (15 ml) cider vinegar

Cut stalk end from broccoli and cut broccoli into flowerets. Clean well.
Steam until cooked but not mushy.

While broccoli is cooking in a small frypan, saute onions, sesame
seeds, and vinegar in butter. Cook over low heat until the seeds turn a
golden color and smell nutlike. This will take about 5 minutes. Combine,
gently, the broccoli and sesame seed mixture. Serve immediately.

Serves 4

SAUTEED COLLARD GREENS

3 tablespoons (45 ml) oil
1 onion, minced
2 tomatoes, peeled, seeded, and chopped
   Salt to taste
½ teaspoon (2.5 ml) dried marjoram
2 pounds (1 kg) collard greens, cleaned, trimmed, and drained well
¼ cup grated Parmesan cheese

Heat oil in a large frypan or saucepan. Saute onions until tender; do not
brown. Add tomatoes and cook for 5 minutes. Add marjoram and season
with salt. Add the collards, cover, and simmer until collards are tender,
approximately 20 minutes. Stir frequently; add a little water if collards
begin to stick. Serve hot, sprinkled with the cheese.

Serves 4

HERBED MUSHROOMS

3 tablespoons (45 ml) oil
1 pound (450 g) mushrooms, cleaned and sliced into threes
2 garlic cloves, minced
  Salt to taste
½ teaspoon (2.5 ml) dried thyme
½ cup (40 g) minced fresh parsley
  Juice of ½ lemon

Heat oil in a saucepan. Add mushrooms, garlic, salt, and thyme. Saute until mushrooms are tender, shaking pan frequently to prevent sticking. This takes 5 to 10 minutes. Right before serving, add the parsley and lemon juice, blending well.

Serves 4

POTATO KUGEL

2 medium potatoes
1 medium onion, grated
1 egg, beaten
½ teaspoon (2.5 ml) salt
1½ tablespoons (22.5 ml) oil, heated
  Warm sour cream

To keep the potatoes from turning color, have all ingredients ready. Preheat oven to 350 degrees F (180 degrees C).

Peel and grate potatoes. Combine all ingredients and blend well. Put the oil into a casserole; pour the potato mixture over the oil. Bake for 1 hour or until kugel is puffed and brown. Serve with warm sour cream.

Serves 4

POTATOES WITH GARLIC

1½ pounds (560 g) potatoes
  2 tablespoons (30 ml) melted butter
  2 garlic cloves, pressed through a garlic press
    Salt to taste

Peel and cut the potatoes into chunks. Cook the potatoes in boiling water until just tender; do not allow them to get soft. Put the potatoes in a shallow baking dish, in one layer. Blend the butter and garlic together. Brush the butter mixture over the potatoes. Sprinkle with salt. Bake, uncovered, in a preheated 350 degrees F (180 degrees C) oven. Turn frequently until golden brown 30 to 45 minutes.

Serves 4

SWEET LIMA BEANS

  1 small onion, chopped
  1 tablespoon (15 ml) oil
 ½ teaspoon (2.5 ml) chili powder
 ¼ cup brown sugar (50 g)
  1 pound (450 g) tomatoes, peeled and chopped
    Salt to taste
  2 cups (330 g) cooked lima beans
 ½ teaspoon (2.5 ml) cider vinegar

Heat oil in a skillet. Saute onion until tender; do not brown. Add chili powder, sugar, tomatoes, and salt. Simmer, uncovered, for 15 minutes, breaking up tomatoes. Add beans and vinegar. Simmer 5 minutes.

Serves 4

SPICED YAMS

2 large yams
2 cloves

Quarter yams and boil with cloves for 15 minutes. Drain, peel, and mash. Blend in the following spice ingredients and serve hot:

Spice
1 teaspoon (5 ml) cinnamon
¼ teaspoon (1.5 ml) cardamom
1 tablespoon (15 ml) cranberry juice

Serves 4

BEANS AND TOFU

SAUTEED CHICK PEAS

1 tablespoon (15 ml) oil
2 cups (400 g) cooked chick peas
1 tomato, peeled, seeded, and chopped
1 tablespoon (15 ml) minced fresh basil or ½ teaspoon (2.5 ml) dried
  basil
½ teaspoon (2.5 ml) dried thyme
  Salt to taste

Heat oil in a skillet. Add the chick peas. Saute for a few minutes, stirring constantly. Add all ingredients, cover, and cook for 10 minutes.

Serves 4

REFRIED BEANS

1 tablespoon (15 ml) oil
1 onion, minced
1 garlic clove, minced
2 cups (400 g) cooked pinto or black beans
½ cup (125 ml) stock from cooked beans
⅛ teaspoon (.50 ml) cumin
  Salt to taste

Heat oil in a skillet, add the onions and garlic, and saute until the onions are tender. Do not brown. Add beans and mash with a fork, adding the stock as the beans become thick. Add the cumin and salt to taste. Blend in well.

All ingredients can be put into a blender and pureed.

FRIJOLES

Add the following to the refried beans:

¼ to ½ cup (20 to 50 g) grated cheese
½ green pepper, minced and sauteed in a small amount of oil
   Cayenne pepper to taste
1 small onion, minced and sauteed in a small amount of oil (optional)

Serves 4

CHICK PEAS WITH TAHINI

Used as a dip with pita or French bread.

¾ cup (150 g) chick peas
¼ cup (50 ml) lemon juice
1 garlic clove, chopped
½ teaspoon (2.5 ml) salt
⅛ teaspoon (5 ml) cayenne pepper
¼ teaspoon (1.5 ml) paprika
½ cup (125 ml) tahini

Garnish
1 tablespoon (15 ml) oil
½ teaspoon (2.5 ml) paprika
1 tablespoon (15 ml) chopped fresh parsley

Cook chick peas and drain, saving liquid. In a blender, puree chick peas, lemon juice, and approximately ½ cup (125 ml) liquid from the chick peas or water. Add liquid slowly, consistency should not be watery. Add all ingredients except garnish and blend, adding more liquid if necessary. The consistency should be runny but not too thick. Pour puree into a serving dish.

For garnish, combine oil and paprika, drizzle over the humus. Sprinkle with parsley.

Serves 6

VEGETARIAN CHILI

1 cup (200 g) pinto or kidney beans
1 cup (200 g) Adzuki beans
1 bay leaf
   Salt to taste
1 teaspoon (5 ml) to 2 tablespoons (30 ml) chili powder, or to taste
½ cup (75 g) minced onions
1 garlic clove, minced
2 teaspoons (10 ml) oil
8 cups (2 l) water

Combine beans and bay leaf in water. Cook beans until tender. Add salt and chili powder.

Heat oil in a skillet and saute onions and garlic until tender. Add to the beans and continue to cook until the consistency is that of chili. Add more water until you have the desired thickness. Takes 3 to 4 hours to cook.

Serve with chopped raw onion on top.

Serves 6

LENTIL AND SPINACH PILAF

1 tablespoon (15 ml) oil
1 garlic clove, minced
½ pound (225 g) spinach, well cleaned and chopped coarsely
1½ cups (250 g) cooked lentils
1 tablespoon (15 ml) chopped fresh parsley
½ teaspoon (2.5 ml) salt
¼ teaspoon (1.5 ml) cumin
3 tablespoons (45 ml) butter (optional)

Heat the oil in a skillet. Saute the garlic over a low flame until it begins to turn golden. Add spinach, and saute for 1 minute. Add lentils, parsley, salt, and cumin, and saute for 5 mintues. Pour the melted butter over the pilaf.

Serves 4

LENTIL SPREAD

1 cup (200 g) well cooked lentils, saving the liquid
1 teaspoon (5 ml) red, barley, or Hatcho miso
¼ teaspoon (1.5 ml) nutmeg
1 tablespoon (15 ml) chopped fresh parsley
   Salt to taste

Puree lentils in a blender, adding cooking liquid until the beans are well blended and smooth. The puree should be thick. Add the miso, nutmeg, parsley, and salt. Puree. Simmer mixture in a saucepan, uncovered, for 5 minutes. Serve warm on bread, in pita bread, or on rice crackers.

This spread will keep refrigerated for a couple days.

Serves 4

TOFU CUTLETS

12 ounces (330 g) tofu, pressed
 1 tablespoon (15 ml) tamari
 ½ cup (70 g) whole wheat flour
 1 egg, lightly beaten with 3 tsp water or milk
 1 cup (100 g) fine bread crumbs
    Oil for deep frying
    Salt to taste

Marinate tofu in 1 tablespoon (15 ml) tamari, turning frequently for 15 minutes.

Cut tofu in half horizontally, then crosswise into ½-inch-thick (1.25 cm) pieces. Pat dry with paper towels. Put flour into a plastic bag. Add tofu, a few pieces at a time, and gently coat with flour. Then dip tofu into the egg and roll in the bread crumbs. Place on a rack and allow to dry for 15 minutes. Shake off any excess crumbs.

Prepare oil for deep frying. Drop tofu, a few pieces at a time, carefully into the oil and fry until golden brown. Drain, serve seasoned with salt.

Top with mayonnaise, if desired.

Serves 4

TOFU AND ONIONS

4 tablespoons (60 ml) oil
1 pound (450 g) tofu, pressed and cut into 1-inch (2.5 cm) cubes
3 onions, sliced very thin
¾ cup (175 ml) stock
½ tablespoon (7.5 ml) cornstarch
½ teaspoon (2.5 ml) tamari

Heat oil in a skillet. Saute onions until tender. Add tofu and saute briefly, heating the tofu.

In a cup, mix the cornstarch, tamari, and stock. Pour over tofu. Simmer, stirring constantly, until the sauce thickens.

Serves 4 to 6

SCRAMBLED TOFU

2 tablespoons (30 ml) oil
1 small onion, minced
1 small carrot, peeled and grated
12 ounces (330 g) tofu, pressed and crumbled
1 tablespoon (15 ml) roasted and ground sesame seeds
¼ teaspoon (1.5 ml) salt
1 to 2 teaspoons (5 to 10 ml) tamari or shoyu

Heat oil in a skillet. Saute onion until tender; do not brown. Add carrots and saute until tender, about 5 minutes. Add all ingredients, more oil if necessary, and saute, stirring constantly, until the tofu is dry and fluffy. Takes about 5 minutes. Serve hot.

Serves 4

GARBANZO BEAN CROQUETTES

These croquettes can be served a number of ways: plain; as a sandwich in pita bread with chopped tomatoes, cucumber, shredded lettuce, and tahini; with vegetables on the side (shredded lettuce, tomatoes, cucumbers, cheese); with a green salad with vinegar and oil dressing.

2   cups (400 g) cooked and mashed garbanzo beans
¼   cup (40 g) bulgar wheat, soaked in hot water for 30 minutes and drained
¼   cup (40 g) finely minced onion
1   garlic clove, finely minced
3   tablespoons (45 ml) whole wheat bread crumbs
1   egg, lightly beaten
½   teaspoon (2.5 ml) salt
1   tablespoon (15 ml) fresh parsley
½   teaspoon (2.5 ml) cumin (optional)
¼   teaspoon (1.5 ml) turmeric (optional)
¼   teaspoon (1.5 ml) coriander (optional)
    Pinch of cayenne pepper (optional)

Combine all ingredients and chill. The spices are optional; however, the taste is subtle and is not as strong as you might imagine.

Heat oil for frying. Make your mixture into small patties 1 ½-inches (3.75 cm) in diameter or 2 ½-inches (6 cm) in diameter. Roll in whole wheat flour. Deep-fry balls or saute patties in oil until golden brown in color. Drain on paper towels.

Serves 2-4

GRAINS

PEARL BARLEY WITH ONIONS

3 tablespoons (45 ml) oil
1 cup (200 g) pearl barley
1 cup (150 g) chopped onions
  Salt to taste
3 cups (750 ml) boiling water

Heat oil in a saucepan. Saute onions until tender. Add barley and saute until barley begins to turn yellow and has a nutty fragrance. Add water, bring to a boil, cover, lower flame, and simmer for 1 hour.

Serves 4

BARLEY–MUSHROOM CASSEROLE

1 cup (50 g) chopped mushrooms
1 medium onion, minced
1 cup (200 g) barley
2½ cups (625 ml) vegetable stock
1 teaspoon (5 ml) salt
3 tablespoons (45 ml) oil or butter
¼ cup (25 g) bread crumbs
¼ cup (25 g) grated cheese, cheddar or Swiss

Heat oil in a saucepan. Saute onion and mushrooms until tender. Add barley and saute until the barley begins to turn brown and smell nutlike. Remove from heat and add stock and salt. Mix. Return to heat and bring mixture to a boil. Cover and lower flame to simmer. Cook until barley is cooked, approximately 1 hour.

Put cooked barley mixture into a casserole. Top with a mixture of the bread crumbs and cheese. Dot top with butter. Bake in a preheated oven at 350 degrees only until the top turns brown. Baking barley too long can cause dryness.

Serves 4

NOODLES WITH CHEESE

4 tablespoons (60 ml) oil
1 pound (450 g) noodles, cooked and drained well
¾ teaspoon (3.5 ml) salt
2½ cups (280 g) cottage cheese (any style)

Heat oil in a skillet. Put noodles in the skillet and cover. Cook, covered, over a low flame for 5 minutes. Stir and continue to cook, covered, for another 5 minutes. Contine to mix and cook until noodles begin to turn light brown.

Remove from heat, add salt and cottage cheese, blending well. Place mixture in a baking dish and bake in a preheated 450 degrees F (230 degrees C) oven until heated through, approximately 10 minutes.

Serves 4

BROWN AND WILD RICE PILAF

Wild rice more than triples in volume when cooked. It also takes longer to cook than brown rice. It is best to cook wild rice separately (see below).

½ cup (100 g) wild rice
2 cups (500 ml) water or stock
1 cup (200 g) brown rice
½ cup (25 g) chopped mushrooms
1 small onion, minced
 Salt
 Oil

Saute wild rice in a small amount of oil until translucent. Add 2 cups (500 ml) water or stock. Bring to a boil. Cover, lower flame, and simmer until done, from 45 to 50 minutes.

Saute brown rice in a small amount of oil until rice begins to turn white. Add onion and mushrooms and saute until tender. Add 1 cup (250 ml) water or stock. Bring to a boil, cover, lower flame, and simmer until rice is done, about 30 minutes.

Combine brown rice mixture with wild rice. Blend well. Serve hot.

Serves 6-8

WILD RICE PILAF

3 tablespoons (45 ml) oil or butter
1½ (300 g) cups wild rice
1 medium onion, minced
½ cup (60 g) thinly sliced celery
1 cup (50 g) chopped mushrooms
4 cups (1 l) water or vegetable stock
2 teaspoons (10 ml) salt
1 teaspoon (5 ml) thyme
1 teaspoon (5 ml) marjoram

Saute rice in oil or butter until translucent; it will take about 5 minutes. Add onion, celery, and mushrooms and saute until tender. Add all ingredients and bring to a boil. Cover, lower the flame, and simmer until rice is done, about 45 to 60 minutes.

Serves 6-8

BULGUR WHEAT PILAF

Cooking time will vary according to the coarseness of the bulgur or cracked wheat. If very coarse, use more stock; if less coarse, use less stock.

3 tablespoons (45 ml) oil or butter
1 medium onion, chopped
1 cup (160 g) bulgur or cracked wheat
2 small tomatoes, peeled, and juiced; chop the pulp.
2 to 3 cups (500 to 750 ml) vegetable stock
Salt to taste

Heat oil or butter in a skillet. Saute onions until transparent. Add wheat and saute, stirring constantly, until the wheat begins to brown. Add tomatoes and stir for a moment. Add stock and salt to taste. Bring to a boil. Cover, lower heat to simmer, and cook until all liquid is absorbed, approximately 30 minutes.

Serves 4

BROWN RICE AND TOFU CASSEROLE

1 medium onion, chopped
  One 2-inch (5 cm) slice tofu, pressed and crumbled
1 cup (180 g) cooked brown rice
  Salt to taste
1 cup (100 g) grated cheddar cheese
½ cup (125 ml) dairy or soy milk
  Bread crumbs

Saute onion in oil until tender. Add tofu and saute for a few minutes. Add rice and more oil if necessary. Saute for an additional 5 minutes. Salt to taste. Remove from heat.

Mix in cheese and milk. Place in a casserole dish. Sprinkle bread crumbs on top and bake in a preheated 350 degrees F (180 degrees C) oven for about 30 minutes or until the cheese begins to bubble

Serves 2

RICE WITH BEAN SPROUTS

1 tablespoon (15 ml) oil
2 tablespoons (30 ml) sesame seeds
1 scallion, including green parts, sliced thin
1 small garlic clove, minced
1 cup (100 g) bean sprouts
1 tablespoon (15 ml) tamari or shoyu (more if desired)
1 cup (170 g) cooked rice

Heat oil in a skillet. Saute seeds, scallion, and garlic until seeds begin to pop and turn brown. Add bean sprouts and stir until hot. Do not allow the bean sprouts to become soft. Add tamari and mix well. Add rice and cook until rice is hot and well blended with all ingredients.

Serves 4

MILLET WITH VEGETABLES

1 tablespoon (15 ml) oil
1 large onion, chopped
1 large carrot, peeled and sliced very thin
1 cup (200 g) millet, roasted with or without oil
3 cups (750 ml) stock
   Salt to taste

Heat oil in a frypan. Saute onions until transparent; do not brown. Add carrots and saute for an additional 5 minutes. Add millet and saute only until blended well with the vegetables. Allow to cool slightly.

Add stock, bring to a boil, cover, lower flame, and simmer until all liquid is absorbed, about 30 to 40 minutes.

Serves 4 to 6

NOODLES AND BUCKWHEAT GROATS (KASHA)

2 cups (400 g) cooked groats
1 cup (50 g) chopped mushrooms
2 small onions, chopped
1 teaspoon (5 ml) salt
2 to 3 tablespoons (30 to 45 ml) oil or butter
¼ pound (100 g) whole wheat noodles, whole wheat and soya noodles, or
   egg noodles, cooked
   Yogurt or sour cream

Heat oil or butter in a skillet. Saute onions and mushrooms until tender. Add groats and saute until well blended. Drain noodles well. Add to buckwheat mixture and heat for 5 minutes, stirring mixture to prevent any sticking to the bottom of the skillet. Serve hot or cold, topped with yogurt or sour cream.

Serves 4

SQUASH BAKE

Oil
1 medium onion, sliced thin
1 garlic clove, minced
2 zucchini, 6 to 8 inches (15 to 20 cm) long, sliced ½-inch (1.25 cm) thick
1 cup (180) cooked brown rice
1 cup (100 g) shredded cheddar cheese
1 tablespoon (15 ml) fresh parsley, chopped
¼ teaspoon (1.5 ml) chervil
    Bread crumbs
    Butter

Heat oil in a skillet. Saute garlic and onion until the onion begins to turn transparent. Add squash and saute until tender. Add rice and more oil if necessary and saute for a few minutes. Combine all ingredients except bread crumbs and butter. Place mixture in a casserole. Cover with a layer of bread crumbs. Dot the top with butter. Bake in a preheated oven at 350 degrees F (180 degrees C) for 30 minutes.

Serves 2

WHOLE OAT GROATS

These are good for morning cereal, as a dessert, and for pie crusts.

1 cup (75 g) whole oats
6 cups (1.5 l) boiling water
1 teaspoon (5 ml) salt

Wash the oats. Dry-roast them in a hot skillet, stirring constantly to prevent burning, until they are golden in color and have a nutty fragrance. Pour water slowly over the oats, add salt, and bring to a boil. Cover and simmer over a very low heat. Can take two to three hours to complete the cooking process.

Serves 1

ROLLED OATS

Excellent cooked the day before and reheated in the morning.

1 cup (75 g) rolled oats
3 cups (750 ml) boiling water
Pinch of salt

Toast oat flakes (optional) in a hot skillet until they are golden in color and have a nutty fragrance. Slowly add 2 cups (500 ml) water and salt. Bring to a boil. Add remaining 1 cup (250 ml) water and bring to a boil again. Lower flame, cover, and simmer, stirring occasionally, until desired consistency is reached, usually, between 12 and 30 minutes.

Serves 1

Variations
Add minced onion into the cooking oats.
Serve sprinkled with cinnamon, bran, or wheat germ.
Serve with slices of fruit.

RICE WITH FRUIT

½ cup (85 g) dried apricots
½ cup (75 g) golden raisins
1 tablespoon (15 ml) oil
½ cup (75 g) minced onions
¼ cup (40 g) minced green peppers
¼ teaspoon (1.5 ml) curry powder
2 cups (340 g) cooked rice (cooked in a stock)
¼ cup (40 g) toasted almond slivers

Soak fruit in water for 30 minutes, drain, and chop. Put aside.

Heat oil in a skillet. Saute onion until transparent. Add green pepper and saute until just tender. Add curry powder and cook for an additional 2 minutes. Add fruit and rice.

Place rice mixture into an oiled baking dish. Bake in a preheated 375 degrees F (190 degrees C) oven for 30 minutes. Garnish with almonds.

Serves 4

INDIAN RICE

This rice is good served with chutney.

 2 tablespoons (30 ml) oil
 ½ cup (75 g) minced onions
 1 cup (180 g) brown rice
 ½ cup (60 g) fresh green peas
 ½ teaspoon (2.5 ml) turmeric
 ½ teaspoon (2.5 ml) curry powder
 2 bay leaves
 1 teaspoon (5 ml) cumin
 ¼ cup (40 g) raisins
    Salt to taste
 2 cups (500 ml) water or stock

Heat oil in a saucepan. Saute onion until tender; do not brown. Add rice and saute until rice begins to turn white. Add all ingredients except stock. Blend well.

Add stock, bring to a boil, cover, lower flame, and simmer until all water has been absorbed, about 30 to 45 minutes.

Serves 4 to 6

SALADS

BULGUR SALAD (TABBOULEH)

- 2 cups (320 g) fine bulgur, well washed
- ½ cup (75 g) minced scallions, or 1 large onion, minced
  Salt to taste
- ¾ cup (60 g) finely chopped fresh parsley
- ½ cup (40 g) minced fresh mint or 3 tablespoons (45 ml) dried crushed mint
- 5 tablespoons (75 ml) olive oil
- ¼ cup (50 ml) fresh lemon juice
- 2 large ripe tomatoes, peeled, juiced, and finely chopped
  Raw lettuce, leaves or chopped

Soak bulgur in water to cover for about 60 minutes before preparing the salad. It will expand in volume. Drain and squeeze out as much water as possible with your hands. Spread out to dry further on a large plate lined with paper towels.

Mix the bulgur with the scallions or onion, squeezing with your hands so that the juice of the scallions penetrates the wheat. Season to taste with salt.

Add the parsley, mint, oil, lemon juice, and tomato; mix well. Season with more salt and lemon juice if desired. The salad should have a distinctive lemon taste. Refrigerate. Serve on a bed of greens.

Serves 4 to 6

SPINACH WITH YOGURT SALAD

- 2 pounds (1 kg) spinach, cooked and drained well
- ½ to 1 teaspoon (2.5 to 5 ml) salt
- 2 cups (500 ml) plain yogurt

Allow the spinach to cool. Season. Add yogurt and mix well. Serve at room temperature.

Serves 4

LENTIL SALAD

1 cup (200 g) brown lentils placed in a saucepan filled with water
1 bay leaf
1 garlic clove, mashed
1 whole clove
1 small onion
½ cup (75 g) minced onions
½ cup (125 ml) olive or vegetable oil
2 tablespoons (30 ml) wine vinegar or lemon juice

Cook lentils with bay leaf, garlic, clove, and onion. Bring to a boil, lower heat, and simmer until the beans are tender. Drain the liquid and discard the onion, clove, bay leaf, and garlic. Salt to taste. Allow to cool.

Put beans into a bowl with minced onions, oil, and vinegar or lemon juice. Marinate for 1 hour in the refrigerator. Drain. Serve on a bed of lettuce leaves or shredded lettuce. Garnish with sliced tomatoes and avocado.

Serves 2

POTATO AND GREEN BEAN SALAD

1 cup (120 g) cooked green beans, cut in half
1 cup (160 g) cooked, cubed potatoes
2 tablespoons (30 ml) minced onions
½ small garlic clove, minced
½ teaspoon (2.5 ml) salt
1 tablespoon (15 ml) olive oil or vegetable oil
½ cup (60 g) thinly sliced celery
1½ tablespoons (22.5 ml) mayonnaise
½ tablespoon (7.5 ml) cider vinegar
   Romaine lettuce

In a mixing bowl, combine the beans, potatoes, onion, garlic, salt, and oil. Mix gently. Marinate, covered, for 1 hour. Gently mix every 15 minutes. Right before serving, add the celery, mayonnaise, and vinegar; mix gently. Serve on a bed of romaine or any green of your choice.

Serves 4

GREEN BEAN SALAD

½ pound (225 g) cooked string beans, cut in halves and chilled
¼ cup (60 g) crushed pineapple
   Watercress

Combine both ingredients and serve on a bed of watercress.

Serves 2

CHICK PEA AND POTATO SALAD

⅓ cup (60 g) chick peas
2 pounds (1 kg) potatoes, peeled and sliced thick
2 large onions, sliced thick
6 tablespoons (90 ml) oil
2 cloves garlic, peeled
1 pound (450 g) tomatoes, peeled and chopped
2½ tablespoons (37.5 ml) tomato paste
   Salt

Soak the chick peas overnight in water.

Heat the oil in a saucepan. Saute the onion until tender; do not brown. Drain chick peas, saving liquid. Add chick peas to onions along with the garlic cloves. Saute until garlic begins to turn color. Add potatoes and saute until they begin to turn golden, turning frequently. Add tomatoes and tomato paste. Cover the mixture with enough liquid, using the liquid from the chick peas plus water to cover the mixture. Blend the tomato paste well. Season.

Bring to a boil, lower flame, simmer, partially covered, until the beans are cooked, about 1 hour. Drain and chill.

Serves 4 to 6

CHICK PEA SALAD

1 cup (200 g) cooked chick peas
¼ cup (30 to 40 g) of each of the following
   grated carrots
   thinly sliced celery
   minced onion
   peeled, cored, and chopped cucumber
   peeled, cored, and chopped apple
1 teaspoon (5 ml) basil
⅓ cup (75 ml) vinegar
1 cup (250 ml) oil
   Salt to taste

Cook chick peas with a small onion stuck with 3 cloves; add 1 bay leaf and 1 crushed garlic clove.

Combine all ingredients except apple. (Do not chop apple until ready to use it.) Marinate overnight. Drain well. Mix in apple. Serve on a bed of shredded lettuce.

Serves 2

COTTAGE CHEESE SALAD OR SPREAD

This salad is excellent as a spread on dark bread or crackers.

1 cup (225 g) cottage cheese
¼ cup (40 g) unsalted sunflower seeds
¼ cup (40 g) minced green peppers
2 tablespoons (30 ml) minced onions

Combine all ingredients. Serve on a bed of lettuce with fresh bread or crackers on the side.

Serves 2

FRUIT SALAD

3 cups (375 g) cored and diced red apples
1 tablespoon (15 ml) lime juice
1 cup (120 g) diced celery
1 orange, pared, sliced, and halved
1 cup (170 g) seedless green grapes, halved
½ cup (75 g) chopped pecans or almonds
1 tablespoon (15 ml) crumbled blue cheese
1 Golden Delicious apple, cored and sliced

Toss diced apples with the lime juice. Place ½ of the apples in the bottom of a 3-inch-deep (7.5 cm) glass bowl. Layer the celery, orange, grapes, pecans, and the remaining diced apple.

Spread a creamy dressing on top. Garnish with blue cheese and apple slices.

Serves 6

For Fruit Dressing, see page 232.
For Cream Dressing for fruit, see page 232.

SWEET BEET SALAD

2 cups (360 g) cooked beets, sliced
½ cup (100 g) brown sugar
½ cup (125 ml) water
½ cup (125 ml) cider vinegar
1 clove garlic, minced
1 teaspoon (5 ml) salt

Put all ingredients except beets into a small saucepan. Heat until boiling. Place the beets in a covered container, and pour the hot mixture over them. Cool at room temperature. Cover and refrigerate.

Turn beets frequently to marinate them if all the beets are not covered by the liquid. Marinate for at least 4 hours or overnight. Drain and serve beets on a bed of greens.

Serves 4

GREEK SALAD

1 clove garlic, cut in half
4 firm tomatoes, quartered
2 small green peppers, sliced into rounds
1 Spanish onion, sliced very thin
1 cucumber, peeled and cut into ½-inch slices
6 ounces (170 g) feta cheese, broken into bite-size pieces
   Greek olives
   Salt
   Freshly ground pepper
1 tablespoon (15 ml) chopped fresh parsley
1 teaspoon (5 ml) oregano
   Wine vinegar or lemon juice
   Olive oil

Rub the garlic on the inside surface of your salad bowl. Combine the cucumber, tomatoes, onion, green peppers, ½ the feta cheese, and about 6 olives. Sprinkle with salt and pepper; mix gently. Crumble the remaining feta on top. Sprinkle with parsley and oregano. Top with 6 more olives.

Pour olive oil, slowly, over the top of the salad. Add a sprinkling of vinegar, but go light on the vinegar. Do not use as much as you would in an oil and vinegar dressing.

Serves 4 to 6

CUCUMBER SALAD

2 cucumbers, peeled and sliced thin
1 cup (250 ml) yogurt or sour cream
3 tablespoons (45 ml) very thinly sliced scallions or 1 small onion, sliced
   or chopped
½ teaspoon (2.5 ml) dill weed

Combine all ingredients. Chill.

Serves 4

AVOCADO WITH SPROUTS SALAD

1 cup (100 g) sprouted wheat
¼ cup (40 g) chopped scallions, including green parts
¼ cup (30 g) thinly sliced celery
1 avocado, cut into small pieces

Combine all ingredients. Blend in French dressing. Serve on a bed of torn greens.

Serves 2

BREADS

OATMEAL BREAD

For a softer crust, brush the tops of the loaves with melted butter while bread is cooling.

```
 2  cups (150 g) rolled oats
2½  cups (625 ml) boiling water
 ¾  cup (175 ml) honey or molasses
 1  tablespoon (15 ml) dry active yeast
 1  cup (250 ml) lukewarm water
 3  tablespoons (45 ml) oil or softened butter
 2  teaspoons (10 ml) salt
 ¼  teaspoon (1.5 ml) cinnamon
 ¼  cup (40 g) chopped nuts
 7  cups (1 kg) whole wheat flour or unbleached white flour or
 3  cups (420 g) whole wheat flour and 4 cups (500 g) unbleached flour
```

Mix the oats and boiling water and let stand for 30 minutes. Add the honey, except for 1 tablespoon (15 ml). Add the oil and salt; mix well.

Dissolve the yeast in the warm water and 1 tablespoon of honey; it will bubble. After yeast is dissolved, add to the oat mixture. Beat in half the flour, the cinnamon and nuts, then continue to beat in flour until you have a medium-soft dough. Turn dough onto a floured board and knead until smooth and elastic.

Put the dough into an oiled bowl, turning the dough over to oil the top. Cover with a damp cloth and let rise, in a warm place, for 1 hour or until it has doubled in bulk.

Turn onto a floured board and knead once more. Divide the dough evenly in half. Place in two 9" x 5" x 3" (23 x 13 x 8 cm) loaf pans, well oiled. Cover with a damp cloth and let rise about 45 minutes or until dough has doubled in bulk.

Preheat oven to 400 degrees F (200 degrees C). Bake the loaves for 5 minutes. Lower the temperature to 325 degrees F (170 degrees C) and bake for 1 hour or until they sound hollow when thumped. Cool on wire racks.

Makes 2 loaves

QUICK BANANA BREAD

2½ cups (350 g) whole wheat flour
 ½ cup (125 ml) honey
3⅓ teaspoons (17 ml) baking powder
 ¾ cup (175 ml) milk
 3 tablespoons (45 ml) oil
 1 egg, beaten
 1 cup (225 g) mashed bananas (2 or 3 very ripe bananas)

Combine all ingredients in a bowl. Do not overblend; mix only until moistened well. Put mixture into a 9" x 9" (23 x 23 cm) baking dish. Bake in a preheated 350 degrees F (180 degrees C) oven for 55 minutes.

BAKING POWDER BISCUITS

2 cups (280 g) whole wheat flour
1 teaspoon (5 ml) salt
3 teaspoons (15 ml) baking powder
4 tablespoons (60 ml) butter or margarine
  Milk

Over a mixing bowl, sift the flour, salt, and baking powder together. Blend in butter with your fingers, then add enough milk—about 1 cup (250 ml)—to make a moist dough.

Put dough on a floured surface. Roll out to ½-inch (1.25 cm) thickness. Cut out biscuits. Bake in a preheated 475 degrees F (240 degrees C) oven for 15 minutes.

Makes approximately 8-10 biscuits

TORTILLAS

2 cups (280 g) corn flour or masa
1 teaspoon (5 ml) salt
1 cup (250 ml) boiling water

Combine the flour and salt. Pour in the boiling water, stirring quickly with a fork until well blended. Work dough with your hands until it does not stick. Make the dough into balls, about the size of golf balls. Flatten the balls into thin circles.

Bake at 350 degrees F (180 degrees C) on an oiled griddle or cookie sheet until dry and beginning to turn brown, then turn tortillas and bake the other side. Keep warm and serve warm.

Makes 6-8

CORNBREAD

2 cups (300 g) cornmeal
½ teaspoon (2.5 ml) salt
2 teaspoons (10 ml) baking powder
2 tablespoons (30 ml) oil
1 cup (250 ml) milk
1 egg, beaten
1 tablespoon (15 ml) sugar

Sift the cornmeal, salt, and baking powder over a large mixing bowl. Make a well in the middle of the dry ingredients. Add the oil, milk, egg, and sugar. Mix well. Pour into an oiled 8-inch-square (20 cm) baking pan. Bake in a preheated 400 degrees F (200 degrees C) oven for 30 minutes.

CORNMEAL SPOON BREAD

1¾ cups (260 g) cornmeal
 3 cups (750 ml) boiling water
1½ cups (375 ml) milk
 3 eggs, beaten
 2 teaspoons (10 ml) salt
 2 tablespoons (30 ml) melted butter

In a large bowl, pour the boiling water over the cornmeal. Add the milk, eggs, salt, and butter. Beat extremely well. Pour mixture into a 8" or 9" (20 to 23 cm) square greased baking dish. Bake in a preheated 350 degrees F (180 degrees C) oven for 45 minutes. Serve hot with butter.

WHOLE WHEAT SESAME CRACKERS

2 cups (280 g) whole wheat flour
½ teaspoon (2.5 ml) salt
6 tablespoons (90 ml) oil
½ cup (125 ml) water
½ cup (75 g) sesame seeds

Combine flour and salt. Beat oil and water together until thick. Add oil mixture to flour and knead with the fingers for 5 minutes. Allow dough to sit for 10 minutes.

Divide dough in half. Roll dough as thin as possible onto a greased baking sheet or onto waxed paper. Turn dough over onto a greased baking sheet. Sprinkle with sesame seeds and salt, if desired. Roll again, pressing in the seeds.

Cut outlines for the crackers and prick all over the dough with a fork. Bake in a preheated 350 degrees F (180 degrees C) oven for 10 minute or until golden brown in color. Let cool before removing from the sheet.

Break apart the individual crackers. Repeat this process with the other half of the dough.

WHOLE WHEAT MUFFINS

2 cups (280 g) whole wheat flour
¼ teaspoon (1.5 ml) salt
3 tablespoons (45 ml) baking powder
3 tablespoons (45 ml) oil
1 egg, beaten
1 cup (250 ml) milk
¼ cup (50 ml) honey
½ cup (75 g) seedless raisins

Sift the flour, salt, and baking powder over a large mixing bowl. Make a well in the center of the flour. Add the oil, egg, milk, and honey, Stir only until flour is moistened. Do not overbeat; batter should be lumpy. Add raisins and mix briefly.

Pour into oiled muffin tins. Bake in a preheated 375 degrees F (190 degrees C) oven for 20 mintues.

Makes 12 muffins.

WHOLE WHEAT PANCAKES

1 teaspoon (5 ml) baking soda
1 cup (140 g) whole wheat flour
½ teaspoon (2.5 ml) salt
1 tablespoon (15 ml) molasses
1 cup (250 ml) buttermilk
1 tablespoon (15 ml) oil

Combine baking soda, flour, and salt in a bowl. Make a well in the center of the flour. In a separate bowl, combine the egg, molasses, buttermilk, and oil, mixing well. Add to flour. Beat until flour is completely moistened. Do not overbeat. Let stand for 5 minutes.

Spoon mixture onto a lightly greased griddle. Turn as soon as pancakes are puffed and full of bubbles.

Makes 12 pancakes

WHOLE WHEAT FRENCH TOAST

3 slices whole wheat bread
1 egg, beaten
¼ cup (50 ml) milk
¼ teaspoon (1.5 ml) salt
  Butter or margarine
  Powdered sugar
  Maple sugar

Combine egg, milk, and salt. Mix well. Dip bread into mixture. Fry on a hot greased (with butter or margarine) griddle or frying pan. Brown each side. Remove from heat and sprinkle with powdered sugar. Serve with pure maple syrup.

Makes 3 slices toast

WHOLE WHEAT WAFFLES

2 cups (280 g) whole wheat flour
4 teaspoons (20 ml) baking powder
½ teaspoon (2.5 ml) salt
2 egg yolks, beaten
½ cup (110 g) butter or margarine, melted
1¾ cups (425 ml) milk
2 egg whites, beaten stiff

Sift together the flour, baking powder, and salt, In a separate bowl, mix the egg yolks and milk together. Add to flour and mix. Add the butter and blend. Fold in the egg whites. Cook on a hot waffle iron.

Makes 8 waffles

WHOLE WHEAT BREAD

  3 cups (750 ml) milk or water
  3 tablespoons (45 ml) oil
2½ teaspoons (12.5 ml) salt
 ½ cup (125 ml) honey or ¼ cup brown sugar
 ¼ cup (50 ml) molasses
  3 tablespoons (45 ml) wheat germ
  2 tablespoons (30 ml) brewer's yeast
  2 tablespoons (30 ml) active dry yeast
 ¼ cup (50 ml) lukewarm water
6½ (900 g) cups whole wheat flour or
  6 cups (840 g) whole wheat flour and ½ cup (40 g) soy flour

In a small saucepan, combine the milk, oil, salt, honey, and molasses. Heat until well blended, stirring constantly. Cool to warm.

Using the measuring cup with which you measured the molasses and honey, dissolve the yeast into the warm water. Let stand until the yeast dissolves and bubbles. Blend all dry ingredients in a bowl.

Combine the yeast with the milk mixture in a large bowl. Stir in half the flour mixture and blend well. Add remaining flour and beat the mixture until well blended.

Turn onto a well-floured board. Knead thoroughly until smooth and elastic. Divide in half and place each half into a well-oiled 8½" x 4¼" x 2½" (22 x 11 x 6 cm) loaf pans. Cover with a damp cloth and let rise for one hour or until the loaves have doubled. Bake at 375 degrees F (190 degrees C) for 50 minutes or until the loaves sound hollow when thumped. Cool on wire racks.

Makes 2 loaves

WHOLE WHEAT DATE MUFFINS

½ cup (60 g) unbleached flour
1½ cups (200 g) whole wheat flour
3 teaspoons (15 ml) baking powder
½ teaspoon (2.5 ml) salt
1 tablespoon (15 ml) brown sugar
2 teaspoons (10 ml) grated orange rind
1 egg, beaten
3 tablespoons (45 ml) oil
¾ cup (175 ml) orange juice
½ cup (90 g) chopped dates

Combine four, baking powder, salt, sugar, and orange rind, in a large mixing bowl. In a separate bowl, mix together the egg, oil, and orange juice. Add the egg mixture to the flour and mix quickly. Add the dates and mix briefly.

Spoon mixture into 12 muffin cups, filling ⅔ full. Bake in a preheated 425 degrees F (220 degrees C) oven for 25 minutes. Remove from tins. Serve hot.

Makes 12 muffins

CHAPATI

Chapati is a very popular unleavened bread in India

2½ cups (350 g) whole wheat flour or 1¼ cups (175 g) whole wheat flour
and 1¼ cups (175 g) corn flour
¾ teaspoon (3.5 ml) salt
Approximately 1 cup (250 ml) water

Mix flour and salt in a bowl. Add enough water, adding it slowly, to make a soft dough that does not stick to your fingers. Put dough onto a floured board and knead, until smooth, for about 5 minutes. Shape the dough into balls about the size of golf balls. Flatten dough in your hands to ¼-inch (.5 cm) thick and place in a heated oiled pan. Cook over a medium flame for 10 minutes on each side until both sides are nicely browned.

Makes 6-8

CRANBERRY BREAD

1 cup (125 g) unbleached all-purpose flour
2 teaspoons (10 ml) baking powder
1 teaspoon (5 ml) salt
¼ teaspoon (1.5 ml) baking soda
¾ cup (100 g) whole wheat flour
¼ cup (20 g) soy flour
3 tablespoons (45 ml) brown sugar
1 egg, beaten
3 tablespoons (45 ml) oil
1 teaspoon (5 ml) grated orange rind
¾ cup (175 ml) orange juice
¾ cup (100 g) chopped raw cranberries
½ cup (75 g) chopped pecans

In a large mixing bowl, sift together the unbleached flour, baking powder, salt, and baking soda. Add the whole wheat flour, soy flour, and sugar, mixing well.

Make a well in the center of the flour. Add the egg, oil, orange rind, and orange juice. Stir to moisten flour thoroughly. Do not overbeat. Mix together the cranberries and nuts. Blend well into the flour mixture.

Turn batter into a loaf pan that has been greased on the bottom. Bake in a preheated 350 degrees F (180 degrees C) oven for 1 hour or until bread is done. Test for doneness by inserting a cake tester or a piece of straw from a broom into the center of the loaf; it should come out clean. Also, the sides of the bread will pull away from the pan.

Cool for 15 mintues. Turn out on a rack. Cool completely. Wrap in foil and chill overnight. Serve at room temperature.

Makes 1 loaf

CARROT BREAD

2½ cups (350 g) whole wheat flour
  1 teaspoon (5 ml) baking powder
  1 teaspoon (5 ml) baking soda
  1 teaspoon (5 ml) ground cinnamon
  ½ teaspoon (2.5 ml) salt
  3 eggs, beaten
  ½ cup (125 ml) oil
  ½ cup (125 ml) milk
  ⅔ cup (165 ml) honey
  2 cups (240 g) peeled and grated carrots
  ½ cup (75 g) chopped pecans

Blend together in a large bowl the flour, baking powder, baking soda, cinnamon, and salt. In a separate bowl, beat the eggs, oil, milk, and honey together. Add to the flour and stir only until flour becomes moistened. Do not overblend. Add the carrots and pecans and fold in gently.

Oil two loaf pans. Pour the mixture into the pans. Bake in a preheated 350 degrees F (180 degrees C) oven for 1 hour. Allow to cool. Refrigerate. Will taste delicious after being cooled.

Makes 2 loaves

PIE CRUSTS

PIZZA DOUGH

1 package active dry yeast
1 teaspoon (5 ml) sugar
1 cup (250 ml) warm water
3½ cups (500 g) whole wheat flour
2 teaspoons (10 ml) salt
2 tablespoons (30 ml) soft butter
1 egg, beaten
  Tomato Sauce (see page 228)
  Mozzarella cheese

Dissolve the yeast and sugar in ¼ cup (50 ml) of the warm water. Let stand for 10 minutes, until the yeast is foamy and dissolved.

Put the flour and salt in a large bowl and work in the butter with a pastry blender or a fork. Make a well in the center of the flour and pour in the yeast mixture, the rest of the water, and the beaten egg.

Mix to a firm dough, which will leave the sides of the bowl clean. Add a tiny bit more flour or water if necessary. Turn the dough out onto a clean working surface and knead for 10 minutes, until the texture becomes smooth and pliable. Then place the dough back in a greased bowl, cover the bowl, and leave in a warm place until the dough has doubled in size, about 1 ½ hours.

Remove the dough from the bowl and punch it down to remove any large pockets of air. Knead for 2 minutes. Divide into 2 or 4 pieces and roll into an 8-inch to 12-inch (20 to 30 cm) circle. Put into greased ovenproof pizza sheets or baking sheets.

Top with Tomato Sauce (page 228) and shredded mozzarella cheese. Bake in a preheated 500 degrees F (250 degrees C) oven for approximately 15 minutes. Crust should be turning brown.

Makes four 8-inch (20 cm) or two 12-inch (30 cm) pies.

WHOLE WHEAT PIE CRUST

1½ (210 g) cups whole wheat flour
⅛ teaspoon (.50 ml) salt
½ cup (110 g) softened butter or margarine
   Approximately ¼ cup (50 ml) ice water

Stir the flour and salt together. Cut in the butter (or use a pastry blender). Mixing with a fork, add ice water by tablespoonfuls until the dough can be formed into a ball.

Roll out on a lightly floured board or between sheets of waxed paper until you have a circle 12 inches (30 cm) in diameter. The dough should extend over the edge of a 9- or 10-inch (23 to 25 cm) pie plate. Turn the edge under and flute the edges with a fork or knife. Prick the bottom with a fork about 2 inches (5 cm) apart, to prevent air pockets.

Bake in a 375 degrees F (190 degrees C) oven for approximately 20 minutes or until lightly browned.

Makes one 9- or 10-inch (23 to 25 cm) pie crust

WHOLE WHEAT PASTRY PIE CRUST

Pastry flour makes a flaky crust.

1 cup (140 g) whole wheat pastry flour
½ teaspoon (2.5 ml) salt
3 tablespoons (45 ml) vegetable oil
   Approximately 3 tablespoons (45 ml) ice water

Stir flour and salt in a small bowl. Add the oil and add enough water, adding 1 teaspoonful at a time, until the dough is very stiff. Roll out on a lightly floured board or between sheets of waxed paper until you have a circle 12 inches (30 cm) in diameter.

The dough should extend over the edge of a 9- or 10-inch (23 to 25 cm) pie plate. Turn the edge under and flute the edges with a fork or knife. Prick the bottom with a fork about 2 inches (5 cm) apart, to prevent air pockets.

Bake in a 375 degrees F (190 degrees C) oven for approximately 20 minutes or until lightly browned.

Makes one 9- or 10-inch (23 to 25 cm) pie crust

FLAKY WHOLE WHEAT PIE CRUST

3 cups (420 g) whole wheat flour
½ teaspoon (2.5 ml) salt
½ cup (125 ml) oil
1 egg
    Approximately 6 tablespoons (90 ml) ice water

Blend the flour and salt together. Beat the egg and oil together. Add the egg mixture to the flour. Add ice water, one teaspoonful at a time, until the dough can be formed into a ball. Divide the mixture in half.

Roll out on a lightly floured board or between sheets of waxed paper until you have a circle 12 inches (30 cm) in diameter. There is enough dough for 2 pie crust shells for a 9- or 10-inch (23 to 25 cm) pie. The dough should extend over the edge of the pie plate. Turn the edge under and flute the edges with a fork or knife. Prick the bottom with a fork about 2 inches (5 cm), to prevent air pockets.

Bake in a 375 degrees F (190 degrees C) oven for approximately 20 minutes or until lightly browned.

Makes two 9- or 10-inch (23 to 25 cm) pie crusts

BROWN RICE CRUST FOR PIE

1½ (270 g) cups cooked brown rice

Pat rice on the bottom and sides of a 9-inch pie plate. Let it dry out in a hot oven for a few minutes and then cool.

Makes one 9-inch (23 cm) crust

SAUCES, DRESSINGS, DIPS, PUREES, AND MARINADES

MUSHROOM SAUCE

Serve this sauce over noodles or cooked vegetables.

- **1 tablespoon (15 ml) butter**
- **¼ (15 g) pound mushrooms, chopped**
- **1 cup (250 ml) sour cream**
- **Salt to taste**
- **Paprika or nutmeg to taste**

Melt the butter in a skillet. Saute mushrooms until just tender, about 5 minutes. Blend in the sour cream, salt, and a sprinkling of paprika or nutmeg. Heat until warm. Do not allow the sauce to boil.

Makes approximately 2 cups (500 ml)

SOUR CREAM SAUCE

This is an excellent sauce for asparagus.

- **½ cup (125 ml) sour cream**
- **1 teaspoon (5 ml) sugar**
- **2 teaspoons (10 ml) wine vinegar**
- **¼ teaspoon (1.5 ml) paprika**
- **½ teaspoon (2.5 ml) salt**
- **¼ cup (25 g) toasted bread crumbs**

Combine all ingredients except bread crumbs. Heat, but do not boil. Add bread crumbs right before serving.

Makes ¾ cup (175 ml)

QUICK HOLLANDAISE

Serve Quick Hollandaise over asparagus, broccoli, or cauliflower.

 2 egg yolks
 ¼ teaspoon (1.5 ml) salt
 ¼ teaspoon (1.5 ml) tabasco
 ½ cup (125 ml) melted butter kept warm
 2 tablespoons (30 ml) fresh lemon juice

Beat the egg yolks until thick. Add salt and tabasco. Add half the butter, a teaspoonful at a time, beating constantly. Mix the lemon juice with the remaining butter and continue to add butter slowly, mixing constantly.

Makes ½ cup (125 ml)

EASY BLENDER HOLLANDAISE SAUCE

This is a good sauce for cooked vegetables.

 ¼ pound (110 g) butter
 1½ teaspoon (7.5 ml) lemon juice mixed with ⅓ cup water
 1½ egg yolks or two egg yolks from very small eggs
    Dash of salt
    Dash of cayenne pepper
 ⅛ teaspoon (.50 ml) dried chervil

Melt butter in a small saucepan. Add the lemon-water mixture and bring to a boil. While butter mixture is reaching a boil, blend the egg yolks, pepper, salt, and chervil in a blender warmed with hot water.

As soon as the butter begins to boil, add it quickly to the eggs. Blend no longer than 10 seconds, or it will thin.

Keep warm in the top part of a double boiler over hot water.

Makes approximately 1 cup (250 ml)

BECHAMEL SAUCE

This sauce is excellent over kasha or millet.

- 2 tablespoons (30 ml) butter
- 2 heaping tablespoons (30 ml) whole wheat pastry flour
- 1 cup (250 ml) stock or milk
  Salt or tamari to taste

Heat butter in a small saucepan, add flour, and cook over a medium flame, stirring constantly, until the flour has a nutlike fragrance, 3-5 minutes. Remove pan from the heat for a few minutes.

Return to heat and add liquid very slowly, to prevent lumps, stirring constantly, until mixture thickens. Add salt or tamari to taste. Cook a few minutes longer.

Makes 1 cup (250 ml)

CREAM SAUCE FOR CREAMING VEGETABLES

- 2 tablespoons (30 ml) butter
- 2 heaping tablespoons (30 ml) whole wheat flour
- 1 cup (250 ml) milk
- 1 small onion, studded with 4 cloves
- ½ bay leaf
  Salt to taste

Melt the butter in a saucepan over very low heat. Add the flour. Heat, stirring constantly, until the flour has a nutty fragrance. Add the milk very slowly, stirring constantly. Add onion and bay leaf and stir the sauce until it is thickened and smooth. Pour into a baking dish and bake in a preheated 350 degrees F (180 degrees C) oven for 20 minutes. Remove onion and bay leaf. Add salt to taste.

Makes 1 cup (250 ml)

Variation
¾ cup (175 ml) of above mixed with ¼ cup (50 ml) heavy cream. Heat and serve.

CHICK PEA SAUCE

This sauce is excellent on grains. It can be put in a blender and pureed.

1 tablespoon (15 ml) oil or butter
1 small onion, chopped
1 carrot, parboiled and sliced thin
2 tablespoons (30 ml) whole wheat flour
1 cup (250 ml) stock from chick peas
  Salt to taste
1 teaspoon (5 ml) tamari (optional)
1 cup (200 g) cooked chick peas

Heat oil in a skillet. Saute onion until tender; do not brown. Add carrots and saute until tender. Add flour and cook until flour has a nutty fragrance. Add stock, a small amount at a time, stirring constantly. Season with salt and tamari. Add chick peas and cook until sauce becomes smooth and thickens.

Makes 2 cups (500 ml)

DHAL SAUCE OR DIP

1 medium onion, chopped
1 clove garlic, minced
1 tablespoon (15 ml) oil
½ cup (100 g) lentils
½ teaspoon (2.5 ml) ground coriander
½ teaspoon (2.5 ml) cumin
2 cups (500 ml) stock
1 bay leaf
  Salt to taste

Heat the oil in a saucepan. Saute the onion and garlic until the onion is tender; do not let the onion or garlic turn brown. Add the lentils, coriander, and cumin. Saute for 2 minutes. Add stock and bay leaf, cover partially, lower flame, and simmer until lentils are well cooked, about 45 to 60 minutes. Remove bay leaf and puree lentils in a blender. Add salt to taste.

Makes approximately 1½ cups (375 ml)

SAUCE FOR PAN–FRIED VEGETABLES

1   tablespoon (15 ml) cornstarch
3   tablespoons (45 ml) cold water
½   teaspoon (2.5 ml) salt
1   tablespoon (15 ml) shoyu or tamari
½   teaspoon (2.5 ml) finely grated ginger root

Combine the cornstarch and cold water; blend until smooth. Add all ingredients, mixing well. A few minutes before the vegetables have finished frying, add sauce and cook until the sauce thickens.

Makes sauce for 1 pound (450 g) of vegetables

SIMPLE PIZZA SAUCE

1   tablespoon (15 ml) oil
1   onion, chopped
1   clove garlic, minced
1   pound (450 g) tomatoes, peeled and chopped, or
     one 16-ounce (450 g) can tomatoes
     Salt

Heat oil in a saucepan. Saute onion and garlic a few minutes until onion is tender. Add tomatoes and simmer until sauce has a thick consistency, approximately 20 to 30 minutes. Season.

Tomato Sauce

For tomato sauce, puree mixture as above, season with salt to taste, and add 1 tablespoon (15 ml) red wine.

Makes 1½ cups (375 ml)

PIZZA OR SPAGHETTI SAUCE

  2 tablespoons (30 ml) olive oil
  2 celery stalks, sliced thin
  ½ bell pepper, chopped
  1 small onion, chopped
  1 clove garlic, minced
  1 can (6 ounces or 160 g) tomato paste diluted in 1 cup (250 ml) water
     6 to 8 tomatoes, peeled, chopped fine
  ½ teaspoon (2.5 ml) oregano
  ½ teaspoon (2.5 ml) basil

Heat oil in a large skillet. Saute celery, peppers, garlic and onions until just tender. Add tomatoes, oregano, basil, and paste mixture. Simmer for 1 hour or longer, until sauce has a thick consistency.

Makes 3 to 5 cups (750 ml to 1.25 l)

MISO ONION SAUCE

This sauce is excellent over grains and tofu.

  3 tablespoons (45 ml) oil or butter
  2 large onions, chopped
  3 tablespoons (45 ml) red, barley, or Hatcho miso, thinned in 1 cup (250 ml)
     water

Heat oil in a large skillet. Add onions and saute until tender; do not brown. Add the miso mixture, cover, and simmer for 30 minutes or until most of the liquid has been evaporated. Allow to stand for 5 hours in a refrigerator or overnight. Reheat and serve.

Makes 1 cup (250 ml)

AVOCADO SALAD DRESSING

This sauce is best used on salads, preferably greens.

1 medium avocado, pitted, skinned, and mashed with ¼ cup (50 ml)
   fresh lemon juice
¼ cup (50 ml) olive oil
¼ cup (50 ml) oil
½ teaspoon (2.5 ml) salt
1 clove garlic, pressed through a garlic press
2 tablespoons (30 ml) minced onions
2 tablespoons (30 ml) white wine vinegar
½ teaspoon (2.5 ml) sugar
   Dash of Tabasco (optional)

Blend the oil into the avocado-lemon juice mixture. Add all ingredients and blend well. Add more salt if necessary. Add a dash of tabasco if you want to make it more spicy.

Makes about 1 cup (250 ml)

TAHINI DRESSING

This dressing is excellent on cooked vegetables.

2 garlic cloves, pressed through a garlic press
   Salt to taste
½ cup (125 ml) lemon juice
1 cup (250 ml) tahini
2 tablespoons (30 ml) oil
   Water as needed
3 tablespoons (45 ml) minced fresh herbs such as coriander or parsley
   Cayenne pepper to taste (optional)

Combine garlic and salt and add remaining ingredients. Combine until you have a smooth paste. Check seasoning. Allow to stand for 1 hour or more, refrigerated.

Makes 2 cups (500 ml)

THOUSAND ISLAND DRESSING

½ cup (125 ml) olive oil
½ cup (125 ml) tomato puree
2 tablespoons (30 ml) lemon juice
2 tablespoons (30 ml) onion, minced
1 tablespoon (15 ml) honey

Put all ingredients in a covered jar. Shake well. Chill.

Makes 1 cup (250 ml)

SOUR CREAM DRESSING

½ cup (125 ml) sour cream
1 tablespoon (15 ml) caraway seeds

Heat cream very gently. Add seeds right before serving. Serve over hot vegetables.

Makes ½ cup (125 ml)

FRENCH DRESSING

6 tablespoons (90 ml) olive or vegetable oil or a combination of both
½ to 2 tablespoons (7.5 to 30 ml) wine vinegar, tarragon vinegar, or
   lemon juice
⅛ teaspoon (.50 ml) salt
¼ teaspoon (1.5 ml) dry mustard
   Herbs of your choice to taste

Combine all ingredients except herbs in a screw-top jar and shake for 40 seconds. Stir in any herbs just before mixing in salad.

Makes ½ cup (125 ml)

GREEN GODDESS SALAD DRESSING

1 cup (250 ml) mayonnaise
1 garlic clove, mashed
2 tablespoons (30 ml) minced fresh chives
2 scallions, including green part, sliced thin
3 tablespoons (45 ml) minced fresh parsley
½ cup (125 ml) sour cream
2 tablespoons (30 ml) tarragon vinegar
   Salt to taste

Blend all ingredients in a blender until smooth. Chill.

Makes 1½ cups (375 ml)

FRUIT DRESSING

½ cup (125 ml) mayonnaise
½ cup (125 ml) whipping cream (heavy cream)

Combine ingredients right before serving.

Makes 1 cup (250 ml)

CREAM DRESSING FOR FRUIT

2 eggs, beaten
¼ cup (50 ml) honey
¼ cup (50 ml) orange juice
½ cup (125 ml) lemon juice
⅛ teaspoon (.50 ml) salt
½ cup (125 ml) heavy cream, whipped
2 teaspoons (10 ml) orange rind, grated
   Garnishes: shredded coconut, chopped nuts, crumbled blue cheese, or
   well-pressed tofu

In a small saucepan, mix the egg, honey, orange juice, lemon juice, and salt. Blend well. Simmer over low heat until the mixture coats a spoon. Remove from the heat. Fold in the cream and orange rind. Serve over a fresh fruit salad and top with a garnish.

Makes a little more than 2 cups (500 g)

FRUIT SAUCE I

Pour this sauce and Fruit Sauce II (see below) over any combination of fruits.

¼ cup (50 g) sugar
½ teaspoon (2.5 ml) salt
½ cup (125 ml) water
1 tablespoon (15 ml) fresh lemon juice
2 teaspoons (10 ml) vanilla extract

In a small saucepan, bring all ingredients except vanilla to a boil. Boil for 1 minute. Add the vanilla and pour over the fresh fruit. Chill. Serve cold.

Serves 4

FRUIT SAUCE II

2 tablespoons (30 ml) sugar
2 tablespoons (30 ml) water
2 tablespoons (30 ml) orange juice
1½ teaspoon (7.4 ml) fresh lemon juice
2 tablespoons (30 ml) Kirsch
Shredded coconut

Combine all ingredients except coconut until sugar is well dissolved. Combine with fruits of your choice. Chill. Serve sprinkled with shredded coconut.

Serves 4

MARINADE FOR VEGETABLES I

3 parts oil
1 part vinegar or lemon juice
1 bay leaf
A large pinch each of fennel, thyme, coriander, and salt

Marinate vegetables for 2 hours in the marinade.

MARINADE FOR VEGETABLES II

3 parts oil
1 part vinegar or lemon juice
   A large pinch each of basil, tarragon, sugar, and salt
⅛ teaspoon (.50 ml) prepared mustard

Marinate vegetables for 2 hours in the marinade.

RAW VEGETABLE DIP

2 egg yolks
1 teaspoon (5 ml) spicy brown mustard
½ teaspoon (2.5 ml) salt
1½ cups (375 ml) olive oil
2 tablespoons (30 ml) lemon juice

Mix egg yolks and mustard and add salt. Add the oil slowly, beating constantly. Blend in the lemon juice and allow to cool.

Combine (250 ml) of the above with 2 minced garlic cloves and ½ cup of minced fresh parsley. Cool overnight or 8 hours. Serve with any of the following raw, chilled vegetables: whole mushrooms, broccoli or cauliflower flowerets, celery sticks, scallions, carrot sticks, zucchini sticks, cherry tomatoes.

Makes a little more than 1 cup (250 ml)

ARTICHOKE DIP I: HERBED BUTTER

½ cup (125 ml) melted butter
½ teaspoon (2.5 ml) crushed fresh tarragon
¼ teaspoon (1.5 ml) minced garlic
1 teaspoon (5 ml) lemon juice

Combine all ingredients except lemon juice and saute until the garlic is tender but not brown. Stir in lemon juice. Serve hot.

Makes ½ cup (125 ml)

ARTICHOKE DIP II: MAYONAISE DIP

1 cup (250 ml) mayonnaise
1 clove garlic, minced
2 anchovy fillets, minced

Combine all ingredients. Chill.

Makes 1 cup (250 ml)

EGGPLANT PUREE

1 medium eggplant
1 tablespoon (15 ml) oil
1 tablespoon (15 ml) minced fresh parsley
2 chopped cloves garlic
2 to 3 teaspoons (10 to 15 ml) lemon juice
4 tablespoons (60 ml) yogurt
   Salt to taste

Cut eggplant in half. Put halves, skin side up, on a piece of foil. Broil under the broiler until skin turns black and blisters and the flesh is soft. Remove from broiler.

After eggplant cools enough to handle, rub the skin under cold running water. Remove all skin.

Cut the eggplant into large pieces. Squeeze with the hands until as much juice as possible is removed.

Put eggplant and oil into a blender and puree. Add all other ingredients and puree.

Or, instead of a blender, use a mortar and pestle or mash with a fork until pureed. Mix eggplant and oil first, then add remaining ingredients.

Makes approximately 2 cups (500 ml) depending on size of eggplant

DESSERTS

APRICOT CREAM

  1 **cup (175 g) dried apricots**
1½ **cups (375 ml) water**
 ⅓ **(60 g) cup sugar**
  3 **tablespoons (45 ml) apricot preserves**
  4 **lemon peel slivers**
 ¾ **teaspoon (3.75 ml) grated orange peel**
  1 **cup (250 ml) whipping cream (heavy cream)**

Bring to a boil in a small saucepan all ingredients except the cream. Lower flame and simmer for 30 minutes or until mixture has the consistency of syrup. Cool. After cooled, puree in a blender.

Whip the cream until stiff. Fold in the apricot mixture very gently. Put mixture into dessert dishes and chill. Serve with sweetened whipping cream, whipped until stiff, on top.

Serves 4

BLENDER APRICOT CUSTARD

½ **cup (90 g) dried apricots**
2 **cups (500 ml) milk**
¾ **cup (175 ml) honey**
3 **eggs**

Put all ingredients into a blender. Blend for 3 to 5 minutes, constantly scraping any unblended material off the sides.

Pour into oiled custard cups or a baking pan. Place on top of a pan of hot water. Bake in a preheated 350 degrees F (180 degrees C) oven for 40 to 50 minutes. A knife inserted into the center will come out clean when the custard is cooked. If it does not, cook longer.

Serves 8

RICE CUSTARD

⅓ cup (60 g) brown rice
2 cups (500 ml) milk
2 eggs
⅓ cup (80 ml) honey
1½ teaspoon (7.5 ml) vanilla
½ cup (75 g) raisins

Cook rice. Mix all ingredients together. Pour into an oiled baking dish. Bake in a preheated 325 degrees F (170 degrees C) oven for 1 hour. Custard is done when a knife inserted into the center comes out clean; cook longer if necessary.

Serves 4 to 6

RICE PUDDING

½ cup (100 g) brown sugar
3 cups (750 ml) milk
3 beaten eggs
⅛ teaspoon (.50 ml) salt
½ teaspoon (2.5 ml) vanilla extract
2 cups (360 g) cooked brown rice

Garnish:
½ cup (75 g) raisins,
¼ cup (20 g) grated coconut,
¼ cup (40 g) chopped nuts,
½ to 1 teaspoon (2.5 to 5 ml) ground cinnamon, or
¼ teaspoon (1.5 ml) nutmeg

Preheat oven to 325 degrees F (170 degrees C).

Beat the eggs, vanilla, sugar, and salt into the milk. Add the rice ingredients. Place in a buttered casserole dish. Bake for about 30 minutes uncovered. The longer it bakes, the drier it will become. Milk should still be visible on the top when it is finished.

Refrigerate. Serve cold. Sprinkle nutmeg, cinnamon, raisins, coconut, or chopped nuts on top.

Serves 6

APPLE CRISP

For a crunchy crust, you must use a shallow baking dish that brings the top of the crisp near the top of the baking dish.

⅓ (45 g) cup whole wheat flour
¼ (50 g) cup brown sugar
⅛ teaspoon (.50 ml) salt
⅓ cup (75 g) butter or margarine
¼ teaspoon (1.5 ml) grated nutmeg
4 cups (500 g) peeled and sliced apples

Mix the flour, brown sugar, and salt. Cut in the shortening to make a crumbly mixture. Add grated nutmeg. Select a 10-inch (25 cm) square shallow baking dish. Put apple slices in the bottom of dish. Cover with crumbly mixture. Bake in a preheated 375 degrees F (190 degrees C) oven for about 40 minutes or until the apples are soft and the top is crunchy and golden brown.

Makes twenty-five 2-inch (5 cm) squares

DATE BARS

1 cup (200 g) brown sugar
¼ cup (50 g) butter
2 eggs, beaten
¾ cup (100 g) whole wheat flour
¼ teaspoon (1.5 ml) baking powder
½ teaspoon (2.5 ml) salt
1 cup (175 g) chopped dates
⅓ cup (50 g) chopped walnuts

Blend the butter and sugar together. Add the eggs and mix well. Sift the flour, baking powder, and salt over the egg mixture. Mix in the dates and nuts, blending well.

Using a greased 8-inch (20 cm) square baking pan, spread in the mixture. Bake in a preheated 350 degrees F (180 degrees C) oven for 20 minutes. Cut into squares.

Makes sixteen 2-inch (5 cm) squares

FRUIT CHEWYS

½ cup (90 g) dried figs
½ cup (90 g) dried apricots
½ cup (90 g) pitted dates
¼ cup (50 g) glaced cherries, chopped
½ cup (75 g) chopped pecans
¼ cup (20 g) coconut, shredded
    Pinch of salt
1 tablespoon (15 ml) honey
½ cup (75 g) finely minced nuts

Put fruits (except coconut) and pecans through a food grinder. Blend in the coconut, salt, and honey, mixing well. Shape into small balls and roll in the minced nuts. Chill.

Makes about 24 small balls

OATMEAL COOKIES

1½ cups (210 g) whole wheat flour
1 cup (125 g) oat flour
1 teaspoon (5 ml) baking soda
½ teaspoon (2.5 ml) salt
1 cup (200 g) brown sugar
2 eggs, lightly beaten
1 cup (250 ml) melted butter
1 teaspoon (5 ml) vanilla
2 cups (150 g) rolled oats
½ cup (75 g) raisins
½ cup (75 g) chopped nuts

Combine the whole wheat flour, oat flour, baking soda, salt, and sugar, making sure there are no lumps in the mixture. Add the eggs, butter, and vanilla. Beat until mixture is creamy. Add the oats, raisins, and nuts; mix well.

Drop the dough by teaspoonfuls onto a well-greased cookie sheet. Bake in a preheated 325 degrees F (170 degrees C) oven for 15 to 20 minutes or until a golden brown.

Makes about 3 dozen cookies

COFFEE CAKE

1½ (210 g) cups whole wheat flour
½ teaspoon (2.5 ml) baking soda
1 teaspoon (5 ml) cream of tartar
¾ teaspoon (3.5 ml) salt
½ cup (100 g) brown sugar
¼ cup (50 g) butter or margarine
1 egg, beaten together with
½ cup (125 ml) milk

Topping
2 tablespoons (30 ml) melted butter
4 tablespoons (60 ml) (or more) brown sugar
1 tablespoon (15 ml) whole wheat flour
Cinnamon to taste

Over a large mixing bowl, sift together the flour, baking soda, tartar, and salt. Blend in the shortening with your fingers. Add the sugar, then the egg mixture. Mix quickly, then beat briefly.

Put into a greased, 8-inch (20 cm) square baking dish, 1 ½ (3.75 cm) inches deep. Cover the top with melted butter, sprinkle with the brown sugar, flour, and cinnamon. Bake in a preheated 425 degrees F (220 degrees C) oven for 20 minutes.

Makes one 8-inch (20 cm) cake

BANANAS IN SOUR CREAM

2 bananas, sliced
1 cup (250 ml) sour cream
¼ cup (50 g) diced oranges
2 tablespoons (30 ml) brown sugar
¼ teaspoon (1.5 ml) vanilla extract
Grated orange peel

Combine all ingredients except the orange peel. Serve garnished with orange peel.

Serves 4

Variation: Add ¼ pound (100 g) of dates cut in halves lengthwise.

SWEET POTATO PECAN PIE

1 unbaked pie crust
2 cups (500 ml) milk
  Grated rind of 1 orange
  Juice of ½ orange
1½ cups (325 g) hot, sweet potatoes, diced
½ cup (100 g) brown sugar, firmly packed
½ teaspoon (2.5 ml) salt
½ teaspoon (2.5 ml) cinnamon
½ teaspoon (2.5 ml) nutmeg
¼ cup (50 g) butter
2 eggs, separated
  Pecan nuts

Line pie plate with pastry dough. Allow to set in the refrigerator until filling is ready.

Combine the milk and orange rind. Scald milk. Add the orange juice, sweet potatoes, brown sugar, salt, cinnamon, nutmeg, and butter. Lower flame and cook until the butter is melted.

Lightly beat the egg yolks. Pour the milk mixture over the egg yolks and beat lightly, mixing well.

Beat the egg whites until stiff. Fold the egg whites into the mixture. Pour into the pie crust. Bake in a preheated 425 degrees F (220 degrees C) oven for 10 minutes. Lower the temperature to 350 degrees F (180 degrees C) and bake for 35 minutes more. Before you continue to bake at the lower temperature, decorate the pie with the pecans, then complete the baking process.

Serves 6-8

INDEX

243

World Almanac Publications
Order Form

Quantity	ISBN	Title/Author	Unit Price	Total
	31655-X	Abracadabra! Magic and Other Tricks/Lewis	$5.95/$7.95 in Canada	
	32836-1	Africa Review 1986/Green	$24.95/$33.95 in Canada	
	32834-5	Asia & Pacific Review 1986/Green	$24.95/$33.95 in Canada	
	32632-6	Ask Shagg™/Guren	$4.95/$6.50 in Canada	
	32189-8	Big Book of Kids' Lists, The/Choron	$8.95/$11.95 in Canada	
	31033-0	Civil War Almanac, The/Bowman	$10.95/$14.75 in Canada	
	31503-0	Collector's Guide to New England, The/Bowles and Bowles	$7.95/$10.95 in Canada	
	31651-7	Complete Dr. Salk: An A-to-Z Guide to Raising Your Child, The/Salk	$8.95/$11.50 in Canada	
	32662-8	Confidence Quotient: 10 Steps to Conquer Self-Doubt, The/ Gellman and Gage	$7.95/$10.75 in Canada	
	32627-X	Cut Your Own Taxes and Save 1986/Metz and Kess	$3.95	
	31628-2	Dieter's Almanac, The/Berland	$7.95/$10.25 in Canada	
	32835-3	Europe Review 1986/Green	$24.95/$33.95 in Canada	
	32190-1	Fire! Prevention: Protection: Escape/Cantor	$3.95/$4.95 in Canada	
	32192-8	For the Record: Women in Sports/Markel and Brooks	$8.95/$11.95 in Canada	
	32624-5	How I Photograph Wildlife and Nature/Rue	$9.95/$13.50 in Canada	
	31709-2	How to Talk Money/Crowe	$7.95/$10.25 in Canada	
	32629-6	I Do: How to Choose Your Mate and Have a Happy Marriage/ Eysenck and Kelly	$8.95	
	32660-1	Kids' World Almanac of Records and Facts, The/ McLoone-Basta and Siegel	$4.95	
	32837-X	Latin America & Caribbean Review 1986/Green	$24.95/$33.95 in Canada	
	32838-8	Middle East Review 1986/Green	$24.95/$33.95 in Canada	
	31652-5	Moonlighting with Your Personal Computer/Waxman	$7.95/$10.75 in Canada	
	32193-6	National Directory of Addresses and Telephone Numbers ,The/Sites	$24.95/$33.95 in Canada	
	31034-9	Omni Future Almanac, The/Weil	$8.95/$11.95 in Canada	
	32623-7	Pop Sixties: A Personal and Irreverent Guide, The/Edelstein	$8.95/$11.95 in Canada	
	32624-5	Singles Almanac, The/Ullman	$8.95/$11.95 in Canada	
	31492-1	Social Security and You: What's New, What's True/Kingson	$2.95	
	0-915106-19-1	Synopsis of the Law of Libel and the Right of Privacy/Sanford	$1.95	
		Twentieth Century: An Almanac, The/Ferrell		
	31708-4	Hardcover	$24.95/$33.95 in Canada	
	32630-X	Paperback	$12.95/$17.50 in Canada	
	32631-8	Vietnam War: An Almanac, The/Bowman	$24.95/$33.95 in Canada	
	32188-X	Where to Sell Anything and Everything/Hyman	$8.95/$11.95 in Canada	
	32659-8	World Almanac` & Book of Facts 1986, The/Lane	$5.95/$6.95 in Canada	
	32661-X	World Almanac Book of Inventions`, The/Giscard d'Estaing	$10.95/$14.75 in Canada	
	29775-X	World Almanac Book of World War II, The/Young	$10.95/$14.75 in Canada	
	0-911818-97-9	World Almanac Consumer Information Kit 1986, The	$2.50	
	32187-1	World Almanac Executive Appointment Book 1986, The	$17.95/$24.95 in Canada	
	32628-8	World Almanac Guide to Natural Foods, The/Ross	$8.95/$11.95 in Canada	
	32194-4	World Almanac's Puzzlink™/Considine	$2.95/$3.95 in Canada	
	32626-1	World Almanac's Puzzlink™ 2/Considine	$2.95/$3.95 in Canada	
	31654-1	World Almanac Real Puzzle™ Book, The/Rubin	$2.95/$3.95 in Canada	
	32191-X	World Almanac Real Puzzle™ Book 2, The/Rubin	$2.95/$3.95 in Canada	
	32625-3	World Almanac Real Puzzle™ Book 3, The/Rubin	$2.95/$3.95 in Canada	
		World of Information: see individual titles		

Mail order form to: World Almanac Publications
P.O. Box 984
Cincinnati, Ohio 45201

Orders must be prepaid by one of the following methods:
☐ Check or Money Order for _____ attached
☐ Bill my charge card (Add $5.00 processing charge for
   orders under $20.00)

Order Total_____

Ohio residents add 5.5% sales tax_____

Shipping and Handling:_____
(Add $2.50 for every purchase up to $50.00,
and $1.00 for every $10.00 thereafter)

TOTAL PAYMENT_____

Visa Account #_____   Exp. Date_____

Master Card Account #_____ Exp. Date_____

Interbank #_____   Exp. Date_____

Authorized Signature_____

Ship to:
Name_____

Street address_____

City/State/Zip Code_____

Special Instructions:_____

All orders will be shipped UPS unless otherwise instructed.
We cannot ship C.O.D.